THE WORLD OF CLASSICAL ATHENS

Text by:

FRANCESCO ADORNO
of the University of Florence

LUIGI BESCHI
of the Italian School of Archaeology, Athens

HENRI VAN EFFENTERRE
of the Sorbonne, Paris

GIOVANNI FERRARA
of the University of Urbino

GIULIO GIANNELLI
Rector of the Scuola Normale Superiore, Pisa

SIE GFRIED LAUFFER
*Director of the Seminar of Ancient History,
the University of Monaco*

PIERRE LÉVÊQUE
Dean of the Faculty of Letters, the University of Besançon

DORO LEVI
Director of the Italian School of Archaeology, Athens

GIANFRANCO MADDOLI
of the University of Florence

ALDO NEPPI MODONA
of the University of Genoa

GIOVANNI PUGLIESE CARRATELLI
*Director of the Institute of Greek History,
the University of Rome*

HOMER A. THOMPSON
*Field Director of the American School of
Classical Studies, Athens*

JOHANNES TRAVLOS
Architect, American School of Classical Studies, Athens

PIERO TREVES
of the University of Florence

JEAN TRIANTAPHYLLOPOULOS
of the University of Athens

THE WORLD
OF CLASSICAL
ATHENS

edited by GIULIO GIANNELLI

335 illustrations in colour

G. P. PUTNAM'S SONS ~ NEW YORK

58368

FIRST AMERICAN EDITION 1970

© 1966 BEMPORAD MARZOCCO, Florence

This translation
© 1970 MACDONALD & Co. (Publishers) Ltd.

Library of Congress Catalog Card Number: 70-99286

Translated by Walter Darwell

First published in Italy in 1966
as TUTTO SU ATENE CLASSICA
by BEMPORAD MARZOCCO, Florence

Printed in Italy

Following upon the eminently successful first two volumes, The World of Ancient Rome *and* The World of Renaissance Florence, *this third volume of the series presents a picture of Greece in the period of her history which has profoundly influenced the whole of civilization: the age of Classical Athens, seen through the public and private lives of her citizens who, from the Acropolis to the Agora, from the time of the Persian threat to the supremacy of Macedon, wrote out for all succeeding ages the civilizing message of the natural dignity of man.*

The reader is offered through words and pictures a panorama of Athenian civilization, a hitherto unpublished Athens as it was, an authentic image of the city stripped of its romantic accretions and based on objective documents, archaeological research and scientific reconstruction. This task has necessitated the collaboration of Italian and foreign scholars, coordinators and research workers, editorial staff and cultural organizations.

The visual sequence of the work, based on the excavations carried out on the site of the ancient Agora by the American School of Classical Studies in Athens under its Director, Homer A. Thompson, who has also contributed a chapter, has been made possible by major contributions from Greek cultural organizations, from private collectors in Athens and by the collaboration of famous museums throughout the world.

The team responsible for The World of Classical Athens — *writers, coordinators, editors and photographers — has thus been enabled to produce one of the most outstanding and beautifully presented accounts of Athenian civilization ever to be published.*

We wish to record our gratitude in particular to Professor Doro Levi, the Director of the Italian School of Archaeology in Athens, for his numerous suggestions and invaluable advice, and to Professor Piero Treves of the University of Florence for his unfailing interest in our labours, and we warmly commend the editorial and the technical staff for the zeal and enthusiasm they showed in the preparation of the work.

THE PUBLISHERS

CONTENTS

2.

For the reconstruction of Classical Athens, ' The Growth of the City' was written by Johannes Travlos and ' The Excavations of the Agora' by Homer A. Thompson and Francesco Adorno. The section on private life in Classical Athens is due to Henri van Effenterre (' Husbands, Wives and Children'), Siegfried Lauffer (' Slaves: « Instruments with Souls »') and Pierre Lévêque (' The Banquet, A Custom of the Age') with the cooperation of Giovanni Ferrara and Gianfranco Maddoli. The chapters on public life were written by Giulio Giannelli (religion, political institutions and the army), Giovanni Pugliese Carratelli (medicine), Piero Treves (education, the economy) and Jean Triantaphyllopoulos (the legal system). The accounts of festivals and games are by Luigi Beschi and of the theatre by Aldo Neppi Modona. The section on Athenian art is by Doro Levi. Piero Treves, Francesco Adorno and Clelia Laviosa have particularly helped in the work of coordination.

THE GROWTH OF THE CITY

The first polis (city-state) of Athens rose on the fortified Acropolis and gradually extended outwards over the narrow plain. It was destroyed several times in the course of the centuries by enemy hordes, Greek and barbarian, yet it rose again, larger and more clearly defined in its two basic centres, the primitive nucleus, scene of solemn and sacred rites, and the public quarter, the hub of a busy commercial life, bounded by the porticoes, temples and public buildings of the Agora.

Around it spread the shadowy grey mass of dwelling houses, built haphazardly ' in the Athenian manner ', that is without any design or unity.

But the face of Athens was etched in symbols of stone, by the temples of Pericles, by the airy profile of the Acropolis, by its bluish limestone, by the perfectly controlled setting of its buildings, and by the warm tones of the marble laid upon it. The Parthenon and the other buildings formed an indissoluble, harmonious entity, a unique symbol of that ' sense of the land ' which is so typically Greek.

If it is true today that anyone who climbs the Acropolis or looks at it from a distance can only guess from these venerable ruins how the lines and the masses were once arranged, it is also true that the eternal countenance of Athens is as unmistakable today as it was when Pericles willed it and Phidias designed it, and as it was finally, linked to the sea and its port by the famous ' Long Wall '.

The *polis* is above all a moral concept which successfully survived the physical destruction of the city.

This is how we must consider Athens, from the moment when the earliest inhabitants of the neolithic age took refuge on the sacred rock, and throughout the five centuries of her history. Rarely was any city destroyed so often or so completely. Only Athens rose again from her ruins to achieve such brilliance, and this because she succeeded through the many centuries of her history in uniting her citizens in a common bond of loyalty.

There are few remains of the first settlement, and our information about the early periods of Athenian history is gleaned from myth and legend, supported latterly by excavations and research into the layout of streets. Some of these streets follow the same direction today: Athens, in fact, has never ceased to be alive. As we walk through the narrow alleys surrounding the Acropolis, we may be treading in the footsteps of ancient Athenians.

The most important pieces of evidence from this first phase of the city's history lie grouped around the Acropolis and the slopes of its rock: foundations of the palace of legendary kings, hypaethral shrines, fountains, wells, traces of the ancient surrounding wall, houses, tombs. There was, however, nothing in that period which could be called an organized group of dwellings, a *polis*.

Athenian history would appear to have begun in the early thirteenth century B.C. and to have evolved normally like that of any other Attic kingdom. The settlement was then limited in extent to the Acropolis and a small area stretching out to the south.

According to Thucydides, the great Athenian historian (*c.* 460-*c.* 400 B.C.), even before the time of the legendary Theseus the city rose on the site of what was later to be the Acropolis. He based his evidence

on the continued existence of important shrines in the area.

There were other shrines situated outside the Acropolis. These were grouped together in the southern sector and included those dedicated to the Olympian Zeus, the Pythion, and to Gaia, the Dionysus *en limnais* (in the marshes).

Recent researches have shown that this part of the old city extended as far as the river Ilissus, and widespread excavations have revealed walls, wells, tombs and, most important of all, numerous vases of

the period. The city traditionally owes its original prestige to Theseus, who united all the townships of Attica into one state with Athens as its capital.

From the second half of the thirteenth century B.C. the Athenians proceeded to fortify their city, at that time bounded by the rock of the Acropolis. A strong wall was built right round the rock on what was known as the 'cyclopean' system, the *Pelargikon* or *Pelasgikon*. In many sectors it was more than sixteen feet wide. The only entrnce was in the western sector, and it was here that Pericles' architect Mne-

Bare, craggy mountains, narrow windswept plains; coasts heavily indented with creeks, bays and inlets; a sky implacably serene for most of the year: this is Attica, the strip of Greece bound to the destiny of Athens and an integral part of the city's life and history. A small area of land between sea and mountain, with a few villages scattered around the city of Pallas and isolated in the meagre country-side amongst vines and olive groves, defended on the north by a few fortifications and, together with Athens, looking outwards, more by necessity than by vocation, towards the sea: Athens and Attica are sacred to Pallas, but Poseidon also has his temples and a flourishing cult there. In the myths, as if symbolizing her destiny, the goddess and the god struggled for a long time for possession of the city, the goddess being identified with her industry and her craftsmen and the god with those whom he taught 'to sail well the seas'. Left: ruins of ancient hill fortifications. Right: ruins of the temple of Poseidon on Cape Sunium (the southern-most point of Attica).

sicles later built the Propylaea (the entrance gateways to the temple precinct). Here there was probably built a second wall, to secure the entrance and at the same time to protect the three most important water-sources: the Asklepieion, the Klepsidra and the spring inside the Aglauros grotto.

After Theseus' time the city generally comprised two sectors: the Acropolis, called the *polis* in official texts of the period, and the lower town, the *asty*, which included the Agora and the residential quarters.

Athens had begun to take on the appearance of an organized city around the sacred rock of the Acropolis under Solon (*c.* 638-558 B.C.) and Pisistratus (d. 527 B.C.).

The definitive grouping of the townships of Attica into a single Athenian state was achieved probably in the early sixth century, in the time of Solon, with the union between the Eleusi and the city of Athens. Later the cult of the Eleusian Demeter brought to Athens, at the same time as the Panathenaic processions, one of the city's greatest festivals, reaching its peak in the time of Pisistratus.

The union with the Eleusi consolidated the strength of the capital, which then began a period of continual expansion to cope with its growing needs. Great building programmes were initiated by Solon and carried out under Pisistratus and his successors.

These extensions created the need for a new outer wall, whose existence is clearly affirmed in contemporary writings. Its exact position is still unknown, however, as the extent of the city in this period has not yet been accurately determined. It would appear to have been built round the Acropolis and its northern slopes, as this would explain the siting of the Agora in this area.

Contemporary records show that the ring of the new outer wall round the Acropolis had a diameter of 800 metres at the most.

The new Agora, also known as the *Kerameikos*, the name of the *demos* (suburb) in whose district it had been built, was situated on the wide open area east of the Kolonos Agoraios, which lay between the Areopagos and the river Eridanus, and which, as excavations have shown, was the cemetery of the old

The Greeks' method of building, imported from Egypt, was with large blocks of stone; they did not know mortar, lime or cement. The stones used in large public buildings were cut into huge blocks parallelepiped in shape, then placed one on top of the other and often held with metal clamps. Left: section of the outer wall of the fortress of Ramnis built in this manner.

Another method of building was with stones cut irregularly into variously shaped polygons. They then had to be fitted together, as in this wall in the Athenian portico at Delphi.

town. It was virtually predestined to be a market-place. Situated near the ancient agora of Theseus, the new square was traversed by the main avenue of the city, the Panathenaic Way, which led from the Acropolis to all the important townships of Attica and was thereby linked to the whole of Greece.

In the sixth century B.C. and until the end of the Persian wars, in the mid-fifth century, the Agora was surrounded by very important buildings such as the Enneakrunos and the walls of Theseus to the south, where Theseus' remains were deposited during the rule of Cimon (deposed 461 B.C.). In the west, running from north to south, stood the temple of Zeus, the temple of Apollo Patrous, the Metroun, the Bouleuterion and the Prytankion.

The buildings greatly enhanced the splendour of the market square, whose limits were marked off with boundary stones. One of these can still be seen stand-

ing in its original position in front of the Prytankion (510-500 B.C.). The altar consecrated to the Twelve Gods was a tall and very important building on the Agora. Built by the grandson of Pisistratus in 521-520 B.C., near the north-west gate, it was the point from which roads led out of the city and all distances were measured. It stood beside the Panathenaic Way, near the cross-roads of the principal thoroughfares.

Pisistratus and his successors were much concerned to beautify the Acropolis. The great quantity of material of architectural interest brought to light by excavations, as well as the very numerous sculptures and inscriptions, enable us to reconstruct the marvel of the Acropolis as it was at this time.

Among the ruins which have been preserved are at least two temples, both consecrated to Athena, the protectress of the city. They were built on the highest point of the Acropolis, on the ruins of an ancient

Mycenaean palace. This was also the site of the most ancient shrines: the ancient peripteral temple (529-520 B.C.), the ruins of which are preserved near the Erechtheum, and the Herkatompedon (570-566 B.C.), which thus preceded the Parthenon and was situated in what became later the Parthenon's north-east corner.

The first Parthenon, of marble, was begun in the period between the battle of Marathon (490 B.C.) and the naval battle of Salamis (479 B.C.). At about the same time the fortified Mycenaean entrance gate was replaced by the grandiose Propylaea. After the battle of Marathon, a small temple and an altar consecrated to Athena Nike (the personification of Victory) were built on the Mycenaean fortifications opposite the Propylaea. This replaced a former altar dedicated to the same goddess and dating back to 566 B.C., the year of the first Panathenaic games.

Although at points fortifications were replaced by the Propylaea and several adjoining shrines, the security of the Acropolis was by no means neglected. The Mycenaean walls and the western outer rampart remained the principal defence of the sacred rock.

Streets were laid outside as well as inside the walls and many people were accommodated in the areas surrounding the city, as evidenced by the several sanctuaries discovered outside the walls and by the famous Gymnasia (cultural centres) of Athens, such as the Academy, the Lyceum and the Cynosarges which were built in the finest suburban areas. It was in such gymnasia that youths were trained in the arts of war and in athletics and received at the same time courses of higher education. They gradually became intellectual centres of considerable importance, and for some thousand years performed inestimable services in the education of young men, making Athens one of the greatest seats of learning in the world.

The most important of the sanctuaries outside the walls were situated on the banks of the Ilissus and were built after the Persian Wars: they were those of the Olympian Zeus, the Pythion and the Gaia. The Athenians would appear to have buried their dead outside the walls from the sixth century onwards. The term *extra muros* as used by Cicero meant a place intended for the burial of the dead.

Ten years after the victory of Marathon, a new Athenian victory at Salamis in 479 B.C. further strengthened the power of the city and added to its glory.

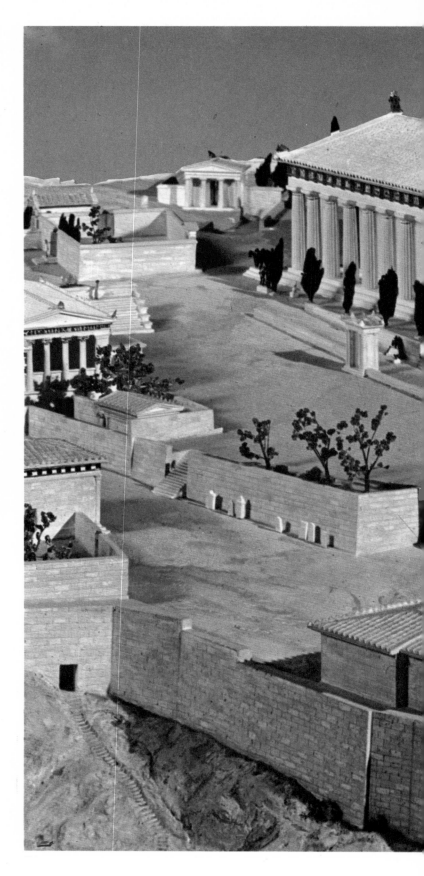

Reconstruction of the Acropolis by W. C. Laidlaw, based on a model by Graham P. Stevens in the Royal Ontario Museum, Toronto, Canada. The Panathenaic procession can be seen wending its way to the Parthenon, which dominates the scene, and passing through the

Propylaea, or entrance portico (bottom right). To the right of the Propylaea is the little temple of Athena Nike, and above it the temple of Artemis. Between the latter and the Parthenon is the Chalcoteca, where votive offerings were kept: vases, sacrificial cups, implements for the cult and arms, especially shields and lances. The large statue (centre) represents Athena Promachos ('Athena fighting in the front rank'). Extreme left: part of the Erechtheum.

The whole of Attica, however, including Athens, suffered an enormous catastrophe by the invasion of the Persians who completed the destruction of the city as they withdrew after their second defeat.

The temples on the Acropolis and the sanctuaries around it were set on fire, as also were the buildings of the Agora. Only a few houses were spared: those which had sheltered the invaders during their occupation of the city. Athens was now an 'open city', as the enemy's chief aim had been to destroy its fortifications. When the Athenians returned to its ruins, their main priority was the immediate rebuilding of the outer wall, and this they accomplished, using stones from the ruins and even from ancient funeral pillars.

The initiative for this reconstruction came from Themistocles, the victor of Salamis, who foresaw further danger from the Spartans and succeeded in rebuilding the ramparts in one year.

The extent of the city during this period was much greater than it had been in the sixth century B.C. This is clearly demonstrated by the dimensions of the new wall, many sections of which have only recently been discovered. The wall was still roughly circular and, surrounding the Acropolis and the Agora, reached a diameter of about a mile, or double that of the old one.

Themistocles also persuaded the Athenians to fortify the harbours of the Piraeus, as he believed in their importance in the development of Athens as a maritime power.

This plan was realized some time later by Cimon who built the Long Walls: the wall to Phalerum Bay and the north wall which protected communications between the city and the harbours at Phalerum Bay and the Piraeus during the war. This protection was extended by the building in 445 B.C. of the south wall parallel to the north wall and 177 yards from it along the side facing the wall to Phalerum. This gave a fortified corridor over four miles long and wide enough to take the road leading from the city to the harbours of the Piraeus.

After the end of the Peloponnesian War (431-404 B.C.), which saw the total defeat of Athens by Sparta, the victors demolished the fortifications of the city,

Opposite: *reconstruction of the Erechtheum (Toronto Museum), one of the most famous temples of antiquity, dedicated to Athena and Poseidon and recalling the quarrel of the god and the goddess over the possession of Attica. Here the salt water sprang out of the ground struck by Poseidon's trident and the sacred olive tree grew out of Athena's lance. Further pictures of the Erechtheum are to be found in the chapters on slaves and on the arts.* Right: *the Erechtheum olive tree.*

the harbours on the Piraeus and the Long Walls. They were rebuilt a few years later (394-391) by Conon, except the wall to Phalerum Bay, where the harbour had fallen out of use.

Almost all the gates of the surrounding wall of Athens existing in the fifth and fourth centuries B.C. have been discovered and identified from their inscriptions as those mentioned by contemporary writers. We know of sixteen, and they were all on the main roads out of the city leading to the townships of Attica or to other localities. Today's roads follow the same routes exactly, routes imposed upon them as the only natural passes through the high mountains surrounding the small plain of Attica.

The Dipylon gate, the main entrance to the city, was situated in the Ceramicus quarter (a district in the north-west inhabited mainly by potters) at the end of the most important roads: those from the Academy, the Piraeus and Eleusis. The latter was the famous Sacred Way and linked Athens not only to Eleusis but also to the rest of Attica, the Peloponnese and other Greek states. The Dipylon gate was also known as the Ceramicus and the Thriasia gate. Not far from it stood the Sacred Gate, through which passed the annual procession to Eleusis.

Between the Sacred Gate and the Dipylon stood the Pompeion, scene of the preparations for the great Eleusinian and Panathenaic festivals and repository of the sacred vessels used on those occasions.

The Athenians were not only concerned with the fortification of their city. Soon after their victory over Persia (449 B.C.) they put in hand a vast building programme beginning with the reconstruction of temples and public buildings. Most of the work was carried out during the rule of Pericles (460-429).

Magnificent temples were built on the Acropolis, replacing those put up by the Persians and immortalizing the age by the perfection of their composition and the incomparable beauty of their statues and carvings.

The architects to whom the task of rebuilding the monuments on the Acropolis was entrusted found their labours easier than in the lower part of the city, where their activities were limited to the Agora.

The new temple dedicated to Athena Parthenos, the Parthenon, dominated the highest point of the Acropolis and was visible from all parts of the city. The temple of Athena Polias was demolished and in its place Callicrates, the leading architect of the period, built the Erechtheum. Mnesicles built the new Propylaea (entrance gates to the temple area) on the site of the old ones, but along a different axis: this was part of the new plan, but it was also designed to set off the colossal statue of Promachos and the temples on either side of it as viewed from the gateways.

The esplanade surrounding these two temples contains the beautiful Calcoteca, the shrine of Artemis Brauronia, several other shrines and altars and a host of statues. In front of the Propylaea, on the Mycenaean bastion, was built the temple of Athena Nike, while round the Acropolis ancient buildings were restored and new ones constructed: on the north slope the shrine of Eros and Aphrodite and the grotto of Aglauros, which had contained a famous spring in the Mycenaean period; at the western end, built in grottoes, the Olympieion, the Pythion and the shrine dedicated to Pan, whose cult originated just after the Persian Wars.

On the south side of the Acropolis Pericles built an Odeion, or wooden-roofed theatre which bears his name, and the famous Theatre of Dionysus. West of the latter was the shrine of Asclepius (god of medicine) and Hygeia (his daughter, goddess of health), founded in 420 B.C.

The plan of the Agora was greatly simplified: it became a large square with new public buildings and temples alongside the older ones which had been refurbished.

On the top of the Colonos Agoraios hill was built, towards the middle of the fifth century B.C., the temple

The Parthenon: detail from a reconstruction of the Acropolis in the Toronto Museum. The pediment and the frieze have been painted in the bright colours which were customary in Classical Greece. Dedicated to Athena Parthenos (the Virgin Athene), it was built by Pericles on the foundations, extended northwards, of the ancient 'great temple' destroyed, together with other buildings on the old Acropolis, by the Persians during their invasion. The plan was by Phidias, who supervised the labour. The building, begun in 447 and given a solemn inauguration in 438, was entirely of Pentelicus marble, though the lower parts were built partly of marble from the ruins of the previous temple. The Parthenon was erected to the glory not only of Athena but of the whole city. It became a Christian church, then a mosque during the Turkish occupation. Used as an ammunition depot by the Turks, it was shelled by the Venetians and blown up in 1687, together with other buildings of both the classical and later periods. For further information and illustrations of the Parthenon see the later chapters on religious life and on art.

of Hephaestus (the smith-god), which is almost completely intact today. The area round this temple was always left free of buildings, and the view from this height down towards the Agora was superb. On the esplanade round the temple various festivals and solemn celebrations were held, the most important being the Panathenaic festivals. It was from this point that the Athenians would watch their athletes competing in races along the Panathenaic Way, starting from the Altar of the Twelve Gods and finishing at the Eleusinion, and from here too they would see the majestic Panathenaic procession wend its way through the Agora towards the Acropolis.

The Ilissus quarter was also developed from the end of the fifth century. This was one of the oldest parts of the city. It had some fine sanctuaries and an idyllic atmosphere, celebrated by Plato in his dialogues.

The two gymnasia near the river Ilissus were renovated, and temples were built throughout the area: to Apollo Delphi, Artemis Agnotera, the Metroun of Agai, Aphrodite in the Gardens and so on. There are still some impressive ruins of the majestic temple to Zeus Olympus.

Part of the reconstruction of the Agora. (Agora Museum, Athens). This famous square, the hub of Athenian life, was dominated by the mass of the temple of He-

Also in the Ilissus quarter stood the temple of Dionysus in the Marshes, the shrines of Apollo Pythios and King Codros, venerated above all kings because he had saved the city during the Doric invasion.

There seem to have been several important public buildings in this area: two Courts of Justice, the Delphinion and the Palladion, are known to us.

Except for the Agora and the Ilissus, all the area around the Acropolis was occupied by private houses.

phaestus, patron of the smiths, the workmen and the craftsmen whose shops were almost all in the immediate neigh-bourhood. The illustration shows, right, *the Stoa of Zeus and,* left, *the Metroun and the Bouleuterion.* Bottom centre: *the temple of Ares. On the reconstruction of the Agora, see below pp. 28 and 29.*

HOUSES AND STREETS

From descriptions left by contemporary writers and from the results of excavations, we know that there was a startling difference between the dwelling houses of Athens, for the most part small and humble, and the magnificent monuments which adorned the city. Actually the Athenian spent most of his day out of doors, in the public places, on the Acropolis, in the Agora or the Gymnasia. The house played a secondary role in his life, and as such it was no more than a number of rooms limited to the needs of the family, grouped round a courtyard, without any luxury or pretension to elegance. This was the case even with fairly wealthy families.

The streets of Athens were generally narrow and irregular, often not more than ten feet wide. Only those leading from the centre of the city to the gates were about fifteen feet in width, and the Panathenaic Way and the Street of the Tripods were about forty.

Athens developed without any plan: the streets were extended irregularly 'in the Attic manner' on the basis of the already existing thoroughfares which had been preserved for centuries.

The reconstructed plan of the city as it was in the fourth century B.C. merely shows the sites of the different types of building: administrative, religious and domestic. It gives no idea of the numbers, but we know from Xenophon (c. 430-355 B.C.) that there were about ten thousand dwelling houses in Athens during his time.

The city's water supply came from wells and from rain water collected in cisterns in the courtyards of private houses. There was the occasional spring on the slopes of the Acropolis dedicated to some very ancient cult, as water had always been a precious commodity for the Athenians.

It was Pisistratus who was mainly responsible for putting the city's water supply on an organized footing, and much of the work done at that time has survived through the centuries of Athenian history.

The scarcity of water, a feature of Athens which has lasted up to modern times, determined the arrangement of gardens, which were naturally rare in the city itself, whereas on the banks of the rivers Cephisus, Ilissus and Eridanus there were fine parks surrounding the Gymnasia of the Academy, the Cynosarges and the Lyceum. The city also had few trees, though this was due as much to lack of space as to lack of water; what trees there were grew round fountains and springs, like the plane trees planted by Cimon near a spring in the Agora.

The shrines also were surrounded by gardens, though these were generally small. Traces of a garden can still be found in the area of the Colonos Agoraios hill around the temple of Ephistos, and there are similar indications around the Tholos (a round building where a committee of the governing council met) and the Temple of Asclepius (the god of healing).

Green predominated also among the tombs in the cemeteries. Burial within the walls was strictly forbidden only from the fifth century B.C. onwards. The Ceramicus was the official burial area and it was here that heroes and famous men were given their tombs. It extended on both sides of the road leading to the Academy which, along one sector outside the Dipylon gate, was 130 feet wide. Other cemeteries were established outside the main gates of the city alongside the main roads.

The development of the city was interrupted by the threat from Macedonia, and particularly when Philip's strength was seen to have increased after the fall of Olynthos (356 B.C.).

The new war tactics of the Macedonians and the use of siege machines compelled the Athenians to rebuild their fortifications in Athens and the Piraeus.

It was not, however, until after the battle of Chaeronea (338 B.C.), when Philip's advance struck terror into the hearts of Athenians, that the main work on the ramparts was completed, and then it was done in haste. Philip turned back and the danger was averted, but the lesson was learnt and the fortifications were finally completed at the end of the century. An outer wall, some thirty feet from the old one, was built round the lower city from the Hill of the Nymphs to the Hill of the Muses. To ward off the siege machines a ditch was dug in front of the wall some thirty-three feet wide and twelve feet deep.

A new wall was built on the Hill of the Nymphs and the Hill of Philopappus to prevent any extension of the city's boundary in those areas.

This preoccupation with matters of defence did not prevent the Athenians from undertaking at the same time a further programme of public works. The happy conduct of the city's finances by the orator Lycurgus allowed the undertaking of a vast plan of building and improvements.

One of the first places to benefit from this plan was the Pnyx hill area. This was laid out on a much larger scale, with a small square on the top and the erection of several new buildings.

At about the same time the new temple of Dionysus was built opposite the theatre of the same name and in the west, near the Temple of Asclepius, a two-tiered portico was erected. In the immediate vicinity of the theatre stood numerous monuments to the choregoi, rich Athenians whose munificence had supplied the theatre with choruses. There were even more of these monuments on the Tripod Way, which led north from the Prytaneum (the city hall) along the foot of the Acropolis to the Odeion and the Theatre of Dionysus.

Under Lycurgus the Agora also had new buildings arranged around the great square: this plan survived from the third century B.C. to the first.

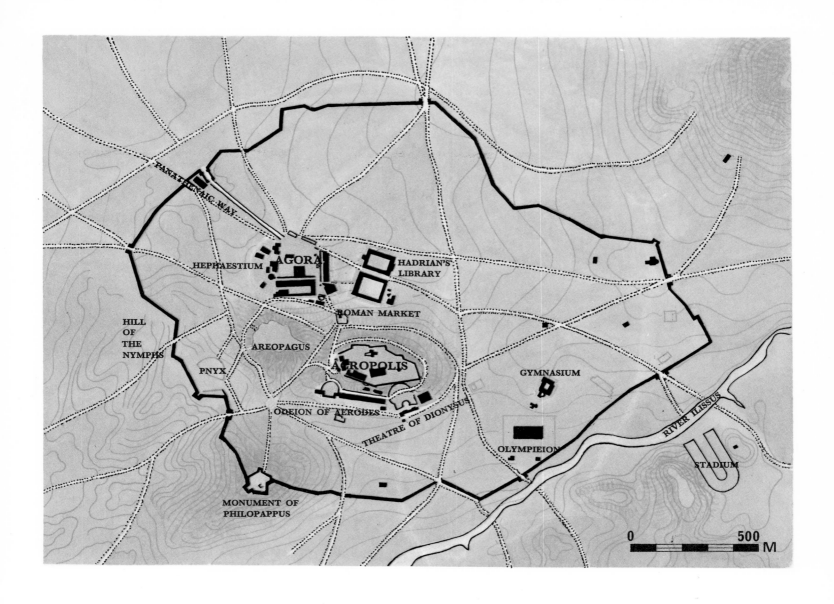

PANATHENAIC WAY

HEPHAESTIUM   AGORA   HADRIAN'S
                                LIBRARY

ROMAN MARKET

HILL
OF
THE
NYMPHS   AREOPAGUS

PNYX   ACROPOLIS   GYMNASIUM

ODEION OF AERODES

THEATRE OF DIONYSUS   RIVER ILISSUS

OLYMPIEION

STADIUM

MONUMENT OF
PHILOPAPPUS

0   500
                           M

Above: *plan of Athens in the second
century* A.D.
Right: *map of the area Athens —
the Piraeus — Phalerum. (Arch.
Travlos).*

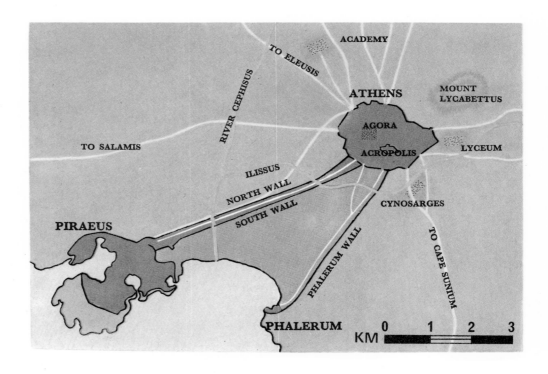

ACADEMY

TO ELEUSIS

RIVER CEPHISUS   ATHENS   MOUNT
                                        LYCABETTUS

TO SALAMIS   AGORA
                           ACROPOLIS   LYCEUM

ILISSUS
NORTH WALL
SOUTH WALL   CYNOSARGES

PIRAEUS   TO CAPE SUNIUM

PHALERUM WALL

PHALERUM   KM   0   1   2   3

4.

The city was still short of space, however, for its growing administrative needs. Its ruling body, the Assembly, had functioned on the Pnyx since the fifth century. Musical and theatrical celebrations had been removed from the Agora to the southern slopes of the Acropolis where the Odeion and the Theatre of Dionysus were built. Lycurgus continued this decentralization of the Agora and built the Panathenaic Stadium near the river Ilissus. This was a large but essentially simple stadium like all those in Greece at this time. Athletic games were thus taken out of the Agora. It was Lycurgus also who completed the Theatre of Dionysus.

Throughout the third and second centuries B.C. Athens continued to be supreme in its fine public buildings and temples.

Its Roman conquerors, overcome by such glory and majesty, continued the construction of fine buildings and further improved the beauty of the city.

Pausanias, a traveller writing in the second century A.D., has left us a magnificent description of the monuments of Athens in his day, and it is largely thanks to this detailed account that most of them have been identified.

The most brilliant period of Athenian history remains, however, the fifth to the third century B.C., three hundred years which turned the little city of Themistocles, Cimon, Pericles and Lycurgus into the beacon which has guided humanity through all succeeding ages.

Athens survives across the years by her lasting influence on man's spirit, symbolized by those of her monuments which have been preserved to us.

THE EXCAVATIONS OF THE AGORA

The Agora was the heart of Athens, the centre of her life as a city-state, of her politics, culture, trade, recreation, work and play. The daily life of all Athenians evolved in the shadow of her porticoes, on the steps of her temples, along side her imposing monuments, her fountains of clear, cool water.

After the polis *there remained only the memory and the legend. On the ruins created first by the Roman Sulla (86 B.C.) then by the Heruli, a Germanic tribe (c. 267 A.D.), there arose a series of anonymous little houses which have only recently been demolished by the excavator's pick.*

The excavations begun in 1931 by the American School of Classical Studies in Athens have restored our picture of the Agora and enabled us to reconstruct it in model form. In this chapter the Field Director of the American School, Homer A. Thompson, traces the outline history of the famous Athens centre and gives the results of the research work undertaken. The administrative buildings, the courts of justice, schools, gymnasia, works of art, shrines, porticos, objects, documents, both illustrious and anonymous, which have come to light are a contribution of the greatest importance to our knowledge of daily life in the city.

The objects and the documents discovered have provided most of the illustrated material in this book.

The Agora, literally the 'Gathering Place', was centre of community life in Athens as in any Greek city state. Here were concentrated the facilities for civic administration and the law. In both early and late times large gatherings of the citizens for political purposes took place in the Agora. It was the scene of the elections to many public offices; the scene also of ostracism. Before the construction of the permanent theatre of Dionysus plays had been given in the Agora, and before the erection of a regular stadium outside the city athletic meetings had been held in its open spaces. Intermingled with the civic buildings that bordered the Agora were a number of shrines of gods and heroes; the annual festivals connected with these sanctuaries enlivened many a day. In early times the Agora had been the principal market-place of the city. Later, merchants and vendors withdrew to nearby streets and lesser squares, but businessmen continued to meet and to arrange their affairs in the shady colonnades of the Agora. Large public fountain houses on the borders of the Agora were sources both of fresh drinking water and of neighbourhood gossip. From the second century B.C. the south side of the Agora was bordered by the Gymnasium of Ptolemy, one of the five famous seats of higher learning in the city. A concert and lecture hall and a library were added to the Gymnasium in the Roman period; they, like the other facilities of the gymnasium, were available to the citizens at large. Close around the Agora crowded private dwellings; interspersed among them were the shops of metal-workers, sculptors, shoemakers and other craftsmen who chose to make their products as close as possible to the point of sale. Several of the public buildings and temples around the Agora were outstanding examples of the architecture of their time. The paintings and sculpture that adorned these buildings and the monuments that bordered 15 thorough-fares made of the Agora a national gallery in the most literal sense of the term.

Little wonder, therefore, that the Agora was thronged with people whose constant movement was the blood stream surging through the heart of the community. 'Every one of the twenty thousand Athenian citizens', remarks a writer of the 4th century B.C., 'went about the Agora engaged either on public or on private business' (Ps. Demosthenes XXV, 51).

Before we consider the individual departments of community life that were centred in the Agora let us review its history. Already in the time of Solon (c. 600 B.C.) the site had been chosen. It was a wise choice: a gently sloping area, self-drained, easy for building, near the middle of the settlement and conveniently situated on the road that led from the principal gate of the city towards the Acropolis. Development was fitful. The great builders were Cimon in the fifth century, Lycurgus in the fourth, the Hellenistic royal families in the second. Then followed benefactions from the Emperor Augustus and members of his family in the first century B.C. The last monumental construction was a library given by the Emperor Hadrian in the second century A.D.

The Agora, like the rest of the city, was devastated by the Persians in 480-79 B.C. It suffered grievously at the hands of Sulla and his Roman troops in 86 B.C. The final blow was dealt in A.D. 267 by the Heruli, a small band of Goths who descended from the Black Sea.

GENERAL APPEARANCE

The model opposite shows the Agora at the height of its development. The restoration is based on the results of the excavations conducted since 1931 by the American School of Classical Studies. We must imagine the Acropolis rising in the distance. The Agora and the Acropolis, the two focal points in the city plan, were connected by a broad processional road, the Panathenaic Way, that ran diagonally through the square. On the west, i.e. the right side, rose the principal administrative buildings, among them the Bouleuterion, the Tholos, the Metroun and the Royal Stoa. From the hilltop on the far right the marble temple of Hephaestus and Athena (so-called Theseum) overlooked the whole Agora.

The south side of the principal square (upper right) was bordered by the Gymnasium of Ptolemy dating from the second century B.C. The Gymnasium was separated from the Agora proper by the Middle Stoa, a double colonnade that faced both ways. This building is partly concealed by a large auditorium given by M. Vipsanius Agrippa about 15 B.C.; it was entered from the south, i.e. from the side of the Gymnasium.

On the east side (upper left) rose the two-storeyed stoa erected by Attalus II, King of Pergamum, 159-138 B.C.

The north side of the square (lower left) has not yet been excavated. From the ancient authors and from inscriptions we know, however, that this side was closed by two other colonnades, both of the fifth century B.C.: the Stoa Poikile and the Stoa of Hermes.

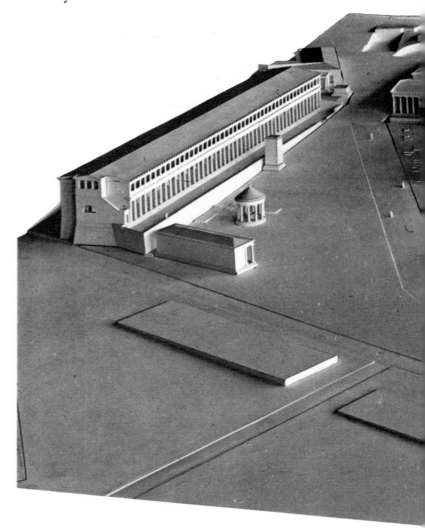

Reconstruction of the Agora and surrounding area as seen in the second century B.C. and based on excavations by the American School of Classical Studies, Athens. The classical part, with additions from the Hellenistic period, is on the right at the foot of the little Hephaestium hill (see also p. 23). This was the site of the public buildings mentioned in this chapter. The background of the Agora was the Acropolis (top left), the Areopagos and the Pnyx (top right), where the popular assemblies met.

Public fountain houses stood at the two upper corners of the square, one of the sixth century B.C. at the south-east corner, and one of the fifth century at the south-west corner.

The once open space within the square came to be crowded with sculptured monuments, altars and temples. Noteworthy among them is the Altar of the Twelve Gods, near the north-west corner of the square; it is recognizable from the surrounding parapet. The enclosure was a place of refuge, an asylum. Because of its prominent and central location it was used also as a point from which to measure distances to places outside Athens. Of interest too is the Temple of Ares that stood near the middle of the square. Built in the fifth century B.C. at Acharnai, a country town of Attica, Ares' temple was transplanted to the Agora in the time of Augustus and re-dedicated to some member of the imperial family. Its resemblance to the Temple of Hephaestus is due to the fact that both were designed by the same architect.

Unlike the Roman Forum, the Agora was never paved. The main thoroughfares were surfaced with gravel. Numerous trees and groves gave the area a park-like aspect: plane trees were planted by the statesman Cimon; a grove of olive and laurel surrounded the Altar of the Twelve Gods; a formal garden bordered the Temple of Hephaestus; certain plants were dedicated to the divinities of the Tholos;

a plane tree stood beside the statue of Demosthenes; a poplar tree was used for the display of public notices. The water needed to maintain the greenery was conveyed in open stone channels that carried the overflow from the public fountain houses down the east and the west sides of the square.

CIVIC ADMINISTRATION

Throughout the long history of the Agora the facilities for administration were concentrated at the south-west corner of the square. The earliest buildings date from the time of Solon (early sixth century B.C.), but many changes and replacements took place before the second century B.C. In that century the group of buildings attained the form that was to persist with little change until the end of the Agora.

The principal administrative buildings were three in number. Most used was the Tholos, a small round structure in which the presiding officers of the Council (*Boule*) had their offices and took their meals. Excavations have brought to light 'barbecue pits' in which the Councillors' meat was broiled, and quantities of their tableware consisting mostly of plain, black-glazed bowls, plates and drinking cups.

The Tholos served also as a bureau of weights and measures; many actual examples have been found

on the site, among them a set of the official standard weights of Athens dating about 500 B.C. Of the Council House (*Bouleuterion*) very little remains, enough however to show that it was a substantial building capable of seating the 500 (later 600) councillors who gathered there for their regular and frequent meetings as the executive body of the Athenian government. The third major building was the Metroun. The name is derived from the Mother of the Gods (meter theon) who was worshipped in the building. In her keeping were deposited the records (on parchment or papyrus) of council meetings and official documents of many other kinds such as copies of treaties, wills and the official versions of the plays of the great tragedians.

In front of the Metroun have been found the remains of the public notice board of Athens. It consisted of a long pedestal on which stood bronze statues of the ten (later twelve) heroes who gave their names to the tribes, i.e. the political subdivisions of the citizen body. The notices were written on gesso-covered tablets (*leukomata*) which were hung on the vertical face of the tall pedestal. A notice pertaining to a particular tribe, e.g. a list of names of men from the tribe who were required to report for military service, would be placed below the hero of that tribe. Among the many other documents here displayed were drafts of newly proposed laws which could thus be studied by all the citizens. The tablets were protected from rain by a projecting cornice and from the fingers of the readers by a fence of chest height.

Around the south-west corner of the square have also been found the ruins of several smaller buildings which served as offices for the boards that administered various departments of civic life: the generals, the public auctioneers, the market controllers, etc. The barracks of the Scythian policemen have not yet been recognized.

In the same general area i.e. around the south-west corner of the square, have been found over 1200 *ostraka*, the potsherds used as ballots in the business of ostracism. On the ballots appear the names of all those outstanding men of the fifth century B.C. who are known to have been voted against as potential dictators (tyrants): Aristeides, Themistocles, Cimon, Pericles, Alcibiades and many others. Having served their purpose the sherds were simply thrown out, or used sometimes for repairing the roads.

LAWCOURTS

Some at least of the many lawcourts known in ancient Athens stood on or close to the Agora. In a delightful passage of a play by Euboulos, a comic poet of the fourth century B.C., all things are said to have been sold together in the same place in Athens:

figs, summoners, grapes, apples, witnesses, roses, honey, lawsuits, myrtle, allotment machines, lambs, water-clocks, laws, indictments.

No building designed as a lawcourt has yet been found, or at least, recognized, in the course of the excavations. On the other hand we know from the ancient authors and inscriptions that the courts sometimes met in other public buildings or sanctuaries, especially those in the Agora. Thus preliminary proceedings in cases concerning impiety which came under the jurisdiction of the King Archon must have been held in the Royal Stoa, among them, probably, the case of Socrates. Fourteen hundred citizens are reported to have been condemned to death in the Stoa Poikile by the Thirty Tyrants in the year 403 B.C. Lawsuits are among the many civic activities that took place in the spacious sanctuary of Theseus along the south side of the Agora. Another of the famous sanctuaries of heroes, the Leocorion, seems also to have been used by the lawcourts in the fourth century B.C. The excavators found among its ruins at the northeast corner of the Agora a number of bronze ballots and other pieces of equipment known to have been used in the courts.

The bronze ballots date from the time of Demosthenes and Aristotle; they correspond precisely with the description by Aristotle in his essay on the Constitution of the Athenians. They are wheel-shaped, of a size to fit in the hand. Some have solid axles for acquittal, some are hollow for condemnation. They were to be held between the fingers in such a way, as Aristotle says, that no one could see which kind was being deposited by the juror in the ballot box.

Among the other furnishings of the lawcourts found in the excavation of the Agora are a number of marble allotment machines (*kleroteria*) used in selecting panels of jurors to serve in the various courts that might be active on a given day. Essential to the working of these machines were bronze identification cards carried by all citizens eligible for jury service; a number of these name-plates have come to light in the Agora.

The most characteristic piece of equipment in the ancient Athenian lawcourt was the water-clock (*klepsydra*) which is mentioned many times by the orators as the device for timing the speeches: so much water for the plaintiff, so much for the defendant. The first actual example of such a timepiece has been found

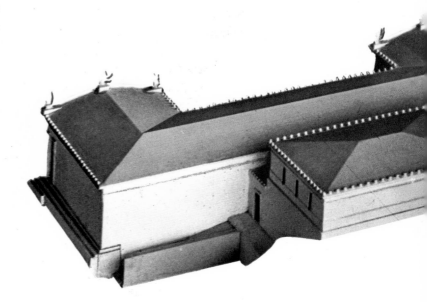

in a well of the late fifth century B.C. at the southwest corner of the Agora. It has the shape of a modern flower pot. A small bronze-lined vent at the bottom could be opened as the speaker began his oration; he could talk only as long as the water ran, three minutes.

EDUCATION

Long before the establishment of formally organized secondary schools or colleges, much informal teaching had been done in Athens. The procedure is known best from the practice of Socrates. This great teacher, as we know from the opening scenes of Plato's dialogues, commonly met with groups of friends and disciples in the homes of well-to-do citizens. Sometimes the setting was the lobby of a palaestra or gymnasium where the young men loitered after their physical exercises. In three cases the place of meeting is given as the Stoa of Zeus (Royal Stoa). Here on the borders of the Agora one could always be sure of a group of listeners. Hence it is little wonder that even after the establishment of regular schools some philosophers continued to frequent the Agora. Diogenes the Cynic in the fourth century B.C., desiring

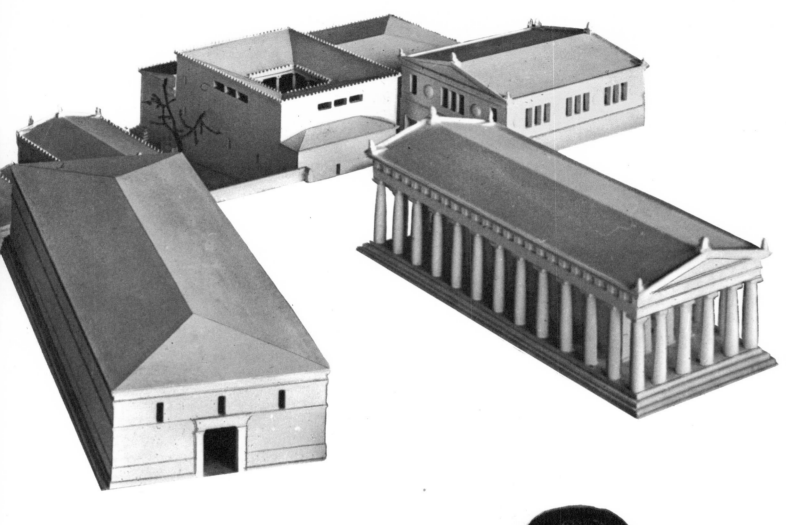

The Stoa of Zeus, the Metroun and the Bouleuterion seen from the little hill of the temple of Hephaestus. The Agora was the city's permanent market and habitual meeting-place of the populace on every occasion. The magistrates and their assistants concerned with the running of the market were to be seen mingling with the crowds. When the Agora was used as a public meeting-place for occasions such as ostracism, it was provided with a wooden surround and entry was strictly controlled on a tribal basis.

33

to demonstrate the virtues of the simple life, took up residence in a large terracotta jar *(pithos)* in the Metroun. In the years around 300 B.C. Zeno, newly come from Cyprus, gathered around him for the discussion of philosophical problems a group that took its name, the Stoic School, from the colonnade where they commonly met, the Stoa Poikile at the north side of the Agora. Even the Apostle Paul when visiting Athens in A.D. 51 resorted to the Agora for his discussions with the Stoics and Epicureans.

In the second century B.C., with the return of peace and prosperity and an expansion of population, there came also a greater demand for higher education. In Athens the many pupils could no longer be accommodated in the three famous gymnasia, the Academy, the Lyceum and Kynosarges, that had been functioning for a long time in the suburbs. Two new gymnasia were established near the middle of the city, and one of these, the Ptolemaion, has recently been recognized at the south side of the main square of the Agora. The establishment took its name from its founder, Ptolemy, King of Egypt. The gymnasium appears to have been set down in an old sanctuary of the hero Theseus, the very embodiment of the Athenian ideal of the athletic and cultivated youth. The close association of hero-sanctuary and gymnasium was in fact normal in ancient Greece. The excavation has shown that the Ptolemaion comprised all the facilities deemed necessary in the Hellenistic world for the training of youth in both athletics and intellectual subjects. A rectangular open space was bordered to north and south by spacious colonnades. Other buildings contained a dressing room, classrooms, drinking fountains, wash rooms, a latrine and a swimming pool. In the inscriptions of the second and first centuries B.C. reference is made repeatedly to 'the library in the Ptolemaion': it was the practice for the class of young men *(ephebes)* at the end of their course to contribute one hundred books to this library.

The gymnasium was intended primarily for the formal training of young men at the expense of the state. But its resources might also be enjoyed by adults, even by visitors from abroad. Thus Cicero *(de Finibus* V, 1) tells of an occasion when he and a small group of friends listened to a lecture in the Ptolemaion by Antiochus, then head of the Academy; in the afternoon the group strolled out to the Academy because it was free of crowds at that time of day.

The popularity of outstanding lecturers in this period was doubtless the reason for the addition of the large auditorium built by the Roman Agrippa about the year 15 B.C. The auditorium was set against the north side of the old gymnasium exactly on the axis of the Agora. Philostratus *(Vitae Sophistarum)* describes two occasions when famous visiting sophists lectured in this building before audiences consisting largely of high-spirited students.

With the passage of time more library space was needed. It was provided, about 100 A.D., through the construction of a new building directly across the Panathenaic Way from the old one. The dedicatory inscription informs us that the new library was a contribution from Titus Flavius Pantainous, one of a distinguished Athenian family. A library notice inscribed on a marble tablet reads: 'No book shall be removed for we have sworn an oath. Open from the first hour till the sixth'. Doodles on the marble columns of the building are doubtless the work of student readers.

The Gymnasium shared the general destruction of 267 A.D. After a century and a half of desolation it was rebuilt on the same site but in the modern manner with three cloistered courtyards and a comfortable bath. In this form it continued in use until the schools of Athens were closed by order of the Emperor Justinian in 529; so persistent was the tradition of higher education in this part of the city.

ART IN THE AGORA

The group of buildings that eventually enclosed the Agora exhibit a pleasing variety in period, scale and architectural order. Several of them were among the best of their kind in the Greek world. Thus the Temple of Hephaestus (the so-called Theseum), which happens to be the best preserved of all Greek temples, is also an admirable example of Doric sacred architecture in its finest period. Though much smaller than the contemporary Parthenon, it bears comparison with that more famous neighbour in respect of craftsmanship, material and the beauty of its sculptural adornment.

The Royal Stoa, erected in the late fifth century B.C. at the north-west corner of the square, has its two ends bent forward at right angles and treated like temple façades. As the first known instance of this

The Odeion, a late construction on the Agora. It was the only covered building available for musical performances. (Agora Museum, Athens).

ingenious design, the Athenian building was repeatedly copied or adapted in other cities of the Greek world.

The huge stoas erected in the second century B.C. along the south and east sides of the main square were each remarkable in its own way. The first was unusual in being divided by a screen wall down the middle so as to serve both the main square and the Gymnasium of Ptolemy. It was only a single storey in height but of great length: 146 metres. Apart from its marble metopes this stoa was all of limestone. The stoa on the east side was smaller in ground plan, being only 116.5 metres in length. But it rose two storeys in height, and each storey contained twenty-one shops behind a double colonnade. The façade was all of marble. One can scarcely doubt that the royal family of Pergamum who contributed this eastern stoa were deliberately trying to outdo their old rivals, the Ptolemies of Egypt, who were responsible for the southern stoa and the Gymnasium. Both the

Hellenistic buildings were to be overshadowed by the great lecture hall built by the Roman Agrippa.

Mention has been made of the rich sculptural adornment of the Temple of Hephaestus. Enough has survived to indicate that the pedimental groups of the temple as well as its outer and inner friezes were all devoted to the glorification of the heroes Heracles and Theseus. The parapet that protected the Altar of the Twelve Gods was adorned with marble tablets sculptured in relief, one to either side of each of the two entrances. Many copies of these reliefs have been recognized. The themes of all four are of a tragic nature: the parting of Orpheus and Eurydice; the daughters of Peleus about to boil their father; Heracles parting from the Hesperides; Heracles, Theseus and Peirithous in Hades. It has been conjectured that the sad atmosphere of the reliefs inspired the name by which the shrine appears to have been known in later times: the Altar of Pity. The very number of the copies indicates that the original reliefs were among the most popular works of their kind.

In addition to such architectural sculpture the Agora was forested with free-standing statues: figures of gods, goddesses and heroes, portraits of outstanding statesmen, generals and men of letters. Perhaps most famous of all was the bronze group of Harmodius and Aristogiton, the two young men who rid the city of the tyrant Hipparchus in 514 B.C. Erected soon after the deed, the original group was carried off by the Persians in 479 B.C. A substitute group was made and put up a few years later. A century and a half thereafter the originals were found in Persia and sent back to Athens by Alexander the Great or one of his generals. Thenceforward the two groups stood together in the Agora until the final disaster. Copies from the Roman period exist, but of the original there remains only a small scrap from the pedestal inscribed with an epigram.

Painting too was splendidly represented in the buildings of the Agora. Especially noteworthy were two series of mural by the leading painters of the second quarter of the fifth century B.C.: Polygnotus (fl.c. 475-445), Mikon and Panainos, the brother of Phidias (B.C. 500). The first series adorned, and indeed gave its name to, the Stoa Poikile (the Painted Stoa), on the north side of the square. This series comprised four battle scenes, two mythical (the Greeks at Troy, the Athenians versus the Amazons) and two historical (Marathon and Oinoe). The other series was spread over three walls of the Sanctuary of Theseus, a fifth century building that was later incorporated in the Gymnasium of Ptolemy. Here the themes were all appropriate to the hero Theseus: (1) the battle between the Athenians (led by Theseus) and the Amazons; (2) the battle between the Lapiths and the Centaurs in which Theseus assisted his Lapith friend Pirithous; (3) Theseus proving his descent from Poseidon by recovering a ring from the bottom of the sea. Of all these paintings not a scrap has survived. Those in the Stoa Poikile were executed on gesso-covered wooden tablets and are reported to have been carried off by some proconsul by 400 A.D. The fate of the other series is quite unknown. We depend for our knowledge of the paintings on brief accounts by Pausanias and on a score of references in various ancient authors. From the tone of these passages it is clear that the works were venerated as ' old mas-

ters '; because of their patriotic themes they also came to be regarded in the nature of ' national monuments '.

The fourth century school of painting was well illustrated by a set of murals in the Royal Stoa. These were the work of Euphranor (fl.c. 360 B.C.), one of the leading Athenian artists of his time. Here again the paintings themselves have vanished, and we depend chiefly on a couple of paragraphs in Pausanias, author of a ' Description of Hellas ', second century A.D. In this series, too, as in the Stoa Poikile, there was a piquant combination of the heroic and the historical. In one panel Theseus was represented together with Democracy and the People of Athens; another pane showed the Battle of Mantinea (362 B.C.) with enough realism to permit the identification of the leaders on either side. On another wall were painted the Twelve Gods.

All these noble works of architecture, sculpture and painting were freely accessible for the enjoyment of all the citizens at all times. They were equally accessible to the artists and craftsmen who lived and worked in the immediate environs of the Agora. The excavations have brought to light the remains of many workshops for the making of statues in bronze, marble and terra-cotta and for the working of metal. They have also yielded evidence of potters' shops; this is not surprising, since the Agora lay in the district known as the Ceramicus, the Potters' Quarter. Here in fact were produced the black-figured and red-figured pottery that was the chief glory of Greek ceramics. It is noteworthy that the later sculpture and the minor arts produced in Athenian workshops frequently betray the influence of the sculpture and paintings on the buildings of the Agora. And a whole generation of Athenian vase painters was deeply affected by the mural paintings of the Stoa Poikile and the Theseum. Nor should it be forgotten that the many illuminating comments which Plato makes both on works of art and on artistic technique were inspired by his everyday contact with these same masterpieces and not less by his observation of the artists whose studios stood close around the Agora.

SHRINES AND FESTIVALS

The Athenian Agora was shared almost equally by gods and men. The excavations have shown that at the height of its development there were a half

The Eliea lawcourt and, in the background, the so-called ' middle Stoa ' dating from the Hellenistic period. Colonnades were a feature of the Agora and permitted citizens of all classes to stroll about or stand and talk at any time of the year, regardless of the sun or the rain.

dozen substantial temples within or close to it: Hephaestus and Athena, Apollo Patrous, Ares and Athena, Demeter, and the south-east and south-west temples of which the divinities are not surely known. Certain important cults were centred on altars unaccompanied by buildings. Such was the sanctuary of the Twelve Gods, the parapet of which has been described above. The altar was founded by the younger Pisistratus in 521 B.C. Fragments of the actual altar and of the stone enclosure wall have come to light and the identification is confirmed by an inscribed dedication found *in situ.* Another altar without temple was that of Zeus Agoraius which has been identified with probability in an imposing marble altar in front of the Metroun. Almost every public building, moreover, sheltered one or more cults: Zeus Eleutherius in the Royal Stoa, the Mother of the Gods in the Metroun, Zeus and Athena in the Bouleuterion, Apollo, Artemis and the Phosphoroi in the Tholos, the hero Strategos in the Strategeum.

Heroes and heroines also received much attention in the Agora. The excavations have produced evidence of the cult of the dead at several points. These local cults were probably associated with some of the early tombs (fifteenth-sixth century B.C.) of which more than two hundred have been found below the classical levels of the Agora. They were no doubt maintained chiefly by individual families, and they flourished especially in the seventh and sixth centuries B.C.

Of all the hero sanctuaries known in the area the most famous was that of Theseus, adjacent to the south side of the square. Theseus was worshipped here, as commonly in Greek cities, in his capacity as hero-founder of the city. According to Athenian tradition it was Theseus who brought about the union of the twelve old communities which resulted in the city state of Athens. In 475 B.C., on the advice of the Delphic oracle, the Athenians brought back the bones of the hero from Skyros where he had died, and for the protection of the relics erected an enclosure within the old sanctuary. On the walls of this enclosure were executed the famous set of paintings described above. Theseus made his ample sanctuary available for many civic purposes. Elections to certain offices were held there. The area was used occasionally for meetings of the Council and for lawsuits.

It was a regular place of asylum, and in an emergency in 415 B.C. it was used as a place of bivouac. Finally, in the second century B.C., much of the area was taken over for the Gymnasium of Ptolemy, but the sanctity of the place persisted.

Annual observances of some sort must have been held in connection with each of these many sanctuaries. Here we are dependent on the evidence of ancient authors and inscriptions which shed tantalizing rays of light on only a few. We are particularly fortunate in the case of the festival of Theseus. A series of ten inscriptions dating from the middle of the second century B.C. gives us many details about the programme of the annual festival, the Theseia. The festival extended over several days and comprised a procession, a sacrifice, a long roster of musical, gymnastic and equestrian contests, and torch races. In earlier days the festival included also a feast in which all the citizens shared at the cost of the state.

Another of the most colourful events connected with the Agora was the passage of the Panathenaic Procession on its way from the Dipylon gate to the Acropolis. This event formed part of the national festival *par excellence*, the Panathenaia, and as such was incorporated in the frieze of the Parthenon. The procession in all its splendour, including priests, magistrates, servitors, sacrificial animals, chariots and horsemen, was seen to best advantage in its diagonal course through the Agora. Here it could be viewed by thousands of citizens, and it was no doubt in part for their convenience that the two huge stoas erected in the second century B.C. were related to the line of the procession in such a way that their broad terraces commanded an excellent view.

LIFE IN THE STOAS

The most striking feature in the plan of the Athenian Agora is the prominence of the stoas, the colonnaded buildings that bordered the square. Nor would any account of the life that went on in this place be complete without some reference to the role played by these buildings.

The basic concept of a stoa is a roof supported on one side by a solid wall, on the other side by a row of columns. Such a structure provided a maximum amount of shelter from the elements at minimum cost. With stoas facing on the square from north, south, east and west the *habitué*, by moving from one to the other, could find comfort at any season of the year, any hour of the day. In winter he would aim at shelter from the wind, exposure to the sun; in summer the reverse. Since the building type was ideally suited to Mediterranean conditions it enjoyed a very long vogue. The basic design remained constant. The scale, however, grew larger: the later stoas are commonly so wide as to require an inner row of columns and, as property values rose, a second storey was sometimes added. Occasionally a row of rooms was placed behind the colonnade to serve as shops or offices. Furthermore the material tended to become richer; marble commonly supplanted limestone in the facades of the later stoas. Some of the Athenian examples, as we have seen, were remarkable also for the splendour of their mural decoration.

The primary function of the stoa was to provide a comfortable setting for the informal social intercourse that has always characterized town life in the Mediterranean. We may illustrate with a brief summary of what is known about just one of the many stoas of the Agora.

The Stoa Poikile still lies deeply buried, yet scores of references in the ancient authors make it seem the most familiar public building of Athens. As the earliest of the stoas in the Agora the Poikile was given the best location; the southern exposure was advantageous in both summer and winter. Reference has been made to the famous murals, the most prominent of which was the Battle of Marathon, a natural choice for the first large public building to be erected in Athens after the repulse of the Persians. Houses and apartment houses stood close to the back of the Stoa. Statues, among them a portrait of Solon, rose in front. The building was sometimes used by the law-courts, and for public arbitration. Proclamations were made here at the time of the Eleusinian festival of Demeter. The building is perhaps best known as the resort of that school of philosophy which took its very name from the Stoa. But still earlier it had been frequented by the Cynic philosopher Crates (*fl. c.* 325 B.C.) who is reported to have embarrassed his pupils by practising a very simple way of life in this very public place.

These few samplings, will perhaps illustrate how, the Agora shaped the political, religious, intellectual, and artistic aspects of life in ancient Athens.

HOUSES AND FURNISHING

In common with other men of ancient times, the Athenian had a very different idea from his modern descendant of what constituted ' home sweet home '. He was used to spending his days out, in the bustle of the Agora, on the temple steps, in the countryside, in a workshop or by the sea, intent on his labours or in pursuit of recreation. The small rooms of his house, often blackened by smoke, closed to the narrow twisting street outside and opening only on to an inner yard for light and air, were really the province of the woman, the smaller children and the slaves. Houses in Classical Athens were for the most part modest dwellings of one or two storeys, cheaply built from poor or even makeshift materials forming an anonymous, uneven patchwork of roofs, broken by indeterminate narrow alleys and overlooked by the architectural miracle of the Acropolis. The Agora, with its porticos and temples, stood almost like an island in the middle of the city.

The rich men's houses were built later and then on the outskirts and in the more picturesque parts of the surrounding countryside. These were spacious buildings, often of elegant taste, with a wide peristyle, adorned with porticoes, gardens and fountains. The Romans were to reproduce them faithfully in Italy and in other Mediterranean lands, and they are preserved for us almost intact by the ashes of Vesuvius, in the Pompeii of 79 A.D.

For centuries, building in the Athenian style meant throwing up new dwelling-houses next to existing ones, without any thought of planning or sense of order which might have brought some respite to the growing sprawl of the old city. Even in a later period the Pseudo-Dichearcus could call the huge area of the city squalid: ' Athens is arid, waterless and, because of its age, badly designed. At first sight a foreign visitor might find it hard to believe that this was once the cradle of what we now call the city of the Athenians '.

The streets in the residential quarters of classical Athens were narrow, irregular and, at least in some parts, evil-smelling. The habit of depositing filth in the streets was one of the worst features of city life and the cause of dangerous epidemics. The houses leaned out with bare walls, interrupted here and by the entrance to a small workshop. There were few passers-by and few voices were heard except at certain times of the day. The men of Athens spent their days out in the bustling Agora and, on certain occasions, in the solemn temples on the Acropolis. Neither their houses nor the narrow streets in which they stood formed an important part of their environment.

The Greek house was a closed world: its only communication with the outside being through a single door, generally to be found at the back. Very occasionally there was an opening in the wall, but this bore very little resemblance to a window. It was typically the house of a man who spent all the day outside, but who guarded jealously within the private world of his family and possessions. Within its four walls lived, or rather was compelled to live, the housewife, the ' enthroned slave ' of Athenian tradition. She was by custom required to take no interest in the world outside.

The writers of the time were very explicit on this point. Aristophanes, speaking of unfaithful wives,

Front entrance of an Athenian house (detail from a reconstruction in the Piraeus National Museum).

classed them with those women who show their faces out of doors. The women, the children under school age and the slaves, both male and female, all spent their day inside the house or, in fine weather, in the courtyard behind. In wet or cold weather they stayed in the rooms overlooking the courtyard, where it was light.

There were very few possibilities of escape from the monotony of this kind of daily life for wives or daughters of marriageable age, even if they were still very young.

HOUSES

Xenophon emphasized the logical construction of a house of his period: ' It is not painted in different colours; the rooms are conceived with the precise purpose of accomodating, in the most functional manner, the objects they are required to contain. The result is that every room seems to await the furnishings destined for it. The most secluded room is naturally that of the master of the house, designed to contain his most precious belongings: cover and fine clothes perhaps. The driest room will contain the corn, the coolest the wine, the lightest the more fragile objects and those which are to be seen, then... the living rooms, furnished with taste, cool in summer and warm in winter. The entire house faces south, thus catching the sun in winter and the shade in summer. The women's apartment is separated from the men's by a solid door fitted with a lock... '. Xenophon goes on further about houses built facing south, emphasizing the advantages but pointing out that they should have the southern wall higher than the northern.

The author is admittedly speaking here about a house built for a middle-class Athenian, decorous and

Two typical buildings from the Classical period with a little garden (Model in the Royal Ontario Museum, Toronto).

suited to a person of considerable means. Of the ten thousand or so homes in the city at this period, most were much less comfortable: some were no more than holes in the rock, like the one which came to be called ' Socrates' prison ', others were rickety constructions with few rooms built on insecure foundations on roughly levelled rock. In such districts the thieves were called ' wall-piercers ', this being their most frequent mode of entry.

In the central sector of the city, houses were of modest proportions, with one or two storeys, either of stone or of clay and covered with tiles or mud-bound thatch. Towards the outskirts, however, things were different. Here, in the quiet open spaces were to be found the houses of the upper-class Athenians, built according to the needs of a Greek family, and more complex in design.

Many houses in Athens were let to one or more families at rents which often made considerable de-mands on the tenants' incomes. Rents in Greece in general were fairly modest in the small towns, but in the cities, and in Athens in particular, they were high because of the concentration of comparative wealth and the constantly increasing number of foreign residents.

Like other ancient houses in many areas of the Mediterranean countries, the Greek house took its air and light from an inner courtyard surrounded by a short arcade. Generally the several rooms within the house were not intercommunicating: each was reached separately from the courtyard, which also contained the household's store of water.

From the outside the house formed a cube of walls almost without any openings. The Athenian had no concept of a window as we know it: indiscreet glances on to the outside world and desperate escapes from the house, such as might occur in Greek comedy, all happened normally through the roof.

A fundamental characteristic of the Athenian house was the clear separation of the women's quarters *(gynaikeion)* from the men's *(androkeion)*.

In two-storeyed houses, which were common nearer the central sectors, the wife, daughters and maidservants usually all slept upstairs, access to which was by a steep and difficult ladder. These were similar to the one described in a speech written by Lysias, a lawyer and orator living in the time of Plato (*c.* 427-348 B.C.): ' I have to say that my small house also has an upper storey. The arrangement of the rooms is the same both upstairs and down for the *gynaikeion* and the *androkeion*. Then a child is born and the mother

Late in the Classical period wealthy Athenian citizens began to build sumptuous houses on the outskirts of the city and the number of these increased in the Hellenistic

begins to feed it... every time she has to bath it she has to come downstairs and is in danger of falling down the ladder. I decided, therefore, to move upstairs myself and put the women on the ground floor'. The upper storey was not always a proper floor, however, corresponding in area to that downstairs as in the case above. Often it was a mere extension

period. They opened on to gardens adorned with porticoes, fountains and plants. The Romans were to copy them for their country villas in the various Mediterranean lands, and some can still be seen in Pompeii. Above: the House of the Vettii, Pompeii.

upwards of certain rooms on the ground floor which the family found indispensable to its daily needs.

Downstairs the meals were taken, guests were received and the most frequently used utensils were stored within easy reach. Often there was no room for the slaves, who were then compelled to sleep in the courtyard in the summer and in the dining room in winter.

The beds were often simple couches which could easily be moved, and there seems to have been no room used exclusively for sleeping.

The capacity of a Greek house was calculated on the number of beds, or rather sleeping-places, it contained. This was common enough to be applied to other things and Pericles, who had a very long head,

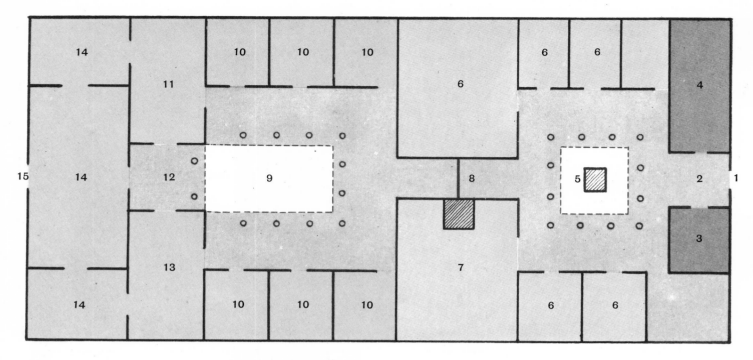

Plan of a late Greek house after Vitruvius: 1. *Door.* 2. *Atrium.* 3. *Caretaker's room.* 4. *Stable.* 5. *Courtyard with peristyle.* 6. *Men's quarters.* 7. *Megaron with fireplace.* 8. *Door or gate of the gynaikeion.* 9. *Gynaikeion peristyle.* 10. *Women's quarters.* 11. *Bedroom of the master and mistress of the house.* 12. *Open room.* 13. *Daughters' bedroom.* 14. *Rooms for various uses.* 15. *Garden gate.*

Vitruvius, who is thought to have lived in the age of Augustus, collected in his ' De Architectura ' a mass of information on all types of buildings of his own and the preceding ages. It is a work of inestimable value.

was described by his enemies as ' the man with the eleven-bed cranium '.

The courtyard also housed the hens and the dog, and many Athenians also kept pigs, even in the most crowded areas.

These are clearly not the houses which the Romans took as models for their villas. The richer Athenian families generally had their houses built around two courtyards surrounded by porticos *(peristilii)*, the men occupying the rooms nearest the street, and the women those facing the courtyard. The *androkeion* and the *gynaikeion* were again strictly segregated by a door or a solid grille.

If the rooms surrounding either courtyard had been extended upwards, this would have been to provide accommodation for the slaves.

In a Greek house of this type examined by Vitruvius, the Roman architect of the mid-first century B.C., the men's quarters were reached by a passageway leading from the porter's lodge to the stables. Around the courtyard, under the porticos, were several rooms for the sons, guests and slaves, and in the

large room for the men, the *megaron*, there was a fireplace. The latter was the living room, where feasts and banquets took place: it was also the finest room in the house.

Opening on to the side porticos of the *gynaikeion* in the second courtyard, were the rooms where the women spent the day, and on to the end portico opened the large bedroom for the husband and wife and smaller rooms for the unmarried daughters. These bedrooms led into the large rooms where male slaves lived.

Taking into account the local variations and adaptations, the remains of Pompeii give a very good idea of what Greek houses were like in Classical Athens.

What has been said above would appear to indicate the importance to the Greeks of the *gynaikeion*, especially in what we might define as the average-size family house. It was here where the women lived and spent almost the whole of the day, and where also the master of the house slept frequently. How frequently, or infrequently, can be guessed from numerous references, especially in the comedies of the period, to the fact that not all Athenian men considered it their duty to spend every night in the matrimonial bedroom. Strepsiades, for example in *The Clouds* (423 B.C.) by Aristophanes, slept with the servants and the sons of the house in a room in the *androkeion*. The *gynaikeion* was, in a word, a closed area in that very private restricted world of the Greek house, rigorously protected from all eyes except those of the head of the family, which explains why respectable ladies were able to wear, in the privacy of their own rooms and secluded from any prying glances, those short flimsy tunics which were worn publicly only by another type of woman. In far-away Sparta these tunics were taken as the symbol of woman's healthy emancipation.

The women's quarters were, from an architectual point of view, the most refined in the house. Floors there were tiled wherever possible, or paved, even in houses where the remaining floors were of beaten earth or mortar. The walls were plastered and sometimes painted.

The *gynaikeion* was the province of the woman of the house, and also the home of the very young children and their nurses.

Marble, bronze, mosaics and stucco work were virtually unknown in Athenian houses in the classical age. They gradually made their appearance in the houses of the very rich in a later period, and certainly not before the fourth century B.C. It was, however, customary to decorate the walls of houses with pictorial motifs and to brighten up the rooms with colour.

The fact that Xenophon, in the passage quoted above, says that a certain house was not painted seems to prove that many others were, and not that painting was exceptional, as some have supposed.

PUBLIC SERVICES

Athens had a poor water supply and many houses had no well or any equipment for raising water. Stopping for water at fountains, a common subject for vase decoration, was a necessary daily task for a people who cared considerably about personal hygiene. There were indeed public baths, built at the expense of the city or of private individuals, but to go there often made one the target of criticism. ' The common

The amis, which could be of terracotta or of metal. (Agora Museum, Athens).

people may go to the baths but not the better classes ' was a saying attributed, but probably wrongly, to Xenophon. There the poor world go in search of warmth. Besides, the upper classes were not in the least prepared for it. ' What good would it do *you* to go to the baths ? You would only burn yourself ', says a character in Aristophanes' allegorical play *Plutus*.

Respectable women never set foot in the women's baths and even a refined *hetaera* (courtesan) such as Phryne kept well away from a place considered to be the rendezvous of prostitutes.

Bathing was therefore done at home, in the most suitable place, and wherever possible there was one particular room reserved for this purpose. It was scarcely bathing as we know it, however, as we see from Attic comedy, in which baths and kitchens are frequently connected because of the problem of heating the water.

In Aristophanes' play *The Wasps*, Philocleon, a foolish father who has taken refuge in the kitchen,

Chair, stool and footrest reconstructed from archaeological findings and vase paintings. The chair was copied from the Grave Stele of Hegeso in the National Museum, Athens, and the stool from a detail on the Parthenon frieze. (Saridis Replicas, Athens).

is thereby suspected by his son of trying to escape from the house 'down the bath plug'. This latter must have been some rudimentary kind of drain. The equipment of a bath-house consisted merely of recipients for the water. It was virtually impossible to immerse the whole body, so that one had either a partial bath or had water poured over one by a slave: the shower method had been practised in Greece since the end of the Homeric age.

A slave or close friend or relative would climb on to a stool and pour buckets full of water over the person to be washed. In the poorer houses, where the floor was often rudimentary or where there was no means of draining away the water, the shower must have presented something of a problem.

The kitchen has already been mentioned. In many families the preparation of food and the washing of the crockery took place in the same part of the house where one washed and bathed. Given the rudimentary ventilation system in Greek houses of the period, it can be easily imagined that walls and ceilings of the smaller dwellings were blackened with smoke, even though, as seems to have been often the case, the fire was actually lit outside and only the burning embers were carried indoors for use in the stoves or small ovens. When the weather permitted, the whole meal was cooked in the courtyard.

Sanitation can hardly have been any better than ventilation. The lavatory was a cramped little room half hidden in the courtyard with a rudimentary seat or, failing this, a ceramic or metal chamber pot, the *amis*. It was not unknown, however, for people to use the secluded corners or a garden or, particularly at night, the streets.

Three-legged tables as generally used in banquets: guests usually ate reclining and each had one of these nearby. The round table is copied from a vase painting in the National Museum, Naples, and the rectangular one from an Attic pitcher in a private collection in Milan. (Saridis Replicas, Athens).

FURNISHINGS

The functional characteristic of Greek domestic architecture noted above by Xenophon is reflected also in the furniture found in the houses of the middle class.

It was natural that importance should be given to the safe-keeping of objects of value, from jewellery to clothing and coverings. The latter were kept in special chests, rather like bench-lockers, at the bottom of which the housewife would lay specially treated fruit. This custom was of very ancient origin, and the fruit most commonly used, the quince, gave a lasting odour to the clothes stored in the chest. It is still customary today, in certain country districts, to store freshly laundered linen with sprigs of aromatic herbs. The chests — the term is purely generic and covers a wide range of shapes and sizes — often came into the household as part of the bride's dowry or as a wedding-gift.

48

Certain wedding-gifts were particularly welcome, especially ceramic objects, not only the *lebeti*, elegant nuptial vases over eighteen inches high and minutely decorated with scenes from history or legend, but also the water-jars, large bowls and amphorae of all kinds which all had a practical as well as a decorative function. The decoration and the craftsmanship were often of a high order.

The *lebeti* had a truncated cone base with a rounded two-handled top fitted with a splendid lid.

The Greek ceramic industry, the most ancient industry to use fire, provided for daily use the most surprising and useful objects which today we are used to manufacturing with other materials: small tables, gratings, stoves, little chairs for children and many other things.

With the linen-chest mentioned above the most important piece of furniture in the master bedroom was the bed. This was very different from the simple easily-moved couches in the *androkeion* provided for the slaves and the young men of the household. In-teresting illustrations of the marriage-bed, and particularly of its decoration, are to be found on vases. It had four solid legs, often carved in the upper parts in the shape of a capital, on which was fastened the frame, generally of strong leather straps. Its particular value lay in the coverings, cushions and in many cases exotic animal skins spread over it.

Wood was the most commonly used material in furnishings. One type of bed was the couch used at banquets, which allowed the user to lie at full length or to sit partially upright.

The Athenians were accustomed to occasional sumptuous meals, or to gatherings at which they spent most of their time reclining. We reproduce a typical piece of furniture used for this purpose reconstructed by T. H. Robsjohn-Gibbings, to whom we are also indebted for the other pieces shown on these pages. These reproductions were made from vase paintings and other archaeological evidence.

The guest, reclining on his couch, had at his side a small table for dishes and wine-cups.

Banquet divan copied from a design on a red-figured drinking-cup discovered at Spina. In addition to cushions, the Greeks also used animal skins, either to cover chairs or as rugs. (Saridis Replicas, Athens).

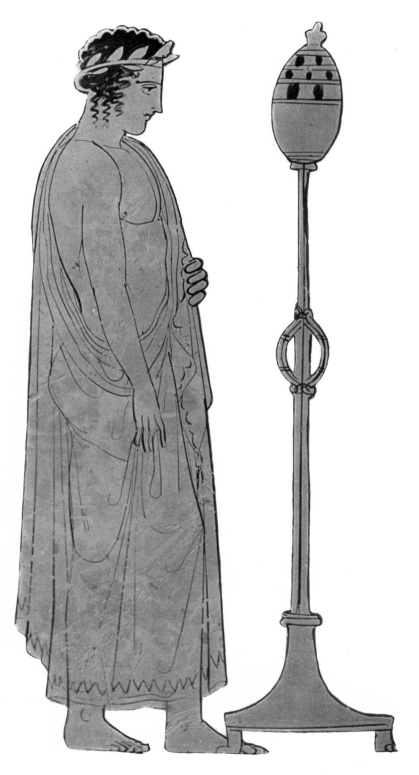

Amongst the ornaments in Athenian houses, especially in the wealthier ones, were incense burners and lebeti. The latter, often the work of skilled craftsmen, were especially elegant and amongst the more important wedding-gifts. (National Museum, Ferrara).

But the couch was not the only piece of furniture used at mealtimes. Greek houses were full of chairs and stools of various styles which could be moved from room to room, from indoors to outside in the courtyard, according to the weather and the season. Some were simple, others were carved and decorated. For sitting down to eat, a small table and a cube of wood with a cushion on it were sufficient, but one type of stool which was in common use had legs, straight or curved, crossing in the middle on a pivot to form an X-shape. The seat was often a stretched skin, so that the stool, which was very light, could be folded up and carried even out of doors.

The more classical style of chair with a curved back, shaped to rest the body in comfort, and with legs curving outwards, was intended mainly for the women of the Greek household, and also for persons of some importance in society. On vases it is this type of chair on which the Gods sit. The comfort and appearance of the chair were often enhanced by the addition of cushions and animal skins.

Every household had its tables, round or square, made of wood, bronze or even marble, of various sizes, almost always three-legged. There was virtually no other kind of furniture on which objects could be placed even temporarily.

Apart from chests which held clothes and precious objects, the Greeks' only furniture consisted of tables and chairs. Of these, however, there was a great variety, from the luxurious chair, carved and decorated like a throne, as on the vase painting opposite, to the simplest bench. The folding stool (above), with its seat of animal skin, was copied by Saridis of Athens from one shown on a bronze buckler in the State Museum, Berlin.

The typical furnishings of an Athenian house in the classical period were therefore beds, tables, stools, chairs and ceramics vases. Some of the wealthier houses contained vases of precious or semi-precious metal, and great bronze braziers, splendidly worked, which gradually superseded the hearth, traditionally to be found in the largest room of the *androkeion*.

The citizen who had no banquet to attend or other function to occupy his evening would retire to bed early. There was, moreover, only the scantiest illumination anywhere. Anyone having to go out into the streets at night used a torch of strips of smoky resinous wood to light his way, while indoors a small terracotta lamp was carried about with two or three burners consisting of wick dipped in oil.

Rooms were lit by oil lamps or by more costly wax candles; on special occasions, such as banquets or other important gatherings, torches were used. Candles and torches were placed in holders which were sometimes elaborately worked.

DRESS IN THE CLASSICAL AGE

In Athens, as in the rest of Greece, the tailor, as we know him today, did not exist. The weaver simply supplied the pieces of cloth or linen from which, with a few stitches and some pins, the women made the clothing both for themselves and their menfolk. This is not to say, however, that with clothing limited to bare essentials people were never elegantly dressed.

It is perhaps because of their deportment or their natural inclination towards elegance that the figures depicted on vases, reliefs and statues, which are the best source of our information about the period, always seem to be men and women dressed, adorned and shod with exquisite yet modest taste. Even so, they occasionally appear to be striving for some originality with the wealth of their pleats, the fullness of their drapery, or the weight, the lightness or the transparency of their material.

The Athenian's lifelong dedication to the achievement of restraint and proportion is expressed in the straight lines of the sack garment, in the folds of the cloak, in the shoes, the adornment, and the jewels.

Among the tasks of the women, who were responsible for the care of the family possessions and the organization of the housework, that of caring for the clothing was not the easiest. The Athenian changed his clothes according to the occasion and the calendar. The housewife's task was therefore not a light one. It was not merely a question of protecting the best clothing from moths (this was done with the aid of pepper pods) but much of the clothing had to be frequently washed. Water was scarce and the queues at fountains and in the wash-houses presented a major problem to the housewife and the female servants.

The Greeks were accustomed to smearing their limbs with grease for their daily exercises in the gymnasium and the women made extensive use of perfumed oils to protect their skins from the use of soda and ashes in cleaning. Frequent laundering was therefore a necessity.

There was clothing to suit every occasion: military habits, gym tunics, solemn ceremonial robes for both men and women, tunics to wear out in the street and short dresses worn by the women indoors or before retiring to bed. In fact it was only within the intimacy of her own house that the married woman would allow herself to be feminine and attractive.

The courtesans, the dancers and the women flute-players were obliged by their calling to change clothes frequently, and thinking and talking about what they would wear and what was new occupied a great part of their daily lives.

CLOTHES

Nowadays it is the cut of our clothes which we consider most important: in ancient times, even for those who dressed most elegantly, cutting material to a particular shape was unknown.

The dress was a long wide rectangle of cloth which could be sewn in parts or drawn in to the shape of the body by a belt or by pins known as fibulas. It was therefore important that the cloth should be well woven and decorated but even more important that the wearer should bear himself elegantly. The rules for draping the material over the body were very detailed, and seen complicated to us. Their explanation will require a certain amount of patience from the reader.

Peasants and manual workers generally wore the *exomis*, a very light, loose garment, pinned up only on the left shoulder and allowing the greatest freedom of movement. It was in effect the simplest form of tunic, usually of dark wool of inferior quality, and was the simplest version of the traditional Greek dress, the *chiton*, worn by men and, with certain modifications, also by women. This too was fastened on the left shoulder, or on both, with fibulas or gatherings, and had the shape of a bottomless sack.

The *chiton* was held in at the waist by a girdle, which allowed the upper part of the garment to stand out in a series of folds called the *kolpos* (breast). A military version had a second girdle, the *zoster*, worn much higher, which allowed a second *kolpos*. When the girdle was loosened the garment became a night-shirt. The *chiton* was widely used in the classical period. In more ancient times, when the Ionian fashion prevailed, many Greeks, especially the aristocrats, wore a long tunic which sometimes had a train with abundant folds. This tunic survived in ceremonial usage, when it was worn by priests, lute-players and competitors in public games.

There was a long *chiton*, called the *chiton podere* ('reaching down to the feet'), and a short one which was only knee-length. The former was often worn by people most frequently in the public eye, such as priests, and on certain occasions by women; the latter was more popular among the ordinary people and among young men, who often wore it without a girdle.

Over the *exomis* or the *chiton* the Athenians wore a cloak, of which there were several kinds: the solemn, rich wide cloak of fine decorated cloth (the *lope* or the *clana*) and the short modest one known as the *himation*.

Whereas the *chiton* and the *exomis* were white or cream-coloured, the cloak was purple, blue, violet, saffron yellow, olive green or of multicoloured stripes. Draping the cloak was no simple matter, and a well-draped one lent a person elegance and style. First of all it was laid over the back and shoulders with the corners left hanging over the front, then with the right arm outstretched the folds were passed over the

Male dress consisted of a tunic (chiton), fastened back on one or both shoulders, and a cloak (himation). They were substantially two rectangles of material adapted to the shape of the body by fibulas, laces or buttons. Sometimes the cloak only was worn. It was common to take up the loose cloth under the armpit on a stick fitted with a cross-piece (Statue of Aesculapius, National Museum, Athens).

left arm and shoulder so that they fell over the back. This the Athenians called 'draping on the right', an action which consisted of taking the hem of the cloak in the right hand, then with the right arm outstretched throwing it over the left shoulder. The accomplishment of this gesture was a mark of style and social distinction: 'In contrast to the man brought up to the philosophical life', Plato has Socrates say, 'who can do nothing servile, the "non-philosophical" man is accustomed to doing all manner of lowly things swiftly and with precision, though he cannot cast his mantle with his right arm, as a free man does, and even less can he compose harmonious words to praise with true hymns the lives of gods and happy men'.

The long chiton (chiton podere), which could be embroidered and decorated, was the dress for occasions of particular solemnity and was only worn by high dignitaries and priests. The way it was worn and draped, imposing moderation of gesture and constant control of movement, denoted the 'class' of the wearer. (From an Attic amphora, National Museum, Ferrara).

Hairstyle of a young man. The curls came down to the neck. (National Museum, Naples).

A characteristic adjunct to the tunic and *himation* was the long stick with a crutch-like rest at the top which enabled the user to lean on it and catch the folds of his *himation* under the armpit. This attitude is frequently depicted on vases of the period and seems to indicate persons engaged in familiar conversation.

Soldiers, and particularly the cavalry, obviously could not wear a garment such as the classical cloak, or *himation*, which impeded movement. They wore instead a very short cloak over their tunics; this was of stiffer, thicker material and was fastened on to the shoulder with a fibula. It was called the *chlamys*, did not cover the body like the *himation* and was never worn without a tunic. In swift movement it swelled out in the wind, its folds giving an effect of great beauty which often attracted the artists of the period.

It is interesting to note that in the great period of Athenian democracy the clothing one wore could have political significance. This is, of course, a factor not limited to this particular age: during the French revolution the wig, for instance, was regarded as a

Thus we see how the standing of a free and cultured man could be judged by the manner in which he draped his cloak.

A person's very bearing was determined by his style of dress. In the most ancient times orators spoke to the people completely wrapped up in their cloaks which hid their arms and allowed only the right hand to emerge, thus forbidding any gesticulation. Later on this custom was considered a symbol of austerity and restraint, and came to be associated with the older way of life. In the time of Demosthenes, on the other hand, the orators wore their cloaks under the right arm and fastened across the chest on the left shoulder, which left the right arm completely free for expansive gestures. Voting by show of hands was also only possible when the right arm was completely free of the draped cloak.

Many Athenians, perhaps in imitation of Spartan customs, which were as austere in matters of dress as in other things, wore their cloaks next to their skins without a tunic. This was considered eccentric for a free man and typical of philosophers.

Young and marriageable women did not cover up their hair. Married ones often wore elegant caps as seen on the left. (Olympia Museum). Right: *woman's hairstyle.*

symbol of adherence to the *ancien régime* and a refusal to accept the new era. The ' political ' style of dress *par excellence* was the simple Spartan cloak, which denoted its wearer's admiration for the constitution and traditions of Sparta, and became a symbol of conservatism and antagonism to democracy. Similarly to wear the *chiton* rather than the long Ionic tunic implied a resistance to the archaic aristocratic traditions of the former feudal age. It was a world in which formalism, the gesture, the dress, were all important, the closed world of the ' little city ', but the city was the greatest in Greece: it was cosmopolitan Athens.

WOMEN'S CLOTHES

It has already been noted that married and respectable Athenian women dressed in public substantially in the same way as men. There were, however, subtle differences. Although the *chiton* was in most cases the traditional dress of both sexes, considerable ingenuity could be shown in the decoration of the material and the cunning use of fibulas and gatherings to create a more coquettish and attractive garment.

One typical female garment, intended for occasions of particular solemnity, had been in existence even before women took to wearing the *chiton*, since the middle of the sixth century B.C. This was the *peplos*, of wool of one or many colours, variously embroidered. Athenian women wore it only over the *chiton*. It was worn in ample folds, draped over at the top to a third of its length and then vertically into two parts. The rear portion could be draped over the head in a kind of hood. It was often held in at the waist with a girdle which kept the pleating well arranged and prevented the wearer's right leg from being exposed as she walked (as happened regularly with men who wore the *chiton*). If not held in at the waist, the garment hung in ample folds known as a *kolpos*. Another method was to have it sewn up half way or all the way down, leaving two holes for the arms. Worn thus it closely resembled a cylinder and created an effect of remarkable symmetry. The closed *peplos* could be worn with a girdle and arranged with pleats

8.

to enrich the drapery and give more body to the garment.

Wool was the material most widely used by the Greeks, whereas flax, a more recent innovation, was reserved for luxury clothing. Wool was thus characteristic of the dress of peasants and most women of the people, including slaves: linen on the other hand was the material used by the well-to-do classes and women of fashion.

The linen tunic, like the *peplos*, was a rectangular piece of material, but the two longer hems were always sewn together and the two upper edges were fastened on each side over the shoulders and along the arms by stitching or sometimes by fibulas. There

Women's clothes in Athens differed from men's only in the material, the design and the skill with which they were draped. For solemn occasions a woman wore a long chiton with a shorter tunic over it. Both garments were decorated with coloured flounces and embroidery (left: from an Attic vase in the National Museum, Ferrara). Their elegance was completed with jewellery, especially earrings. Indoors women wore light short tunics, attractive and elegant, like the type known as amorgine, from Amorgos. The commonest colours were red and yellow. When she went out on her daily business, the well-mannered Athenian woman covered her short tunic with a long woollen cloak. Opposite: woman wearing cloak (the Capitoline Museums, Rome) and girl in short tunic (the Vatican Museums).

58

was a girdle which formed a deeper *kolpos*. Sometimes the linen tunic was pleated by hand, Athenians not being familiar with the flat-iron.

Linen being somewhat lighter than wool, while the woollen *peplos* was usually sufficient protection by itself, the linen tunic required in winter the covering of a cloak, a shawl fastened over the shoulder, a round cape or a simple *peplos* used as an overcoat.

As we can see from vases, bas-reliefs and statues, women's dress, though essentially quite simple, allowed considerable variation, retaining nevertheless the characteristic of Athenian and Greek dress in general: austerity and simple elegance.

Courtesans, women flute-players and dancers were naturally not concerned with austerity, though they did not despise the *peplos* or the *chiton*, especially if these were elegant and well-made. They did not hesitate, however, to appear in public or among foreigners clad in the short tunic of light material known generically as the *chitonia*. This is the kind of garment referred to by Aristophanes when he speaks of 'the bright yellow *krokoté* and the short close-fitting tunic of Amorgo'.

ACCESSORIES AND JEWELLERY

In a sunny country such as Attica the parasol and the fan naturally enjoiyed extensive use. The fan was a simple flat sheet, usually of wood, in the shape of a heart or a leaf, of which the stalk formed the handle. It was probably green, blue or white in colour, though if pretending to elegance it would be gilded. The parasol, similar to our modern umbrella, consisted of a circular piece of material stretched over ribs converging on a ring which could slide up and down the handle. It could also be trimmed with a fringe. If large, it was carried by a slave who walked behind the lady, shading her. In religious processions it had the same function as the baldachin today of both protecting and exalting the person it covered. During certain religious rites such as the Panathenaic processions the *Canephori* (maidens from noble families carrying on their heads baskets containing sacred implements) were each followed by the daughter of a foreigner resident in Athens holding a parasol over her.

The pleated tunic caught up in one or two folds round the waist was considered particularly elegant, and the best material for this was light wool or linen. These were worn especially by the hetaera (courtesan) and the flute-player. (Detail from an Attic vase, National Museum, Ferrara). Opposite: two kinds of bracelet. Above: a small ointment jar. (Benaki Museum, Athens).

The dowry of a Greek woman always contained one or more finely wrought mirrors, often of silver or another precious metal. If in other ages the mirror has come to be thought of as the symbol of female coquetry, in Athens it was considered the woman's accessory *par excellence*. Men, in fact, never used them. To renounce the companionship of her mirror meant, to a Greek woman, growing old: 'On reaching the age of fifty Nicias, much given to the arts of love, hung up in the temple of Cypris [Venus] her dancing-shoes, her locks of hair, her shining bronze mirror of exquisite workmanship and her rich girdle', reported a writer of epigrams in the Palatine Anthology, a collection of short elegiac poems collected by Constantine Cephalas (*c.* 917 A.D.).

With the mirror went the comb, used for the frequent touching-up of the elaborate hair-styles worn by ladies during the day. Excavations have revealed large numbers of these combs in a reasonable state of preservation. They were often of excellent workmanship, in box-wood, gold, silver or bronze and could be worn in the hair, as is sometimes done today.

In addition to the mirror and comb the ladies and young girls of Athens used make-up: rouge, cosmetics and perfumes, for which the craftsmen of the period made exquisite little boxes and vases.

For the Greek woman, as for women of all ages, her toilet was of fundamental importance, a complicated but pleasurable daily ritual to which the maidservants made a valued contribution. If the lady decided to wash her long hair, her servants poured the warm water over her head as she knelt down, and then rubbed her hair dry. Then followed the skilful art of make-up with colouring and brushes large and small for the eyes, the lips, the cheeks, the arms and the shoulders. The colouring was applied only after the skin had been given a uniform texture by the use of a kind of white lead, plastered on quite liberally by elderly matrons. This white lead, obtained by dissolving in water compresses of lead carbonate, served not only as a foundation cream but also, when put on thickly, as a means of covering up early wrinkles and any imperfections of the skin.

The ladies of easy virtue tended to be more liberal with their paint, as is illustrated by the story of Phryne who, during a banquet, proposed to the many courtesans present as a 'revelation of the truth', a good face-wash! Phryne evidently knew what she was doing, because her own skin was the only one to survive the ordeal and remain fresh and glowing, when the complexions of the others melted away into stains of pink and grey.

If Greek women paid considerable attention to their make-up they were nevertheless very particular about the cleanliness of their skin. The make-up was removed with soda or ashes, then the skin was smeared with scented oils.

Dress was completed by jewellery. Gold work reached a stage of refinement in the time of Pericles when the delicate pendants and necklaces came to replace heavier types worn since the sixth century. Bracelets of gold or silver were common, and were worn not only round the wrist, but also between the elbow and the shoulder. They could be plain rings decorated with a figurine or in the shape of a serpent coiled round on itself.

Elegant Athenian women had their ear lobes pierced and wore on them ear-rings of all kinds. The disc of precious metal, variously ornamented, was very common, and there were gold or silver rings which could also be worn as amulets round the ankle or calf. The snake design was also worn in miniature as an ear-ring. As might be expected, ear-rings, necklaces and bracelets could make up a valuable dowry for a married woman. Jewellery was kept in a small casket, such as is commonly seen in vase paintings. These caskets were all similar in shape but distinguished by their intricate design and good taste. In vase paintings and funerary bas-reliefs the slave-girl handing the jewels to her mistress seems intensely aware of her part in a feminine ritual of particular importance.

If respectable ladies were proud of their jewels, the courtesans considered them not only as objects of adornment but outward signs of their triumphs. In an oration 'Against Neaera', a particularly valuable source of our knowledge of the amatory life of the ancient Greeks, the three types of gift which meant the most were clothes, jewellery and slaves.

HATS AND SHOES

Hats as we know them played no part in women's dress in classical Athens. A beautiful face was set off, according to custom, by a coquettish hairstyle or a wig. The hair could be held in place by a net or a coif, especially at night, or covered with a very fine veil on solemn occasions. In cold weather Athenian women covered their heads with a fold of their tunics.

Men usually went about bare-headed, but hats could be worn in the country or when travelling. The commonest types of masculine headgear were the *pilos*, tall, roughly cone-shaped, sometimes with a peak and variously ornamented, and the *pilidion* (a little *pilos*), a felt or woollen cap worn also by old men at night. The *pilidion*, without peak or ornament, was worn particularly by slaves and working-class men. No Athenian of standing would have ventured out wearing such common headgear, unless he wanted people to think that he had lost his wits. Solon reputedly did just this, feigning madness by going into the Agora wearing a *pilidion* on his head, so that he could freely express his own political opinions.

The traveller usually wore a *petasos*, a broad-brimmed hat of felt or straw with a lace to fasten it under the chin: this also allowed it to be pushed back and carried on the shoulders.

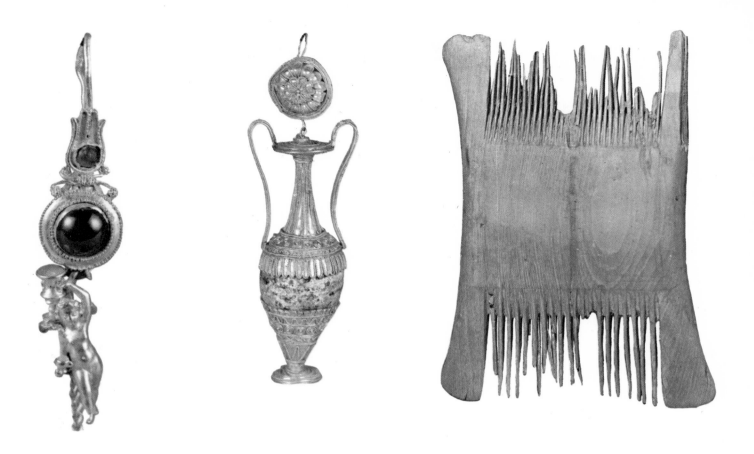

Opposite: *a small silver mirror with dedication. The mirror, often finely worked, was a typical feminine instrument and would be part of the young bride's dowry. Men, as a rule, scorned them. (Kannellopoulos Collection, Athens).* Above: *two earrings and a comb. (Agora Museum, Athens).* Below: *an Athenian woman begins her toilet as her maid holds out the mirror. (From an Attic vase in the Kannellopoulos Collection, Athens).*

The classical himation, as adapted by the following Hellenistic age. Now an imposing cloak, fittingly draped, it also covers the head (statuette from Tanagra, The Louvre, Paris).

Men and women cared about footwear. Walking about barefoot was restricted to indoors where the floors were mainly of beaten earth. Outside it was considered odd and expected only of beggars or eccentric philosophers like Socrates; to wear coarse ugly footwear such as heavy shoes or clogs was even considered a sign of low intelligence. In Sparta, on the other hand, total abstinence from footwear of any kind was considered to be excellent training for bodily strength.

A great many names of types of footwear have come down to us, and we can distinguish several different kinds on vase paintings. The difficulty is to reconcile the one with the other. Shoes were made to measure, that is to say the cobbler cut the sole directly round the client's foot as he (or she) stood on a table.

The sandal, which was very widely used, was a plain sole of cork, wood or leather held on with thongs to the ankle or the big toe. Instead of the sandal, travellers wore a soft half-boot, laced up in front with or without a turnover top. The *cothurnos*, of Asiatic origin, had a high sole and was cut to the same shape for either foot, hence the nickname 'Cothurnos' given to the statesman Theramenes accusing him of having a foot (the same one) in both camps. The *cothurnos* became well known as the characteristic footwear of tragic actors.

Women's shoes were more varied and elegant in design: bedside slippers, every kind of sandal, elegant half-boots for outdoor wear. The leather for these could be black, red or white. To add to their height, women wore inner soles between their heels and the soles of the shoes; they seem not to have known the high heel.

A fine pair of shoes did not seem to have been quite enough for those who sought elegance in the short tunic. The most fashionable ladies wore a flexible metal ring in the form of a snake around their ankles as an amulet, or wide, vividly coloured ribbons bound round their legs up to the knees and adorned with different motifs. The same kind of ribbon could also be worn as a trimming round the border of the tunic or the cloak.

There were also rudimentary kinds of stocking: rudimentary, that is, when compared with our modern silk or nylon.

The *typical Greek headwear with the wide circular brim was the petasos. It was fixed to the head at the middle by a tape and was worn throughout the Classical age, but almost entirely by men. Women began to wear it in the early years of the Hellenistic age.* Below and top left: *two types of petasos. (Bas-reliefs from the Agora Museum and the Acropolis Museum, Athens).* Top right: *hairstyle of a rural god. (Capitoline Museums, Rome).*

FOOD AND DRINK

Before the word 'vegetarian' was invented, the Greeks claimed to be 'eaters of leaves'. Their first two daily meals consisted merely of a salad, some figs and a handful of olives, and it was only for the last meal of the day that they ate anything substantial. Even then, this was fish and rarely meat, and it was eaten without the sauces and dressings associated later with Roman and oriental cooking. It was unusual even for wealthy Athenians to have a resident cook: if one was required for a special occasion he was hired and had to be paid very generously both for his services and for his reputation, real or imaginary.

The kitchen was therefore the province of the woman of the house, who was assisted by the slaves, and the cooking was simple and homely to maintain an economical budget and to keep the family in sound health. Many of the so-called recent discoveries of the dieticians were already being practised in Classical Athens. Fish was so common that it came to be called by a word meaning 'anything which could be eaten with bread'. Lean pork was prescribed for the diet of athletes as the most nourishing and easily digestible meat and the best suited to their physical requirements.

Food served at banquets was naturally richer and more varied, but even the greatest epicures among the Greeks rarely indulged themselves to excess. If a Greek did let himself go in a symposium *(banquet, but mainly for drinking) the wines of Rhodes, Chios and Lesbos might be said to be worthy of a little intemperance.*

Most Athenian husbands had to go out in the morning to the Agora to do the shopping.

The wife, or the most expert of the women slaves, did the cooking. The husband thus followed the same morning routine: first the usual frugal *akratisma* (breakfast) of bread dipped in a little undiluted wine with perhaps a few olives or a couple of dried figs, then out into the usual streets, where he saw the usual well-known faces, to the Agora. Once he began to mingle with the crowds and walk among all the merchandise and the fine buildings he would linger to exchange a few words with his friends or join the fringe of some group of people to see what was going on. What a good idea it had been of Cimon's to plant all those plane trees and poplars in the market square: their shade was most welcome in the heat of the day. The women, as we have said, stayed at home; it was not done to bring a respectable woman, or even a slave, into an atmosphere such as this. All these men,

freemen and slaves ready to undertake any kind of work, all these salesmen and their hundreds of clients, all those idlers in search of novelty and those youths whose behaviour would scarcely recommend them to the best society... There was little danger for the husband, apart from being swindled by some dishonest trader, and even then he could seek the protection of the *agoranomoi* (the justices responsible for the market) who might fine the offender and take steps to see that there was no repetition of the offence. He could also wander freely in the labyrinth of the commercial quarter, in the fishmarket, amongst the cheese-vendors, in the peaceful quarter where wine was sold, amongst carts and tents, where objects were laid out for sale either on the ground or on the steps of some large building, getting himself knocked about in the crowd, stopping to greet the barber or the perfumier in their shops, which at this hour would be full of idlers exchanging gossip and slander, and

Jars (Agora Museum, Athens). In addition to oil, wine and water, flour, greens and other vegetables were stored in jars. Beans, chickpeas and lentils, olives and figs were basic foods in Greece.

every now and then going to buy something for the lunch and dinner at home. If he had made a lot of purchases and could afford to, he would stay on in the Agora and send the provisions home by a messenger. He might even have his shopping done for him by his *agorastes*, his slave who could be trusted to choose well and buy economically the family's provisions.

It was not unusual to see in the Agora the shining uniform of a soldier intent, not on military duties, but merely on acquiring three or four fish and a few coppers' worth of figs. He would be like those comic soldiers in Aristophanes' *Lysistrata* who strutted about the market place armed to the teeth, one with a shield and a terrifying Gorgon's head on his breast-plate, looking for their favourite fish, another using his helmet as a vegetable-basket and a third brandishing a bukeler and javelin in one hand and grabbing handfuls of ripe olives with the other, much to the terror of the wretched tradesman.

GREEK COOKING AND ITS INGREDIENTS

If we follow one of these husbands — a man who has become domesticated more out of necessity than inclination — or an *agorastes* as he wanders among the provisions laid out for sale, we shall get some idea of what made up a Greek dish, what variety of products and ingredients went into the daily meals of a family or on to the festive table.

He would have to stop opposite the many rows of vegetables on show: there must always be a stock of beans in the house, fresh ones in season, dried ones for making a *purée*, for roasting or for grinding into flour. The tradesmen also did well with their lentils and chickpeas in their many varieties of white, black and red. White chickpeas, his favourite, had been recommended by no less an authority than Hippocrates (*c.* 460-357 B.C.). As for the *purée* which the Greeks called *etnos*, it was reputed to have been the favourite food of Hercules, and many a Greek

Weighing sylphion for export to Greece (from a cup showing Arcisilaos, King of Cyrene). The sylphion was a plant found in Cyrenaica and known to the Romans as 'laserpitium'. Its juice was used in Greece for cooking and as a medicine. (Ridder Museum, Paris).

child who refused to eat this mash of beans or lentils would be exhorted by his mother to follow the example of the great hero of antiquity.

Beans could be shelled or left in their pods to be cooked and eaten with other greenstuff. This formed such an important part of their diet that a comic poet called the Greeks *phyllotrogoi*, 'eaters of leaves'. A good raw salad and a plate of cooked greens must have been very similar to what we eat today, as the Athenians also used dressings of vinegar, aromatic herbs and oil. There was probably a greater variety of herbs, judging by the catalogue made by the naturalist Theophrastus (d. *c.* 287 B.C.) who gives us their difficult scientific names. This variety, which in practice was only relative, did not mean very much to the poor, who ate principally herbs, but in some cases, as Chremylus, a character in Aristophanes' *Plutus* tells us, were compelled to eat shoots of mallow instead of bread and dried radish leaves instead of scones. Herbs in Greece could be used for anything: a lettuce

would make a fine salad and, when required, cure the poisonous bite of an animal. For sweetening, the Athenian used carrots, and for adding a bitter taste chicory which grew wild in Greece and appears to have been brought into the country from the East. Asparagus, turnips and cabbages were common, and the onion could boast of great antiquity as it was mentioned in Homer. The leek, according to Hippocrates, had valuable laxative qualities. Hesiod (the eighth century nature poet) and Theophrastus (the third century botanist), mention the asphodel root cooked in embers and seasoned with oil and salt. This was a frugal but very appetizing dish, sometimes eaten with figs. The Athenians did not, however, live on vegetables alone if they had a little money to spare, and by the fifth century at least they seem to have been able to vary their diet considerably. They tended to moralize about the austerity of ancient times, when fish and meat were almost unknown, but the gradual levelling-out of the various social strata, in which the

69

very poor became less poor and the wealthy less wealthy, brought a better average standard of feeding, and meat and various kinds of fish became part of everyone's diet.

When considering Greek cooking it is advisable always to distinguish between the simple, hastily prepared meal of the normal family and the festive banquets at which the food was richer and more abundant. Nevertheless, in Periclean Athens the average family often ate a good dish of pork, a meat which they never ceased to praise for its ease of digestion. Beef, which had been the favourite meat for centuries previously,

now began to take second place. The taste for pork was perhaps conditioned by the advice of the physicians who recommended it for athletes. The school of Hippocrates warned people against the dangers of eating beef, although this had been the staple diet of the powerful Heracles, the mythical founder of the Dorians, and advised instead the lighter meat of the pig, more suitable for those engaged in physical exercise. The wealthier families ate sucking-pigs, fattened up with a special diet, and reserved the normal pork for the slaves. Nothing was wasted: care was given to cooking the various parts of the animal in different ways so that it could all be eaten. The usual method was for the husband to buy it boiled from the *efthopoles*, the butcher who sold meat ready and prepared for cooking. There was little demand for goat's meat or mutton, but hare was occasionally found on a good table, as we learn from the many references in Aristophanes. It seems to have been eaten as an *entrée*, lightly turned on the spit whilst the scented wine was still in the jars, the fish roasting on the grid-iron and the ring-shaped loaves baking in the oven.

The wealthy also ate fowl and game, including highly-prized peacocks, which were regarded as a great speciality, pheasant, woodcock, thrush and other small birds. The Theban merchant in Aristophanes' *Acharnians* walks about strung with ducks, crows, partridge, wrens, cormorants, geese... until they call him 'the storm which exterminates the birds'. Aristophanes describes how these birds came to their end. Pisteteros says to Evelpides in sorrowful tones: 'They throw stones at the birds as if they were madmen, and do not respect even the temples, where snares are laid, traps and nets to catch them. The birds are then hawked round to the passers-by who feel their flesh and, if they are satisfied, buy them. They are eaten roasted, sometimes as many as seven at a time. Sometimes they are sprinkled with grated cheese, oil, sage, vinegar and a kind of sweet thick sauce made of various substances beaten together: they pour it on thick and it reminds you of anointing the dead...'.

The Athenians also ate shellfish and molluscs — fish in general became so common in the cheaper varieties that the word *opson*, which properly meant anything from vegetables to meat and fruit which could be eaten with bread, came to mean fish, as this was the food which commonly accompanied bread.

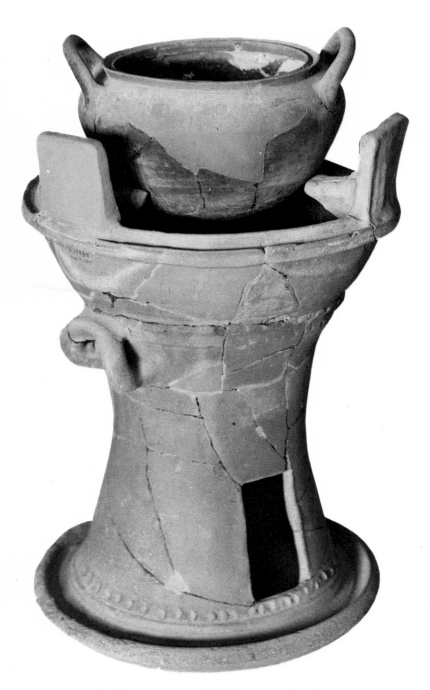

Cooking-stove as used in the courtyards of houses in Greece and throughout the Mediterranean countries. Outdoor cooking was preferred to avoid filling the house with smoke. (Agora Museum, Athens).

The woman in Greece was responsible for the cleanliness of the house and took care to see that the pots and pans were neatly arranged in a row. Above: pan, sieves and ladle. (Benaki Museum, Athens).

Votive cup.
(National Museum, Ferrara).

Votive pig.
(Eleusis Museum).

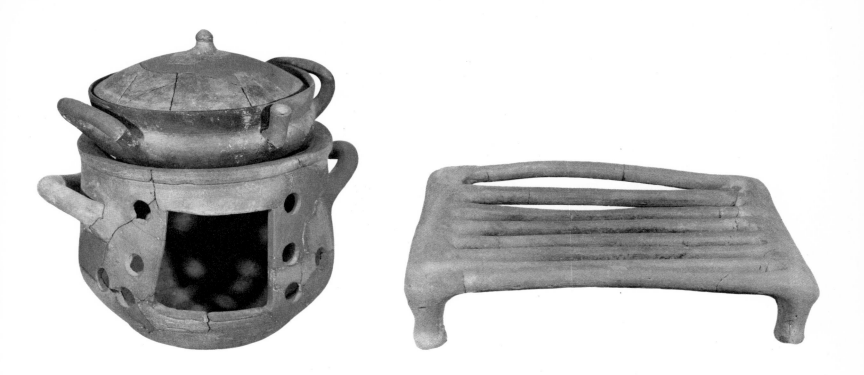

Some kitchen utensils preserved in the Agora Museum: oven, tureen, pot with heater and grill for sausages. Sausages were a particular delicacy for Athenians who, according to an ancient tradition, ate them especially during the Apaturie, the feast of the phratries, between October and November. Venison and veal were also eaten on solemn occasions, though not to any large extent, and they were not as much appreciated as hare. Below: stag and bull. (National Museum, Florence).

73

The modern visitor to Greece will discover that the current word for fish *(psari)* is derived from the ancient *opson*. Fish and bread being the commonest food of the Athenians, the fish market was the busiest part of the Agora. Cheap fresh sardines, smoked and pickled fish of all kinds sold by the *tarichos* (fishmonger) were eaten by all, but a rarer dish was the freshwater eel, especially from Lake Copais. ' Hey you! ' calls out Diceopolos to the Boeotian merchant in Aristophanes' *Acharnians*, ' if you really have the best fish of all, eels, let me see them! '. The merchant opening his basket says solemnly to an eel: ' Oh first-born of the fifty virgins of Copais, arise, come forth and greet this stranger! '. Whereupon Diceopolos is overjoyed: ' Oh, my beloved, you whom I have so desired are here at last. Quick, slaves, bring an oven and bellows and you, friends, observe this choice eel which I have longed for six years and which has finally come to me! Greet it, fellows. I offer you charcoal, but quickly, take it within... Not even

death can separate me from my beloved when she is cooked and served with beetroot! '.

There were cheeses of all kinds from the thousands of sheep and goats which grazed in Attica, and their names are too numerous to mention. They were all eaten with bread. Homer had called men ' flour eaters ', and for the Athenians of the fifth century B.C., wheat and barley were still the basic foods. The commonest type of bread, whether baked at home or bought outside, was the *maza*, made of barley flour baked in the oven and given different flavours according to the liquid with which the dough was mixed. This was the bread given every day to the State pensioners by the Prytaneum (City Council) in accordance with the wishes of Solon. The round loaf of real wheaten bread, the *artos*, was usually reserved for festivals; it could be bought daily, though it cost much more, as wheat was scarcer than barley.

The commonest drink was water and there was also milk, but it was wine which elicited incomparable praise from the Greek poets. One did not have to be a poet to appreciate the virtues of wine, the ' gift of Dionysus '. Attica did not produce enough for her own consumption and Athens imported considerable quantities of highly prized wine from Rhodes, Chios, Lesbos and Thasos in those large sealed amphorae which have been preserved in such large numbers, with the merchant's name or the country of origin stamped on the handles. As this precious liquid travelled about the Mediterranean it had to have some preservative added, and the ingenious wine experts of Greece used several substances, the commonest of which was salt water. It is possible that the modern Greek resinated wine, *retzina*, may be traced back to these ancient origins. Ancient wine was very strong and heavy and was seldom drunk at table undiluted. It was mixed with generous proportions of water in a large bowl called a *krater*, from the same root as the verb *kerannumi* to mix. The modern Greek word for wine is *krasi* which clearly derives from this custom.

DAILY MEALS AND FESTIVE MEALS

Reference has already been made to the light morning meal called the *akratisma*, the first of three which each Athenian took every day unless, as could happen, he had to skip one because he could not afford it.

An Athenian cook had to adapt himself to the tastes of his clients in a city where heavy port traffic brought people from all over Greece. Those from Rhodes, for example, liked to begin their meal with a large cup of hot wine diluted with water used in cooking the fish. Above: *bronze cup. (Benaki Museum, Athens).* Below: *fish from an Attic vase. (National Museum, Ferrara).*

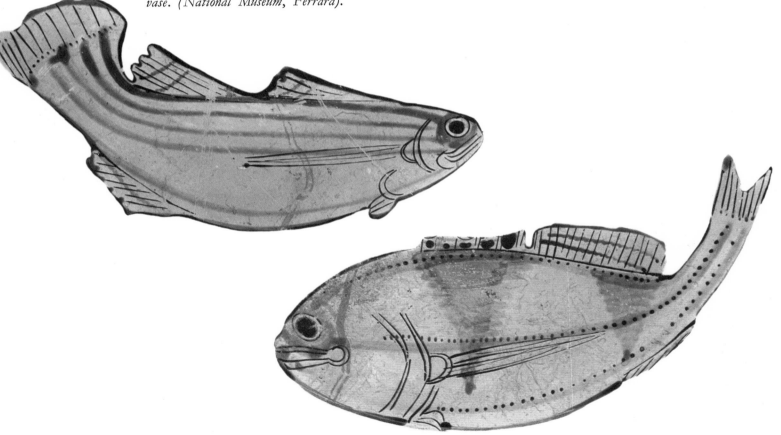

Sucking pig, like fish, was considered most nutritious and easily digestible. In religious rites, the blood of the pig was thought to have purificatory virtues. Sacrifice of a young pig. (From an Attic vase in The Louvre, Paris).

In Homer's time the first meal was called the *ariston*, and was followed by the *deipnon* and the *dorpon*. In succeeding ages and in Periclean Athens, the terminology was changed and the first meal, which was very light, became the *akratisma* (from *akratos*, undiluted wine in which bread was dipped), the midday meal was called the *ariston* (the *prandium* of the Romans), and the evening meal, which remained the most important and, starting at dusk, lasted sometimes well into the night, was called the *deipnon*. We know very little about the *ariston*, which seems to have been a fairly substantial meal in some cases, as reference is made occasionally to the use of provisions acquired during the morning shopping. If the husband did not return in time for the meal to be prepared there was nothing to eat. When the popular tribunals were sitting, it was possible to put the pots on the stove at the time when they were expected to rise for the midday break, but it was never possible to eat before twelve and sometimes the meal was delayed until one o'clock.

The meal which demanded most attention by the women and the female slaves who, even Plato admits,

were better at this than the men, was the supper, or *deipnon*. This was the most substantial meal of the day and the one to which the master of the house, however restricted his means, would invite his guests. These invitations were frequent, as no good Athenian liked eating without friends present, and whenever he could he would ask his wife if one or other of them could come to supper. There were also occasions on which other members of the family came, and the occasional festival, sacrifice or public banquet also relieved the monotony of the simple meal at home. There were too associations such as the *eranos* or the *thiasos* which existed just to bring their members together at a table: each one brought his own provisions in a basket (foreshadowing perhaps our modern picnics) and paid a small sum to the association for the facilities it afforded. On a fine summer's day they would go to the Piraeus and feast on fresh fish. This must have happened very frequently as they coined a verb *aktazein* (from *akte*, a river bank or coast line) which meant 'to go for a picnic by the sea'.

The typical Greek meal which deserves our particular attention was, however, the banquet. This

76

would be given by some wealthy host to his friends. Even his casual acquaintances, met perhaps only in the street, would be invited, and there would be no shortage of gate-crashers either. The unwanted guest might also be brought by an invited guest as happened at the banquet of Agaton when Socrates turned up with Aristodemos, much to the embarrassment of his host who did not care to show his displeasure for fear of offending the philosopher. The gate-crasher is a common figure of fun in the comedies of the time.

The banquet was served by a number of men-slaves under a *trapezopoios* or *trapezokomos*. The lady of the house stayed behind the scenes, occasionally even in the kitchen, as women were not admitted to a banquet except at a wedding feast. If other exceptions were made it was not to accommodate wives. In funeral scenes recorded in bas-reliefs there are frequent representations of banquets which show women reclining next to the men on *klinai* (couches): these were courtesans. If women from the family appeared they were never shown reclining but always seated beside the head of the family.

A slave moved around among the guests with a bowl for washing the hands. This was a necessary precaution as all food was eaten with the fingers, though for liquids there were spoons, and during the meal the fingers were again cleaned with pieces of bread which were then thrown to the dogs.

The menu, or *grammatidon*, was in two parts: the first part consisted of solid food and the second mainly of wine accompanied by spicy titbits and fruit, usually dried, to maintain the thirst. There was an interval between the two parts, during which the tables were removed. These were small and portable, and were placed one in front of each guest at the beginning of the meal. The guests then washed their hands again, put garlands round their necks, sprinkled themselves with perfume and helped themselves to some undiluted wine from a large jar which had been brought in. They then drank to Dionysus, to the sound of songs and flutes and the *symposium* proper began (the word comes from *sun* and *pino*, 'to drink together'). The wine drunk after the initial libation was taken diluted.

Guests, invited and uninvited, and their host then chose a *simposiarchos*, or King of the Feast, who watched over the mixing of the wine and decided how many cups Diphilos, Callias and Ermogenes ought to drink.

Wine was kept undiluted in large jars from which it was drawn as required. (National Museum, Ferrara).

Every banquet, even for the most secular festivities, carried its religious overtones in the libations which were drunk. The food was made eatable by the intervention of fire, and in fire there was the divine spark; a god was therefore present at every stove and oven and at every table. It was to him that a libation was drunk. Every meal, therefore, even those taken outside the family, was a sacred act, and social and political groups, in an age when politics and religion were less distinguished from each other than they have been since, considered certain meals taken together to be the outward sign of their common religious faith.

Thus in Athens, members of the *phratries* (kinship associations) would gather together periodically round a table, and the city itself would organize public banquets, the success of which was in some way held to reflect the prosperity of the city itself. A law attributed to the great Solon decreed that every day there was to be held in the city a public meal to which only pure-bred Athenians could be invited. The law was vigorously observed and the citizens participating were chosen by lot. They were known as 'parasites' from *para siteo*, 'to eat with someone'. The word acquired its pejorative meaning only at a later date. Anyone walking about the Agora at a certain time who happened to pass by the *tholos*, would notice a smell of cooking: this was the meal being prepared for the members of the city council, who were obliged to eat together.

'The State sacrifices many victims', said Xenophon, 'and the people take part in the feasts, dividing amongst them the consecrated meats'. Perhaps it was not all that enjoyable to have a public meal or eat at the city's table for the 'parasites' as at one time a law had to be passed threatening severe punishment to anyone attempting to avoid his duties of eating at the public board once chosen to do so. The food itself may have been alright, but what annoyed the Athenians most of all was having to put up with all the ritual, with its tiresome pedantry, before the food could be served. It could have been enough to dull the appetite of most when, after all this ceremonial, one was served with meat cooked in accordance with the religious rites which forbade, amongst other things, the use of salt. The cook's professional standards would have to give way to his religious conscience, and this seems to have been the case especially in the Kerykes family, of noble Athenian origin, which for generations provided the priests who performed the sacrifices and the cooks who cut up and prepared the meat for the table. Yet once the strict requirements of the religious meal had been satisfied, down to the last prescribed portion of meat and drop of wine, what was to prevent one from seeking consolation in a rollicking secular banquet?

NATIONAL AND IMPORTED CHEFS

The religious feast hardly allowed a cook to show off his art to the best advantage. There were, however, many cooks who could not face the combined challenge of the oven and the demands of a fastidious client for sumptuous private banquets. The cooking in small families was done, as we have seen, by the woman of the house or by the most expert among the female slaves. When the number and the quality of the guests required something out of the ordinary it was customary to seek the help of a professional chef. There were several written treatises on the culinary art dating back to the fourth century B.C., and many interesting fragments of these have come down to us. Few people could read and understand them however, and the services of a *mageiros* were therefore essential. Here was a man who had devoted his life to the art and who placed his services at the disposal of anyone who could afford to pay for them.

Cooking utensils were very similar to those used today. Terracotta pitchers and bowls, sometimes quite plain, were to be found even in the poorest houses. (Agora Museum, Athens).

The eating and drinking vessels used at table in Greece were often of great value and rare beauty, some of them being signed by the artists who made them. Above left: *two-handled bowl from a private collection in Rome.* Right: *cup signed by artist. (Kannellopoulos Collection, Athens).*

Although official voices would have us believe that Athenian cooking was frugal until a late period — Herodotus contrasts its simplicity with the luxury of oriental meals — the figure of the cook which occurs so frequently in ancient comedies is sufficient proof of his popularity in Periclean Athens. 'It is not given to everyone to cook the *glaucos* [fish] as I do!' boasts a chef in a fragment by Cratinus; and in a dialogue between Xantia and a servant of Proserpine in Aristophanes' *The Frogs*, the accomplice in an escape from the house through an air-vent in the kitchen is the *mageiros*, apparently busily engaged in removing the cooked fish from the oven. The poet Simonides of Amorgos (*c.* 640 B.C.) has a passage in which a cook declares that he can do his job 'not badly', and a fragment by Sophocles (496-406) contains a boast by another that he can 'cook with skill'. It is understandable that these men should be conscious of their superiority, as they had studied hard to achieve their skills, which were considerable when compared with those of the average housewife. Some later comic poets describe vividly the schools of cookery which sprang up around some wizard of the pot such as a certain Soterides, one of whose pupils was a *mageiros* in a comedy by Euphorion. Soterides managed to

cook in the middle of winter for King Nicomedes of Bythinia, who lived a long way from the sea, an 'oyster' which he concocted with great skill out of a turnip. Hence the poet's conclusion that a great chef and a poet have at least one thing in common: they are both practitioners of subtle devices.

In a comedy by Sosipatros a professional chef speaks disparagingly of those persons who claim to be cooks but really know nothing about it. 'Whoever wants a good cook should see that he is trained from boyhood and has the capacity to learn and remember all he is told'. This race of chefs is dying out, however, and, he goes on, there are only three names left: Boidon, Cariadis and himself. These three studied under no less a great master than Sicon, a man of wide culture who taught his pupils astrology, architecture and strategy, all indispensable skills for the confection of a dish! The chef also had to be *au fait* with ancient ideological trends. The one who cooked for the (female) Dancers of Posiddipos (an epigrammatist) recommended his pupils, at the introduction of the course, to cultivate a boldness of behaviour, an obscurity of speech and an awareness of changing tastes. Giuba, a chef, in *Samothrace* by Athenaeus (*c.* 200 B.C.) was of the opinion that history was linked

79

to the development of cooking. He demonstrated this with examples from the past as far back as the ages when men devoured each other. One could follow up the idea of Athenaeus and recall certain episodes linked with characters in history who conquered not only the hunger of the guest (the chef is often identified in ancient times with the general called upon to fight and to be victorious) but also gained victory and lasting fame in the annals of mankind.

Many of these master-cooks were Athenians, men on the spot, as it were. In the comedies of the time they were represented wearing a mask, the *maison*, so called perhaps from the name of the actor who first wore it. They had studied in Athens and repaid the city by practising their art within its walls. Many others, however, came from abroad and sold their services in Athens, where they were called by the curious name of 'cicadas' (*tettix*), perhaps because this insect was considered by the Greeks to be an excellent appetizer!

Foreign chefs were highly esteemed and those known for any speciality were soon sent for when the occasion arose. The culinary art as practised in ancient times seems to have transcended most frontiers, as is evidenced by the wide variety of well-known authors of treatises on gastronomy: Sophron, Simonides of Chios, Tindaricos of Sicio, Zopirinos, Heraclitus of Ephesus and Parmenion of Rhodes. The latter wrote the famous 'Culinary Instructions' which earnest apprentice chefs are said to have studied over many a lampful of midnight oil. There were also the famous seven true wizards of the kitchen, each celebrated for one speciality, such as Agidis of

Rhodes (fish), Nereos of Chios (salt-water eels), the Athenian Charidis (mixed salad wrapped in fig-leaves) and so on. Some even came from Sicily to Greece, such as Polemon of Megara who took pains to point out that he was from Megara Iblea and not Megara Nisea.

HIRING A COOK

A cook in Classical Athens was originally in the slave class but was able, through his art, to progress up the social ladder. He would have command over all the slaves of the household and would achieve a position of some authority in the wealthier families. Not all, however, were employed full-time. Many would gather in the *mageireion*, the place in the Agora where, shuffling about behind their display of cooking utensils and accompanied by a few scullery-boys, the cooks who hired out their services would wait to be engaged by one of the many bourgeois husbands who had invited guests for the evening and wanted to put on a special meal. The husband would listen to their sales talk, in which the cooks would compete for his attention, take note of their several specialities, haggle over their charges and finally decide. The cook who was hired would give his name to the *gineconomos*, the magistrate concerned from the late fourth century B.C. with a citizen's private affairs, as a guarantee to the client. The client would now be returning home satisfied and, followed by a small squad of cooks, doubtless relishing in anticipation some exquisite repast.

HUSBANDS, WIVES AND CHILDREN

The prevailing moral climate in Classical Athens permitted constant and frequent evasion of conjugal duties, but the family remained the fundamental institution of the city-state. Men and women attained the state of marriage not out of love or of interest alone, but rather out of a carefully reached decision by their families to which their own wishes could be subordinate. The wife had a destiny and a mission of her own which centred on the children, on the running of the new house and on an absolute devotion to her husband. 'It is the true mother', Socrates said in his Memorabili, *'who divides her own substance with the child, brings it into the world with great suffering, nourishes it and cares for it. And she receives nothing in exchange. The little one does not recognize the breast which feeds it and does not know how to ask for what it wants. But the mother does...'. These are words which have expressed as well as any others throughout the centuries that mixture of innate understanding and generosity which unites the generations through the cell of the family. And few documents express better than a funeral stele the perpetual need for reciprocal charity which marriage entails, even at its most successful, and the combination of anxiety and confidence which unites a man and a woman within a family. These are the things which rescued the ordinary life of Classical Athens from the mediocre, the humdrum and the inconsistent in the sphere of marriage and the family, and restored to childhood, to love and to the link between the generations their rightful and eternal place.*

Judging by the names of the various 'complexes' which psychoanalysts have traced back to Greek antiquity, from Oedipus to Narcissus, it might be thought that sensuality was rife in Athens and throughout the Hellenic world. Phaedra, Medea, Clytemnestra and other Greek heroines have provided the theatres of all succeeding ages with models for those passions which torment the human soul and destroy family life: sensual folly, depravity, criminal jealousy. In fact ordinary life in Classical Athens bore no relation to its representation in the theatre. There were, of course, crimes of passion and deceived husbands and wives, but no more so than anywhere else, and these were not particularly evident on the surface of life.

'Private' life was very private indeed. The golden age of Athens was very different from all those periods called 'courtly', or from the delicate and often violent sentimentality of the age of the early Greek lyric poets, or from the ostentatious passionate intrigue of some ancient civilizations. There was nothing which resembled the repeated marriages of Imperial Rome, the scurrilos life of the Medici or the Borgias or the divorces in America! The motive for marriage was more than love or interest alone, and divorce was rare. The funny story and satirical farce were more appreciated than private scandal. If a woman chose to break with conformity and custom, society was prepared to show tolerance. 'The courtesan for pleasure, the concubine for the home and the wife for legitimate offspring and the upbringing of the family!' was the easy-going dictum of the pseudo-Demosthenes. In brief, serious matters such as trade and politics were dealt with outside the home, in the Agora, on the Pnyx, on the steps of the temples or the theatre or in front of the doors of the courts.

To speak of marriage and family life in Classical Athens is like describing the reverse side of a piece of scenery or the very ordinary back stage of a theatre.

Ancient historians did not venture to do it, comic authors were too inclined to caricature; lawyers intervened only when things went wrong! Whom shall we believe? We have to rely on pictures, on objects, on the keen observation of the craftsmen who portrayed over and over again around the drinking-cups and on the sides of the *lekythoi* the most typical scenes of family life. The rules of the genre forbade any reference to setting or landscape, and this is a great pity. The craftsmen were limited to repetition of the stereotypes which were most popular with their clientele, most of whom were foreign. All things considered, however, Attic vase paintings are our most reliable sources of information.

These vase paintings give us an excellent idea of the lives of young men and women before marriage and in the period of their first love.

YOUNG PEOPLE

The two sexes were rigorously separated, the boys spending most of their time out of doors and the girls staying at home. The boys devoted their time to learning all that might be useful to them when they reached manhood; they worked, studied, trained or amused themselves according to their social class. The girls stayed at home, not, however, as recluses, but helping the mother in her household tasks, which convention held to be her exclusive domain. Running the household with the help of the slaves, spinning, weaving or sewing in the doorway or the passageways of the house, chattering the while amongst themselves, fetching from the fountain the few pitcherfuls of water necessary for the still primitive hygiene of the family — these were in themselves sufficient tasks to occupy any girl in the brief period between puberty and marriage. These were years which in any case passed quickly: even before the age of fifteen an Athenian girl could become a good wife. Judging by the conversations between man and wife reported by Xenophon (*c.* 430 - *c.* 355) in his *Oeconomicus*, the *fiancée* was required to have neither education, science or culture; modesty, obedience and economy were the qualities best appreciated. The favourite scenes depicted on vases take on a certain grace and reserve when the *fiancée* is present: measured gestures and deference from the servants and

a gravity of bearing which is emphasized by the ample folds of the dresses, but which is equally evident in a little naked slave-girl. However banal or even futile their occupations may seem — bathing, dressing, doing their hair, tidying up the room, chatting — these young women assume a dignity which is not entirely the craftsman's art.

For a woman, diversion was to be found only in the practice of religion. Family ceremonies and official festivities must have been the great moments which relieved the monotony of daily life. Preparations went on a long time beforehand: embroidering the *peplos* which the maidens from the noblest families offered to Athena in the Panathenaic processions; preparing the sacred bread and the offerings to the gods and to the departed; going over again and again the complicated dance steps which would form part of the ritual. There were lively round dances of child-like simplicity, which have come to light only recently in the temple of Artemis at Brauron, slower dances in which the girls danced hand in hand, and Dionysiac rites when a Bacchic delirium gripped the revellers. These were occasions for the women to go out and, perhaps, to begin some amorous adventure. One notable seducer of married women, Gratosthenes, was killed by an irate husband who was ably defended by the great rhetorician Lysias (born *c.* 450 B.C.). More usually, however, family life was spent quietly and happily on feast days. Some votive steles dedicated to Artemis and Asclepius show Athenian families on feast days dressed up in their best clothes looking for all the world like modern bourgeois promenaders!

MARRIAGE

Marriage arrangements were the concern of the parents. The young people, or the girls at least, had little say in them. A marriage was for social and financial convenience and to ensure the best conditions for the continuation of the family line. Many people other than the future bride and bridegroom had an interest. A wedding had an atmosphere, if not of religious devotion, at least of tradition, ritual, and almost of magic. It was a time when the families concerned faced the unknown and the conjectural, and this is why in certain ceremonies there were elements

Women spent most of their time shut up indoors. Looking after the house and bringing up the children left them little time for going out, but they found opportunities to dress and to adorn themselves elegantly and even with a certain coquetry to please themselves and their husbands. (From an Attic vase in the National Museum, Ferrara).

of crudeness and brutality born of ancient deep-seated fears. As she approached this crucial time of her life the girl was no longer called *parthenos* (virgin) but *nymphe* (*fiancée* or young bride). The appropriate gods Artemis Limnatis (of the marshes) and Heira Teleia (the Pure) were invoked by ritual formulae. Ancient wisdom considered marriage a decisive step in one's life: 'If you succeed with your first wife, rejoice in your good fortune', the legislator Carondas is supposed to have said, 'and if not, it would be folly to tempt your luck with another!'.

The question as to whether the young couple might be suited to each other therefore hardly mattered. Their suitability was something more difficult to foresee than the financial advantages which might arise from the contract. The legal act was performed orally in most cases, but before witnesses, and this gave the marriage its legitimacy. The bride's father or guardian 'gave her away' to her betrothed and stated the amount of the dowry he had bestowed on her. The patrimonies of the bride and bridegroom were usually not merged, as difficulties of separation

would arise if the marriage turned out to be sterile, if the husband died or the wife was driven out of the home and sent back to her family. The parents thus took every precaution. On the other hand there was no shortage of dowry-hunters. Here is an excerpt from a comedy: 'The dowry will be one talent. And I'll not take her? Could I live and turn down one talent? Could I sleep and let this occasion pass me by? But I should deserve the torments of Hell if I did not respect that talent of silver'.

In certain cases the civic authorities intervened in this eminently private business of the marriage arrangements: this was to protect girls who had been left as orphans and only children and had inherited the family property. In these cases the girls were given away by their nearest relative, and the marriage was supervised by the *archon* (the Chief Magistrate after whom the year was named). If this marriage was unsuccessful it very quickly ended up in the lawcourts. Some of these discussions about marriage settlements must have been quite sordid, but then the Athenian never hesitated to speak his mind on money matters.

When everything on the financial side had been satisfactorily arranged the wedding could take place. After the betrothal ceremony the bride was 'handed over' and left her own home for that of her husband. This was a family celebration which had nothing to do with the religious or the civil ceremonies. The gods of the household were held to preside over the various rituals and only parents and friends were present. The ceremonies were performed by a god-parent or by a close friend of the bride and bridegroom, while the prosperity of the young couple was toasted in wine which had to be handed round by a youth both of whose parents were living. Weddings were naturally festive occasions, and a family would be proud to show off its wealth and the number of its relations. By Solon's time it seems to have been necessary to curb over-spending and sumptuary laws were passed limiting the expense of both weddings and funerals. This was as much to achieve a more democratic egalitarianism as to protect the family against itself. It was also perhaps an attempt by the *polis* to legislate for a taxable return. One essential feature of the wedding was the procession which accompanied the bride from one house to another, and here too other rites were celebrated.

The rites of farewell, propitiation and purification were held on the previous day. The bride wore a veil covering the whole of her face and was attended by her female friends and parents. All went in procession to the fountain of Callirhoe (wife of Alcmaeon) to draw the water for the nuptial bath in a special jar with a long neck. The same vase, called a *loutrophoros*, was placed on the grave of those who had died unmarried, perhaps to ensure that it would be there if needed in the after-life. Wedding gifts were sent to the home of the bride and taken to that of the bridegroom the day after the wedding in a last procession, which would include also the bride's own furniture. Everything which followed was ritual, magical or symbolical: sacrifices, offerings, wedding feast, songs and the exchange of greetings. All this was aimed at ensuring the fertility of the union, the prosperity of the new home and protection from ill fortune which ever threatened, to the Greek mind, the man who was too happy. Flowers and garlands were chosen

The box in which women kept their most precious possessions was a frequent feature of vase paintings. Often finely wrought, it would contain the jewellery brought as a dowry, the mirror and the cosmetics. Left: *vase. (Capitoline Museums, Rome).* Above: *detail of vase. (Kannellopoulos Collection, Athens).*

Athenian women were frequently reproached in comedies for seeking relief from their loneliness in the odd cup of wine. Above: a vase for keeping wine. (Agora Museum, Athens).

with great care. Baskets of fruit were offered, sesame seeds were scattered on the floor and torches were lit to revive the latent energies of Life and Nature. The shouts of joy of the guests, the bacchanalian dancing at the door of the nuptial chamber, and the ritual invocation 'Hymen, god of weddings!' shouted in chorus in hymns and songs, all sprang from the same ancient traditional beliefs and have their counterpart in other civilizations. Life would thus continue. A new generation would perpetuate the cult of the ancestors and the usages and customs of the family. The husband's fraternity was informed of his marriage and some time after the ceremony he stood all the members a drink. One day they would welcome his son amongst them.

The weddings referred to above took place between young people whose families, rich or poor, were all citizens of Athens. In the past certain aristo-

cratic families had contracted unions outside Attica. Megakles, head of the great Athenian family of the Alcmeonidai, won the hand of the beautiful Agariste, daughter of the tyrant of Sikyon, the Dorian city on the gulf of Corinth. He had to contend with rivals from the greatest families in Hellas. In the age of Pericles, however, such unions were frowned upon, although Pericles' mother, another Agariste, was related to the same Dorian family. A law of 451 B.C. allowed citizenship to be granted only to those persons born of Athenian parents legitimately united in matrimony.

The author of this law, Pericles himself, contracted an irregular union with Aspasia of Miletos who bore him, before 440 B.C., a son called Pericles. It was only after a great deal of trouble that the young Pericles was granted the citizenship of Athens in recognition of his father's great services. The great statesman was very much in the public eye: not so, of course, the ordinary citizen, whose activities would scarcely give rise to much jealousy. Every time that the civic list came up for revision, virtually the same number of names were struck off, which would seem to point to a certain tolerance in the application of the law. There were doubtless accommodating witnesses, and bribery and corruption were not unknown. There was no such thing in those days as the identity card.

As well as the legitimate marriage 'by promise' there appears to have been another more rudimentary form of union which, though having no legal standing, was in practice as binding. The poor, who could not afford a marriage settlement, could not afford either the expense of a legal marriage. Foreigners resident in Athens also raised their families outside the framework of laws which did not apply to them. Slaves, although having few rights, did in fact often lead a family life of their own. There is no doubt either that many Athenian men had concubines in the house who were not all slaves. There was a certain instability in Athenian family life due to the repeated absence of the men at sea, in frequent wars, or maintaining contact between Athens and the various peoples in the Aegean, on the shores of the Adriatic and in the Crimea. The distant traveller could lie with impunity, and those arriving at the Piraeus often came from far-away places. Many a complicated story of doubtful parentage and accident of birth would prove virtually impossible to unravel. Demosthenes had a client, born of a legal union, who sued his bastard brothers as they had received preference over him in the matter of being registered on the civil lists. It would seem that many Athenian families suffered the ambiguity of uncertain relationships.

THE YOUNG COUPLE

It would be interesting to see into the intimacies of the married couple's new life together and to know something of their feelings. Xenophon gives us a somewhat idyllic account of the subject in his *Oeconomica*, written when he was approaching fifty and had retired from the army to live in the country. The work deals with the management of households and property and, in the persons of Ischomachus and his young bride, seems to recall the happy married life of the author and his wife Phylesia. Speaking of his wife, Ischomachus says: 'When she became used to me and put aside her shyness sufficiently to speak to me I asked her: 'Tell me, my dear, do you now understand why I married you and why your parents gave you to me? You know that I could easily have found others to share my bed. But after much reflec-

tion, I for my part and your parents for yours, on the best partner we could find for our house and our children, I chose you, and your parents chose me amongst the best parties available'. He then follows with interesting proposals for the upbringing of the children and for a true community of living within the family. Ischomachus' young wife then asks ingenuously: 'How can I help you? What can I do? Everything depends on you! My duty, as my mother has told me, is to be honest and true...'. Encouraged by this submissive attitude, Ischomachus then goes on to expatiate on the theme of 'the wife at home, the husband out of the house', and draws up in a few pages a 'Manual of the Perfect Housewife', which is full of interest. His 'Praise of Order in the Household', however, smacks a little of the retired Field Marshal.

Discretion, delicacy, smiling efficiency and tenderness: these are the qualities of the young wife as depicted by Xenophon. Aristophanes used other colours, however, to depict the womenfolk of Athens, as he mocked the easy-going traditionalism of some of those who would aspire to city government: 'They wash their wool in hot water in the old-fashioned way: they squat in front of their grid-irons as they have always done; they carry their loads on their heads,

Bowl with lid representing scenes from the gynaikeion. (National Museum, Ferrara).

as they have always done; they celebrate the *Thesmo-phoria* [a fertility festival] as they have always done; they bake cakes as they have always done; they nag their husbands, as they have always done; they cook themselves little titbits as they have always done; they prefer their wine undiluted, as they have always done'. We must remember that this speech came in a comedy (*Women in Parliament*, 392 B.C.), and that misogyny was a favourite source of fun. The darts of Aristophanes doubtless found their target, just as there were many who would recognize themselves in the kinder judgements of Xenophon. The truth most likely lay somewhere in between.

There seems no doubt that the ancients considered the vocation of men and women in the home to be contrasting and not complementary. 'The man must concern himself with work in the fields, with the market and errands in the city: the woman with her wool, making bread and doing the household tasks', wrote one Stoic philosopher. In classical Athens, in fact, husband and wife commonly had one or two slaves each, even in the poorer families and where there were more than this the time would be fully occupied in supervising the slaves' duties. It was quite common for the husband and wife to do no work at all in the house, and the running of the household was a division rather of responsibilities than of work. It is not surprising, therefore, that such a system should tend to make husband and wife indifferent to each other in the home, as they were absorbed in matters so diverse that they had little need to consult each other, and eventually might find that they had very little to say to each other at all, as Socrates once observed.

Men and women tended to lead different lives in general in ancient Greece and this separation began in childhood. Boys and girls were never educated together. Girls never went into a *gymnasium*. Women went to theatres only when they could be given separate seats. Men met in their public life, in the navy, in the army, during physical training and at banquets. Religious festivals also kept men and women apart. Some festivals were reserved for one sex only, such as the *Haloa* (a feast to protect the germination of grain) and the *Thesmophoria* (for fertility) in which, apart from certain officials, only women took part. When men required the services of women they had recourse to courtesans or female slaves as servants,

dancers, flute-players or companions at feasts. The only time they kept company with respectable women was at family celebrations, and even then the women were served at separate tables. Men and women could meet fleetingly in the streets; the women wore veils like Muslims but there was no law against rendezvous and the exchange of greetings.

It was also possible for men and women to work in the same place. Many of the poorer women of Athens had to work to eke out an existence and they commonly had stalls in the market or sold perfume and garlands of flowers to the passers-by. They also worked in the fields, naturally, but it is surprising to find them engaged in certain types of craft work, usually organized into small groups.

This habit of separate living seems to have carried into the privacy of the house. Certainly, as the comic poet Philiscus said, 'there is nothing like conjugal love to make you change your ideas!' and we know

what capital Aristophanes' Lysistrata would have made of this argument. Yet comic characters such as Strepsiades, who complained that his wife acted as she pleased, and Philocleon, who spoiled his daughter to such an extent that he spent on her most of the money he earned as a court judge, are not the only ones to resent the interference of women. We do not, however, have a great deal of reliable information on the relationship between husband and wife in Classical Athens. The very vocabulary of love, affection, devotion and tenderness is rather deficient in Greek, though there are words enough for passion, and the stronger kind of passion in particular. Such words as there are to describe marital relationships are crude rather than refined. If we are to believe Xenophon's *Symposium*, there were people in Athens such as Niceratus who ' was passionately in love with his wife and she with him ', but at the end of the work an erotic dance is performed which ' makes the unmarried guests swear to take a wife without delay and sends the married ones galloping home to enjoy their own wives '.

PRACTICAL FAMILY LIFE

Fortunately it is easier to reconstruct the family's practical life than the intimate life of the young married couple. The subject is simplified by the division of labour inside the home and the relative simplicity of the daily round.

The man took charge of everything which pertained to life outside the home: work, with certain exceptions, politics, with no exceptions, legal matters, business affairs, errands, shopping. Often his wife saw him only at breakfast and in the evening when the supper was ready. This was the only meal of any substance which the Greek took, and he relaxed at

' *She was chaste, spun the yarn and looked after the house* ', said a Greek in grateful tribute to his faithful wife. Spinning and weaving were almost exclusively feminine pursuits in Athens, carried out mainly in the house but also occasionally in workshops. (Painting on the back of a cylix, Capitoline Museums, Rome).

12.

the same time. There were also evenings spent with friends and banquets which lasted well into the night. The rich and the popular who liked this kind of evening entertainment spent very little time at home.

The woman was therefore left alone for the greater part of the day with only the company of relatives, slaves and children. She does not seem to have been very much occupied or even concerned with what we know as housework. The ' scenes from the *gynaikeion* ' which appear on vase paintings show by preference the woman at her bath, doing her hair or dressing. Cleaning the house was doubtless considered menial and to be left to the slaves. It is significant that in all the advice he gave on how to run the home, Ischomachus never spoke of a broom.

A housewife's principal duty seems to have been to keep everything in order and supervise the work of others. The symbol of her authority was the small casket of keys which she carried about with her: it appears on representations of funerals carved on steles in Attica. The woman was married so that she could be the guardian of the family property and this duty began immediately after her wedding, as children and their attendant demands only came later, if the gods were willing. She had to stay at home to see that no ill befell the household. Locks were primitive and houses were built very close to each other. Everywhere there were underfed slaves and petty thieves who, if caught pilfering, had nothing to lose. In these conditions it was risky to go out, and a woman in the house was a good insurance. Provided, of course, that she was not the least trustworthy of them all. Hesiod (eighth century B.C.) advised frankly that one should not trust those women ' who brazenly show their thighs and whose headspinning chatter is only aimed at relieving you of your savings! '. To be a good supervisor and a good organizer, fearful of not having enough to go round and therefore economical in everything — these were the qualities a husband expected in his wife. It was also in her own interests to see that the patrimony, in which she had an interest, was preserved intact.

In our modern economy with its plentiful output of goods we have perhaps lost the sense of closely planning our supply of food and other necessities. It we need anything, we can always ' pop around to the corner shop '. This was impossible in ancient times. The security of life and the survival of the family in many cases literally depended on the supplies of daily bread. To control household consumption, prudently but without excessive parsimony, was no easy task. Let us not forget either the irregularities of the calendar which modern researches have brought to light. However hard the *archon* might try, the official year did not always coincide with the seasons, and we can imagine a poor family's anxieties in the last days of a month when it was found that a day or two more had to be added to bring the sun and moon-based calendars together. Every household lived, in part at least, on the produce of its own fields and orchards, so that division of labour and distribution of products throughout the year demanded skill and discernment. The arrival of provisions in the market was subject to external events such as peace on the frontiers between Megara and Boeotia, or the arrival in port of ships bringing grain from Egypt or the Black Sea, and it was never wise to rely on these supplies being regular. So the duties which a husband left to his wife were among the most delicate and important. ' Overseer and controller of the household ' she was called, and this was the Athenian woman's proud boast through the mouth of Praxagora, the outspoken wife in ' The Assembly of Women '.

WOMEN IN CHARGE OF THE HOUSE

It does not matter that Ischomachus lived in a wealthy household: the master of the house earnestly recommended his wife to distinguish between the ordinary and the exceptional, to ' put aside on the one hand a part of what is to be consumed month by month and on the other that which is calculated on a yearly basis, for thus is consumption better controlled '.

Assisted by the most intelligent of her slaves, the housewife therefore counted, collected together and stored up all the family provisions. There were jars for the cereals, the oil, wine, olives and preserves, and boxes for the clothes, the materials and the covers. The clothes worn at festivals and the husband or the son's military uniforms had to be sprinkled with pepper against moths and stored away. The various shaped vases needed for daily use had to be put back in the larder or in their recesses, and the fine cups and valuable crockery, the pride of the house, hung up by their handles on hooks on the wall. The most precious articles were hidden away in the *thalamos*, the bedroom, which could be quite elegant, and in which the wife awaited her husband. This was the most private, and therefore the best protected, place in the house. It took an intelligent woman to remember where everything went. Xenophon shows us Ischomachus' youg wife completely flustered because she was unable to lay her hands on something her husband had asked for.

Of all the possessions entrusted to the care of the housewife, none were more precious than the slaves. When there were only one or two, as in the poorer Athenian family, a very humane relationship often sprang up between them and their masters. A speech by Demosthenes mentions a nurse, a freed slave, who returned in her old age to live out her time with her former master. She was taken by surprise and beaten to death trying to defend the family property and possessions against marauders. The family had been sitting quietly in the courtyard, where the wife, the children and the old woman were about to eat, when the robbers broke in: a moving scene, doubtless a little dramatized for the cause the orator was pleading, but vary plausible nevertheless. Every care was given to the old nurse until the doctor, hurriedly summoned, said that there was no more hope. It was one of the wife's duties to look after slaves who were ill. When Ischomachus told his wife this, she showed a sense of dedication, which would appear to belie other reports we read of wives who considered it their duty to look after slaves rather like a farmer's wife looks after her hens: merely for what she can get out of them. She did, however, have to keep her slave girls shut up ' so that they didn't have babies without permission! '.

The housewife organized the work of all the servants, and this was no mean task in a large and wealthy household. Just as in fact, each house was to a certain extent self-sufficient as far as food requirements were concerned so, in another sense, it was a production unit which could turn out objects of value and importance. Much craftwork could be done on the premises, under a lean-to shed or a workshop attached to the house. This was under the supervision of the husband and does not concern us for the moment. The housewife was responsible traditionally for one particular kind of craftwork: weaving. Men's and

One of the most important tasks of the women was to do the laundering. Cloaks and more substantial woven clothes would be sent to the dyer, but the finer clothes would be washed at home. (National Museum, Ferrara).

women's clothing, linen for the bath or the kitchen, covers, cushions — all these could be made at home. Wool and goat hair were the usual raw materials and every household knew how to spin and weave them. Linen also was used for finer and more expensive cloth. Cotton and silk were imported already manufactured. The wool was washed in hot water to remove the grease, dried and then carded with combs, or on an *epinetron*, a rough piece of baked clay, semi-cylindrical in shape and designed to be held over the knee. Some of these instruments have come down to us, and one of them, the *epinetron* from Eretria (a town in Euboia) is justly renowned for its sumptuous decoration. It shows a bust of Artemis and, along its sides, mythological scenes recalling famous married couples, Thetis and Peleus, Cadmus and Harmonia, Alcestis and Admetus. Thus it might be said that these legendary husbands and wives offered their protection to the work symbolized in the *epinetron*. The wool was then spun with the distaff and spindle, objects which were often symbolically deposited in the tombs of faithful housewives.

One of the favourite themes of the poets of the Palatine Anthology is that of the three sisters who dedicate to Athena their distaff, shuttle and wool basket, and offer to Artemis a fabric with a triple hem. Penelope spent long years at her loom weaving, as we known from a painting on a Greek cup in the Bologna Museum. There were Penelopes in every house in Athens who worked away slowly at their looms, simple vertical frames with rollers from which the weft threads hung down, drawn taut by a series of weights. The work was done mainly by slaves, the housewife distributing the wool, deciding the design and colours, inspecting the daily output and directing the teaching of the young ones. Dyeing and washing appear to have been done outside in specialized workshops employing mainly men. The finishing and any further washing of the cloth was done at home by the women, then the material was folded and put away. These activities are portrayed in many vase paintings of the period.

The remaining duties in this catalogue of housekeeping tasks performed by the women were filling

and trimming the lamps and fetching water. The age of the tyrants had brought a good system of water supply to Athens, without which the high concentration of buildings within the city would have been impossible.

The Pisistratids endowed Athens with many public fountains but this did not mean that there was an abundant supply of water all the year round. There was nothing in Greece which corresponds to the gigantic Roman aqueducts. For bathing and washing, for the kitchen and the table, water had to be fetched in jars and three-handled pitchers called *hydraia*, which

Where there was no well in the house, the women had to go to the fountain for water. Just as the man met his friends in the Agora, chatted with them, or discussed politics and other problems, the woman met her neighbours at the fountain and gossiped about eternal feminine trivialities such as clothes, hairstyles, friends, children and, if she were unmarried, of boyfriends. Going to fetch the water was a good excuse to get away from the gilded cage of the house and occasionally to further some amorous intrigue. Above: gargoyle from fountain. (Corinth Museum). Opposite: women at the fountain. Left: restored Attic pitcher. (Villa Giulia Museum, Rome).

93

the girls carried elegantly on their heads or their shoulders. This gesture was immortalized by the Athenian sculptor Phidias (early fifth century) with his male *spondophori* (libation carriers) in the Panathenaic procession. Judging by the pictures on their pottery, the Athenians must have had to economize on water: a simple flat bowl on a marble stand was sufficient for the ablutions of several women; a small jar was enough for daily cleansing; a complete bath was a luxury, and could turn the house into a quagmire. Bathing was much more a country habit: in the town it was more reasonable to wash small areas at a time. There was always a crowd at the fountain: free women and slaves coming and going from early morning onwards, all mingling without distincion of class. It was not always a very suitable place for well brought-up young girls, and they were to be discouraged from making too frequent visits.

This, then, was how the married woman in Athens spent her day, which brought her innumerable small jobs and great responsibility. Accustomed as she was to her husband's absence, she not unnaturally fell victim to certain temptations, one of which was gossiping with her friends and neighbours. The arrangement of the houses on hillsides with terraces and courtyards made this innocent diversion very easy. News spread rapidly, covering very quickly a whole district as it was carried by slaves and children. The women had shrill voices: the same word in Greek was used to describe the 'melodious' song of the cicada, the female voice and the noise of a saw. The writers of comedies have left many amusing accounts of Athenian gossip-mongers: we can note the poor intellectual quality of their speech, but at the same time admire their sound common sense and the forthrightness of their language, which was far removed from the rhetoric and sophistry of some of the men. The extraordinary frankness of their spech was often very comical in itself. As in the *Arabian Nights*, the women of Athens were not afraid to call a spade a spade.

THE FAMILY IN TIMES OF MORAL CRISIS

It does not follow that Athenian women were necessarily more immodest than others. It is a fact that there was a high standard of morality within the

family at the beginning of the fifth century B.C. but during the fourth century it evidently began to decline somewhat after the Peloponnesian War. Mention of decadence has become commonplace in histories of the period, and one hesitates to cast doubts, but it does appear to be based on very subjective judgements: those of the misogynist Euripides and the lucid, but begrudging Thucydides. It might be suspected that the latter exaggerated signs of moral decay, if indeed there were any, in the city, but it must be remembered that Athens had banished him during a war in which he had lost a battle. In contrast he can find warmth and nobility enough to describe the good old days. In the fourth century we listen only to the philosophers such as Plato, who took their theories for reality, or to orators, such as Demosthenes, not given to flattery or charity towards their adversaries.

Typical Athenian well-head. (Agora Museum, Athens). Made of stone or marble, it was buried deep in the ground, as seen in the illustration opposite of a slave drawing water. (On a cylix, Capitoline Museums, Rome).

Model of an Athenian fountain. Slave-girls from the wealthier families came not only to draw water, but also to do the laundry, as in the public wash-house of today. (Sikion Museum).

Between the gloom of the fifth century and the philosophy and rhetoric of the fourth stand the writers of comedies, such as Aristophanes, who were naturally given to exaggeration. These then were the several sources from which attempts have been made to establish the essential lines of a historical 'evolution' of Athenian morality. The economic organization of the city was unchanged, the social structures remained the same; the weight of civil war hung over divided Hellas, but was accepted as a necessary evil. This does not mean that life went on completely without changes, without crises, but their effect on ordinary family life must not be exaggerated. The 'angry young men' with their affected way of life, symbolized by Alcibiades at the end of the fifth century B.C., were virtually the same as the young rebels of the time of Pisistratus a century earlier, whom the vase paintings portray in red. Is there really much difference between the kind of society described by the pseudo-Demosthenes in 'Against Neaera', and that in the 'Characters' of Theophrastus? Aspasia is shown as a woman of brilliant intelligence and Phryne as one of simple beauty. Is it not perhaps their lovers who are reflected in their image? One was the mistress of a great statesman and the other of a pleasure-loving orator and a somewhat easy-going sculptor. In the eyes of the public they were both courtesans, and no excuses for their behaviour were sought. A man was allowed the greatest freedom, in law and, in fact, even when married. There was open homosexuality in the *gymnasia* where the foundations were laid for the educational theories and the military training of a large section of Greek society. There were complaisant musicians and actresses in the various clubs and assembly-rooms, whose presence at banquets was a *sine qua non*. There were concubines who could be more or less bought for service in the family, and submissive slaves, who were not unlike a human booty of war at the mercy of their conquerors' whims. There was thus little occasion, unless it were out of avarice, for a man to restrain his instincts, and even the wisest among men, even a Socrates enjoyed sexual freedom.

None of this, however, applied in any way to the married woman. It has been popularly supposed that there was equality between the sexes in Classical Athens, but this idea arose from the exaggerated claims of comic writers and the laconic writings of philosophers. In the matter of the fidelity and the honesty of the wives, Athens was as demanding in the fourth century as she had been at the time of the battle of Marathon (490 B.C.). The law still allowed the deceived husband to kill the lover, not only of his wife but of his concubine, if caught in the act. This law never fell into disuse, and the lawcourt oratory which has come down to us never reveals any change of attitude to the question. The husband had a duty to preserve the purity of his family and descendants and the dignity of his house. Euphiletus (a character in Lysias' 'On the murder of Eratosthenes'), a deceived husband who avenged himself by killing his wife's lover, told how his married life began: 'When I had decided to marry and had taken a wife, this was my attitude towards her: to avoid annoying her yet at the same time not to allow her too much freedom. I watched over her, therefore, as much as possible, and this I consider was just. When our child was born, however, I ceased my vigilance over her and entrusted her with all my possessions, as I now deemed that we were united by a stronger bond. And she was a model wife...'. The poor man thus believed that he had done all in his power to ward off the trouble which befell him. He does not hesitate to tell his judges that he would be happy if they could judge him by the same feelings which they would have had themselves were they in his position. Such an appeal would not go unheard, which seems to indicate that the law held family life to be seriously affected by the wife's adultery.

One of Aristotle's disciples said that 'love is the sickness of idle souls'. Could an Athenian housewife's preoccupation with her domestic duties and the education of the children be said to have protected her from its temptations? Or did she seek consolation elsewhere for the neglect of her husband? If we are to believe the comic poets, she took refuge in wine. There is no doubt that Athenian women frequently got drunk. Sobriety was a highly appreciated virtue, which would seem to imply that it was not all that common. It should be remembered that the woman's duty was to superintend the household, and that the husband would complain less about the wife's addiction in itself than about her depriving himself and his friends of the family provision. There was no coffee in those days either, or any distilling of alcohol. Wine was a most excellent tonic.

DIVORCE

The family life we have referred to was that of the average couple who generally lived together, if not happily, at least resignedly. There were others, however, whose marriages broke up through incompatibility of character, through questions of money, ambition, cruelty or sterility. What was their fate? A husband could divorce his wife as it pleased him, by a simple statement of repudiation in front of a witness. He then renounced all claim to the material advantages which his marriage had brought him and had to hand back the dowry to his father-in-law or his wife's nearest relative acting as her guardian. If he failed to do this, he had to provide her with an income equal to one sixth of the dowry which he would raise by mortgaging land or property. This would cause many a husband to reflect on the wisdom of a divorce, especially if the wife had given him the children which they had hoped for on their marriage. Certain families did not scruple to conceal some of their patrimony, and the young Demosthenes was deceived into believing that a certain family had been impoverished by having to pay alimony, whereas in fact there had been no divorce at all.

Only when the divorce was sought by the wife did it require a certain time for official formalities. These cases were much more difficult and far less common than cases in which the initiative came from the husband. The couple had to apply to the *archon*, the protector of family rights, to have the divorce registered. Such interference by the *polis* in private affairs was possible only in the gravest circumstances. It is not easy to imagine what grounds the wife would plead, as we know that a great deal of licence was allowed in the conduct of husbands, and even gross cruelty would probably not be admitted as a suitable reason. A close examination of the documents seems to point to money difficulties and rarely, if ever, to alienation of affection, as affection played so small a part in many of these marriages. To the Athenian husband every solution or combination of solutions was

A woman's most important occupation was the care of the children. Sons, who ensured the continuation of the family, were the fundamental reason for marriage. A husband could reject a sterile wife. (Vase painting, National Museum, Ferrara).

possible. The most 'elegant' was to hand over your ex-wife to a friend, as Pericles seems to have done.

Public opinion did not regard favourably either women who divorced their husbands, or their parents, brothers or other relatives who were left with a now unmarried woman on their hands. It was therefore in everyone's interests to marry her off again as soon as possible, in which case she could then simply pass from one household to another. This does not seem to have happened very often, however, as we find Demosthenes saying quite firmly about marriage: ' It is not to be taken lightly: it is the lives of our sisters and our daughters which we are entrusting to others; on these occasions every precaution must be taken '.

THE CHILDREN

Marriage was intended to ensure the continuity of the family and was thus more of a social institution than a legalized love-match. Its purpose was procreation, and the wife's barrenness must have been the most frequent motive for its repudiation. The Athenians, like the rest of the Greeks, seem to have practised a form of family planning. Boys were wanted more than girls but too many mouths to feed was in any case to be avoided. Two methods were practised, both of them legal: the exposure of new-born infants, and abortion. Otherwise the Athenian was a good husband and a good father. Literary texts draw a discreet veil over little babies, but there are many descriptions of happy family lives involving children.

Two aspects of the birth of a child in Classical Athens are of interest: the physical and the ritual. The first concerned only the women: the mother, her female relatives and knowledgeable neighbours who could be relied upon to help together with a more or less competent professional midwife. There were also the goddesses who presided over the event, such as Artemis Locheia or Eileithyia. The doubtful conditions of hygiene, the frequent extreme youth of the parents, the repeated and frequent pregnancies and many other causes must have brought a terrible toll of stillborn babies without the need for voluntary abortion. This, in any case, could not be performed without the father's consent. Children who were sickly or malformed, or simply any unwanted female children, were exposed at birth. Sometimes a barren wife or a professional baby-snatcher would try to rescue a rejected child, but most of these died. To their families, these exposed babies had just never existed, and the fathers had probably never seen them.

The ritual connected with the birth of a child was the festival of the Amphidromia and was begun a few days later. It was a ceremony of purification for the mother and all those who had assisted in her labour, and a ritual by which the child was officially recognized as a member of the family. The ceremony took place around the hearth, which symbolized the striking of roots and the continuity of time. The baby was carried round the hearth and then placed down on the ground nearby. When it was lifted up, it could then receive its name; it was no longer a simple product of animal nature, but a human being and an accepted member of the family. Its father no longer had the right to get rid of it. If it was male and the firstborn, it received the name of the paternal grandfather, of whom it thus became a symbolic reincarnation. In the following autumn, at the Apaturia, the civic festival of the phratries (assemblies of closely-linked families), the child was presented by the father to the members for official enrollment, thus ensuring his future status as a citizen of the *polis*.

This was the equivalent of our registration on the civil or voters' lists, and was the occasion for congratulations to the member who had thus attained the dignity of a father. His wife and the legitimacy of his offspring were now beyond suspicion. One virtue of this public act was that the legitimacy was made manifest throughout the neighbourhood. There was the case of a certain Frastor who tried to register a child he had had by a well-known courtesan. His neighbours would have none of it, and so Frastor, in his anger, sued them in the lawcourts. When he was required to declare under oath that his wife was a citizen and that he was legitimately married to her, he did not dare to perjure himself and abandoned both his ' wife ' and the child. There are many similar examples in ' Against Neaera ' which demonstrate how the city of Athens, without any central records organization or police force, was able to maintain the integrity of its civic life merely by self-discipline within its many social groups under the vigilance of its inhabitants. There might have been a slackness of morals within the privacy of a citizen's family life, but this was not allowed to intrude into public affairs.

CHILDHOOD

We are well informed about the early years of a child's life, spent entirely in the *gynaikeion* (women's quarters) where vase-paintings show us women going about their toilet. When we do see children, they are usually being tightly wrapped up in swaddling clothes until they resemble nothing more than shapeless bundles. When the artist is really interested in children he shows them being prepared for the bath, one slave getting the water ready and another handing the baby to its mother who has just put down the lyre which she was playing. The Athenians, who seemed unfeeling at the birth of a child, and, later, when they put young people to hard work, nevertheless appeared to surround the child of tender years with much care and affection. It was not unknown for the father to attend to the needs of a small baby. There were good precedents in Homer: Peleus had held the little Achilles on his knee and tried to give him (very clumsily) his feeding-bottle, and Hector had picked up in his arms the young Astyanax, who was terrified by the crest of his father's helmet. The statue of Hermes by the Athenian sculptor Praxiteles in the Olympia Museum shows the god smiling affably at the young Dionysus as he hands him a bunch of grapes.

In the majority of cases the early years of a child's life were spent in the care of a nurse, an essential member of the household, as it was she who ensured the continuity between the generations. The young wife would often bring into her new home the faithful slave who had brought her up and who, whilst continuing to look after her, would take care of her children later. The nurses were usually slaves, though

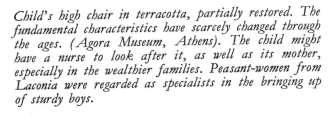

Child's high chair in terracotta, partially restored. The fundamental characteristics have scarcely changed through the ages. (Agora Museum, Athens). The child might have a nurse to look after it, as well as its mother, especially in the wealthier families. Peasant-women from Laconia were regarded as specialists in the bringing up of sturdy boys.

not often so by birth. They could be lower-class freeborn women such as could be part of the booty of war, when women from captured cities were sold on the market or taken captive by pirates. It was the fashion for the better-class Athenian families, who were always inclined to favour the Spartan way of life, to send for the peasant women of Laconia, who were strapping and generous wet nurses and knew what it took to make strong men. The remedies these women used in cases of illness were often of foreign, and therefore doubtful, origin and this, combined with the primitive hygiene of those days, must have made a young child's life precarious, to say the least. There were baths in wine or urine, poultices of unlikely composition and various concoctions to complete a badly-balanced diet during weaning, which often came late. At the basis of this there was, however, a constant care and preoccupation for the child's welfare which often produced miracles. Recourse was also had to magic in the form of amulets, strangely shaped stones and sachets of mysterious powders which warded off sickness and the evil eye.

Children did not like being parted from the company of the women who had brought then up. The nurse became a familiar figure in the classical theatre because her presence in the family was taken for granted, even if she were a slave and even if the hero, like Orestes in *The Choephoroe* (' The Libation Bearers ', a play by Aeschylus, 458 B.C.) was long past the age of swaddling clothes and feeding bottles. The nurse was moreover the only guarantee of the authenticity of the child's descent. Substitutions were possible, especially in the larger and wealthier households. Orestes himself would not have escaped from his mother's hatred had it not been for the devotion of his nurse who substituted him for her own son.

GAMES

If the father took only a remote interest in the early upbringing of his children, as most of his day was spent outside the house, this upbringing was not always entrusted entirely to women. The way the houses were built and the gentle climate brought a swarm of children out on to the doorsteps of the houses, the outer stairways, the terraces, the yards and the streets. They would play, often naked or wearing a minimum of clothing, with anything that came their way. They made their own toys with bits of damp clay and a piece of wood or material. There would also be many domestic animals around, dogs especially, but also cats and cockerels (not fully domesticated at this time and often trained for fighting), pigs, rabbits and weasels. There were also the children of the slaves with whom they were firm playmates. These things are not mentioned in contemporary documents, as they were doubtless held to be of no importance. Plato, however, had recognized the educative value of games, and he knew of the Spartan custom of encouraging children to form organized bands which the State would then supervise. In his *Laws* he gives valuable and kindly advice on how to carry little babies, on cradles, on ' songs which are veritable charms ', on the need of children between the ages of three and six to amuse themselves, and on ' games which arise of their own accord, and which children discover by themselves as soon as they are together '.

Children played with knuckle-bones, tops, yo-yos, hoops and every kind of stick. Girls had dolls which they dressed; the dolls could be made to sit down and move their heads by a very simple system of articulation. Excavations of the tombs of children have revealed numerous toys, bereaved parents evidently

thinking that their little owners should not have to go into the next world without them. The most exciting game for all children, both boys and girls, was to 'do what the grown-ups do' in which they could give free rein to their instict for imitation and prepare themselves for the adult world. This was no doubt the reason behind the work which was given to young children. The same word *pais* was used for both a child and a slave, which makes one think that young people were often used for menial tasks, rather in the same way as we have our stable-boys, bell-boys and so on. There was no legal minimum age for working, and a good part of the labour must have fallen on the shoulders of the young as well as on the slaves. This is why so many toys in Athens were miniature reproductions of real things. The little boy who arranged his toy sheep or his little vases soon learnt to drive donkeys and goats in front of him the whole day long or pass heavy baskets of clay for vases in the claypits of Cape Colias, seven miles south of Athens. 'What a long time', Socrates said to Glaucon in the *Republic* of Plato (427-348) 'must the sons of vase-makers watch and wait before they venture to make vases themselves'. It is difficult to believe that they stood watching with arms folded; it is more likely that they took post as manual labourers or as errand-boys.

From quite an early age the young boys of Athens took part in some of the festivals of the *polis*. From the age of three they had their place in the festival of spring, flowers and new wine, called the Anthesteria. Everywhere in the city the wine-jars were opened, people went to banquets, families invited their friends, drinking parties were held, there was a procession in which Dionysus, mounted on a float, was paraded past the citizens, and everyone thought of the dead now that spring was beginning again. The festival resembled our modern carnival. The small children wore crowns of flowers and were given toys. They seem to have done their best to join in the fun, as we can see from a plump little boy shown in a painting as he crawls towards a table laden with good food, watched by a very dignified cock which is taller than he is. Every time a family held a celebration or took part in the festivals of the *polis* it can be assumed that there were little children there as well. Some of the children were given certain functions to perform. In the festivals of Athena and of Dionysus they acted as bearers of the appropriate symbols.

Torch bearers, runners and dancers did not have to attain their majority before they could express in the world of ritual what their youth symbolized: hope in the family and the 'spring of the *polis*'.

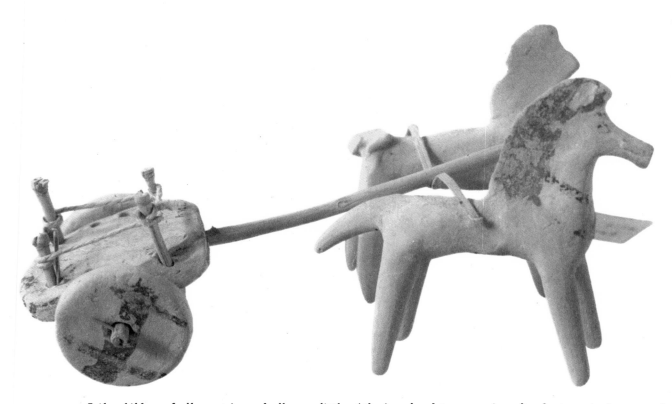

Like children of all countries and all ages, little Athenians loved toys, running after hoops, spinning tops, throwing and catching balls. There were toys of all kinds: jointed dolls for the girls, soldiers, horses, sheep of wood or terracotta for the boys. Opposite: bronze statue of a child at play from the Archaeological Museum, Athens. Above: a little votive cart from the Museum, Corinth.

THE AUTHORITY OF THE FATHER

In the world of civic affairs and politics, however, childhood and youth had no rights and no influence. Paternal authority was very real. The father could no longer dispose of the life of his children, as he once could, but he still had considerable powers, such as being able to sell into slavery a daughter who had allowed herself to be seduced. This total, exclusive authority of the head of the family was a very important element in that balance of functions between the two sexes within the household. According to Plato there was a saying in Athens: ' We gather all our wealth between four walls and entrust it to the management of our wives '. But it was the husband who took all the important decisions concerning the family possessions, the women of the household and the children. Whilst he was alive his power was absolute. Attic orators show us the husband consulting with his friends and arguing with them about what he should do at home far more frequently than they report his conversations with his wife on the same subject. If he was called away on a journey or to war he would entrust these necessary decisions to a friend or a relative, in the presence of a witness, and his wife and children would have to accept the trustee's authority. With the setting up of his own home the husband acquired a new civil status. He was now free from any power his father had over him, and virtually out of reach of the patriarchal tyranny of his grandfather. The legal basis of the regime was the small or the conjugal family; this did not, of course, exclude respect for the old or the obligation to feed and look after them which was provided for under the law of Solon. The patrimony was administered solely by the husband who had absolute right over the marriage settlement and over the possessions of his children under majority age, except in the case of divorce when he was obliged to return the value of his wife's dowry. He was the sole legal representative of his wife, his children until they attained their majority, and his slaves, of whom he was the legal owner, as they were counted among his property. The orator Isaeus (*c.* 420 - *c.* 350) the teacher of Demosthenes (383-322) said that a child could not bequeath his property ' because the law expressly forbids him to enter into any contract, as is also the case with women, if the value concerned is more than that of a *medimnos* of barley '. This quantity was worth two or three drachmae and was clearly intended to limit the wife's financial responsibility to the amount which would be spent in the house daily, to the small amount her husband would allow her, or to matters of minimum importance.

GOOD HOUSEKEEPING

We should remember, however, that in Athens, which was a rich city by ancient standards, there was much less actual currency in circulation than one might perhaps expect, and the greater part of the family property could not easily be converted into cash. There were fields, or perhaps a farm, in the country, houses, workshops and slaves in the city, furniture and jewels, household equipment including valuable vases, but doubtless very little money. With the development of trade in the Piraeus in the fifth century B.C. ' banks ' were opened everywhere and with them the opportunity arose to increase one's capital. There were private investments, loans, often without interest, to neighbours or friends, and long-term promissory notes. Sea-borne trade seems to have brought in considerable profits. Only enough cash was left at home to cover the more immediate necessities.

All the drachmae, the minae and the talents mentioned by the orators of antiquity, all the money which was called the ' blood and the soul of mortals ' was mostly so many figures in accounts, representing the value of assets. When the slave had to be sent to the market to do the family shopping, the houswife was often hard put to it to find the few necessary oboles. Coins representing the sub-divisions of units were much scarcer than the units themselves, and it was frequently necessary to resort to forms of barter, to daily credit and to discounts for prompt settlement.

But, one might ask, were there not also rich families in Athens? Indeed there were. In certain lawsuits concerned with inheritances, or discussions on financial matters involving an exchange of goods, details of this wealth were often quoted: ' the property in the deme of Phyla, which could well be worth one talent ', ' the house in the city near the statue of Dionysus in the Marshes, let and bringing in an income of one thousand drachmae ', or ' the slave, an

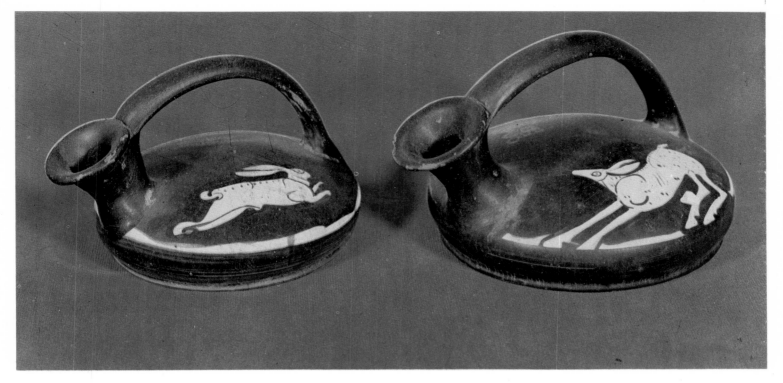

The Athenian household contained receptacles of all kinds, some of them precious, painted with figures or friezes, and used to store food or liquids. They could form part of the table service, or contain perfume, or, like these two askoi, be used for balsam. (National Museum, Ferrara).

expert laundress, whom he is putting up for sale in the market'. If, however, there was a banquet to be provided for at home, a daughter to be married off, or a relative ransomed from pirates, or if a jealous fate had designated one for one of those costly public offices in the city such as the *trierarchia*, which involved the fitting out of a trireme, or the *choregia*, which meant recruiting and supporting a theatre chorus, then it would be necessary to take out an immediate loan. Ready money on this scale was no more easily available to the rich than small change was to the poor, and the expense of the *trierarchia* was considered crippling.

It must be remembered that the family had so to order its affairs that it could function as a self-supporting unit. Inviting friends to a banquet meant ensuring that enough food had been stored away and sufficient wine had been drawn. The shepherd had to send down the roughly cured skin of one of those sheep which grazed up in the hills around Athens before the cobbler could be given the raw material and asked to make a pair of fine shoes for the wife or the daughter. When the Athenian admiral Timotheus saw arrive at his house in the Piraeus two im-

portant foreign visitors who had come to give him their support in certain difficult political matters, he was compelled to send a slave to his banker to borrow cloaks, covers, two silver cups and a hundred drachmae. This was, of course, a single example and Timotheus was not by any means a model husband, but it does suggest that frequent borrowings were necessary between neighbours and friends to make good the deficiencies of the system. It was a sacred duty to welcome a guest, considered to be sent by Zeus, but there seems little evidence of preparations being made beforehand. It was customary to record mortgages on the boundary stones of property in Attica. Many of these were for limited amounts and seem to have been pledges to pay an amount fixed in advance. They were clearly not the transactions of small property owners who had been ruined and were getting deeper into debt before finally losing all their possessions. The owners were usually persons of considerable means who found this the only way to raise some ready cash, perhaps for some family matter or a dowry.

Xenophon's *Oeconomicus*, or the 'Management of a Household and Property', was therefore a completely new science to the Greeks. It was taken up later by Aristotle (384-322), who developed it into some thing resembling the economics we know today.

SUCCESSION

We learn more about the administration of family property from what happened when a person died, when questions of inheritance and succession arose. As far as material things were concerned, the death of the wife meant very little. If there were no children, the husband lost no time in looking for another partner. If there were children and he did not wish to remarry, the problem was solved by the old nurse taking over the children and the concubine carried on with the housework, together with the slaves. The death of the father of a family was a much more serious matter. This immediately put his wife under the tutelage of his old guardian or another man, who could be his oldest son if there were no other near male relative. A man could designate in his will another man to become his widow's new husband, an arrangement which could have its compensations if there were a large dowry.

It was, however, the future of the patrimony which was at stake. Athenian custom sought to reconcile, in a way which could cause the least harm, the traditions of ancient Greek law, which tended towards preserving the unity of the heritage, perpetuating the family line and continuing the cult of the ancestors, with the more modern 'democratic' aspirations towards equality of rights and individual free-will. Masculine privilege had existed since ancient times, and this had put the daughters in an unfair position compared with the sons, given priority to the men over the women, and generally put the relatives on the father's side before those on the mother's, right down the line of succession. There was also a very ancient system known as the *epicleratos*, a legal fiction justified on religious grounds, by which a daughter marrying a close relative of her late father lost her share of the inheritance to any son she bore. This ensured that the patrimony continued unbroken down the family line. Although these ancient usages continued, there were many attempts to override them. It is true that an equal division of the inheritance between sons and daughters tended to break up the patrimony into small lots, but to try to avoid this by having only one son was too dangerous. There were frequent wars, not to mention plagues, illnesses and other dangers, which meant that sons often died before their fathers. It was not uncommon to adopt another son when the male succession had died out.

Adoption could be certified in due and proper form, like the declaration of a birth in front of the phratry and the deme of the adoptive father. More often than not, however, adoption was an attempt to legalize the illegitimate, or a device to get round some awkward or unwelcome arrangement in a will. In cases such as these, there was no hesitation in contesting it in the courts on the plea that it was the act of a man in his dotage or at the mercy of some adventuress.

It could happen that the succession fell to children under age who had to be entrusted to guardians. This meant the intrusion into the family circle of a more distant relative, or even of a stranger, friend or neighbour whom the dying man in his last days had considered the right person to look after his children.

Demosthenes' father had entrusted his two young children and their mother, just before he died, to two of his nephews and a childhood friend. As the patrimony was one of the most important in Athens and the guardians were incapable, or perhaps too capable, the young Demosthenes had to go to law to recover his own inheritance and use it to defend that of his mother and sister. Such was the beginning of his career.

It was frequently the case that the trustees turned out to be dishonest and embezzled the property of their wards. The task was often made easier for them when the husband had handed over in his will his widow or daughter in marriage. Attic law seems to have favoured the right of the individual to act in accordance with ancient custom, which weighed heavily on the family. Once it became possible to have recourse to public appeal in a court presided over by the *archon*, things became progressively easier.

FUNERALS

The death of the husband or wife, or of an aged relative surrounded by filial affection, or of a young member of the family prematurely taken away by

The Greeks spent part of their day in pastimes. Amongst the most popular were dice and bones, the latter being the smoothed-down knuckle-bones from the ankle of a goat. Knuckle-bone games are still found today: guessing their number, throwing them into a hole, or using them like dice with their four faces. (Agora Museum, Athens).

illness or war, was much more than a question of financial settlements or legal wrangling for the average Athenian family. The fatalism of the Greeks and their sense of the inevitable were generally too strong to provoke any revolt against death. This was the human condition, and in the classical age there was none of that sugary sentimentality we find in the epitaphs of the following Hellenistic period. It was, however, a time of great grief for the family, and through their mourning we can see a very dignified and moving side of Athenian life. Their grief was expressed audibly and visibly: the body was laid out in the lobby of the house amid the lamentations of the family and the neighbours, while the women wailed and wept, tore out their hair, scratched their faces or sprinkled themselves with ashes. These excessive manifestations, so typical of the south, eventually became a matter of public concern. Athens, in common with other cities, attempted to bring them under control by limiting the mourning to only the closest relatives. This was not very easy, however,

as there was more to these noisy expressions of grief than mere mourning of the departed. It was also necessary to ward off any evil which might arise from contact with the dead. The house and everything in it was held to be contaminated, and required to be purified by special rites when the mourners returned from the funeral. This in itself was not enough to revive the life spirit which had been defiled by the presence of the corpse: the spirit had to be conjured up again by noisy lamentation, music and funeral banquets. The invocation of the dead, the funeral lament *(threnos)*, the praise of the departed, all had symbolic value and the funeral ceremony itself, as well as the later cult of the dead, had one fundamental motive: to ensure that the corpse was really dead, that it was not left unsatisfied or avenged or improperly buried, in which case it would surely return to earth and torment the living.

The funeral procession usually took place at night. The corpse was carried outside the walls of the town to a cemetery such as the one in the Ceramicus district.

There it was burnt on a pyre, and the ashes were then collected in an urn, or it was buried. Burial was the more ancient custom and it still survived in Classical Athens. Libations of wine, milk and perfumed oil were poured on the deceased. Later a monument was erected to the deceased: a cippus (section of a column without capital), a stele or a simple flagstone. On each anniversary, or on special feast-days, the relatives returned to decorate the tomb with strips of woollen cloth, to place on it flowers and wreaths and to bring new offerings in specially shaped ritual vases. These vases were of two kinds: the *lechithoi* which had finely painted scenes of mourning against a white background, and the *loutrophoroi* with their figures, painted in red, of the young girls whose premature death they recalled.

The scenes depicted on the vases and sculptures of the steles show that there was another side to the family life as described by the orators and comedians, a side which had nothing to do with money, personal defects or ridicule. Suffering had brought with it a refinement, husband and wife were closer together and the last farewells of a bereaved family sometimes have a dramatic intensity, as on the stele of Damosistratos or that of Theanos in the Athens Museum. There is a similarity between the look in the eyes of Ctesileos as he gazes at his wife, sitting in the already hieratic position of those whose death has made them heroes, and that of the old man, the father on a stele said to be by Ilyssos, who seems to be praying before his dead son, lost in the prime of his life, while a little slave-boy and the dead youth's favourite dog look on, each expressing in his own way his sorrow and bewilderment. These reliefs with one or two figures, and sometimes also the portrayals of family reunions, as on the Phainippos stele in the Louvre, admirably express the normal sentiments of an Athenian family. The steles do not always show men and women reunited, perhaps because of some reticence on the part of the artist in showing conjugal relationships, even in death. The stele of Mnesaretis is quite as moving, although it shows just two women. The difference between their ages is clearly shown; this was a period in which art chose to represent the essential, the fullness of humanity and not the transience of existence. The artist sought to emphasize the solidity of the family bonds and death never appeared with the twisted, strident features we find in Etruscan art.

SLAVES: 'INSTRUMENTS WITH SOULS'

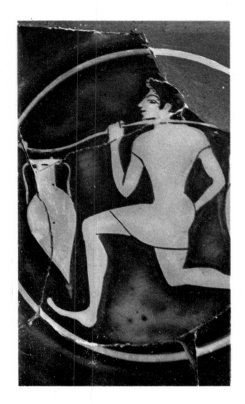

'Instrument with soul', according to Aristotle's definition, 'human merchandise' according to the law, the slave was a fundamental part of life in Athens. Private and public slaves carried out a wide variety of tasks according to their training, their abilities and to the trust put in them. They dug out silver in the Laurion mines in the southern tip of Attica, worked as labourers alongside free men on public works, ran businesses, worked as craftsmen, servants, cooks, sailors, teachers and administrators. Some of them were even employed in the public service, and in the fifth century it was the slaves who formed the first city police. Slave women worked as waitresses, laundresses, wet-nurses, spinners of yarn, or were exploited by their owners for the oldest profession in the world.

Formerly slaves had been prisoners of war, or captured by pirates, or left exposed to die as little children. In Athens they were generally treated better than they would have been in most other cities of the period. They could earn wages, often equal to those of free men, and once they had paid their master for their board and lodging, they might even be able to put a little aside and eventually buy their own freedom. It was not unknown for this 'human merchandise', these 'instruments with souls' also to take part in certain religious festivals and mystery rites.

Slavery was a fundamental component of society in Classical Athens. In earlier periods of Greek history there had been slaves as a consequence of defeat in war or of indebtedness, and there are examples of these in Homer. The sixth century, however, saw slavery put on a commercial basis when money began to replace bartering and the big cities with sea-going trade such as Melos (Milo), Chios, Aegina and Corinth took on an importance equal to that of great inland trading cities. Man was not considered to have a natural right to liberty; anyone falling into the power of a foreigner could be considered immediately as a slave to be bought and sold.

The expropriation of the possessions of citizens in debt and their degradation into slavery was stopped under a law of Solon in 594 B.C. It was really not until the fifth century that the great influx of slaves arising from overseas trading began to reach the country districts in Attica.

Where did the slaves come from? The main source was Attica's continual warfare. Slave dealers went in the wake of armies and bought up the prisoners, whom they then sold at great profit. During the Persian War, in the battle off the mouth of the river Eurymedon along the coast of southern Asia Minor (467 B.C.), the Athenian commander Cimon took 20,000 prisoners, all of whom were sold into slavery. Many Athenians themselves were taken off as slaves after their surrender outside Syracuse (413 B.C.). Another source of slavery was piracy, which infected the whole Mediterranean until put down by the Romans. Plato, for example, was captured by pirates when returning from Sicily and taken for sale to the market of Aegina, where he was ransomed by a friend for a considerable sum. Unwanted children could by custom be abandoned at birth and anyone who found them and brought them up could keep them as slaves. Most slaves in Athens, however, were 'barbarians', a term used to designate all non-Greeks, and came particularly from countries to the north and east where the sale and exchange of these unfortunate creatures was particularly rife. One Athenian, according to a document of 415 B.C. had sixteen slaves and these came from Thrace (five), Caria (three), Syria (two), Illyria (two) and Colchis, Scythia, Lydia and Malta (one each).

The customs duty levied on a slave was two per cent of his sale price. Strict standards were imposed in the market: the proprietor guaranteed the slave to be free from defects or illness unless declared, and failure to make such a declaration rendered him liable to give the purchaser his money back. The purchase had to be made public by the town crier or by written notice, so that if the slave already had a legal owner from whom he might have escaped, he could be returned and the sale stopped. The price varied from 100 to 200 drachmae depending on the age, the physical condition and, above all, the particular aptitudes of the slave. A boy would fetch 70 drachmae, a specialized craftsman 300, which was also the price of an attractive girl slave. Nicias, one of the wealthiest mining contractors in Athens, paid 6,000 drachmae for a highly qualified Thracian slave whom he employed as a technician.

During the fifth and fourth centuries B.C. these prices, which it is impossible to evaluate in terms of today's money, remained almost constant. Relatively speaking the prices were quite high when it is realized that the average income of an Athenian who had to live by his own means was about 15 drachmae a month. It is evident that only persons of considerable means could employ slaves in any number. Very many Athenians did not have these means and, like Socrates, provided personally for themselves and their families without the help of slaves. Others had one only. The orator Aeschines had seven. A man owning fifty, like Demosthenes' father who employed them in his workshops, was considered very wealthy. Nicias with his thousand must have had the most.

The total number in Athens at this time can be estimated only approximately. There were probably some 300,000 people in the whole of Attica in the time of Pericles. Of these about 40,000 men were of military age: together with their families they totalled some 150,000. There were about 50,000 foreigners (free men) and the remainder, about 100,000, were

slaves. The figures for Athens were of course proportionately less.

THE WORK OF SLAVES

The work done by slaves was very varied. Few were employed in agriculture, as the small Attic farms were run almost entirely by their owners who themselves worked the fields and took the produce to market. There were also many one-man workshops in the crowded quarter between the Areopagus and the Pnyx which did not need slave labout either.

As manufacturing and trade expanded, however, a larger labour force became necessary and employers increasingly had recourse to slaves. There were medium-sized industries (*ergasteria*) employing twenty or thirty slaves as apprentices or specialized workers (*cheirotechnai*) in the production of metal utensils, furniture, leather goods, textiles, pottery and other craftwork. The more trustworthy and intelligent slaves sometimes had supervisory jobs and occupied positions of administrative responsibility. The administrator of Pericles' household and property, for example, was a slave.

Women slaves worked especially at spinning, laundering, and similar occupations, or were employed in prostitution. When an undertaking employing slave labour failed and was sold, the slaves went with it and figured on the stock as 'living' goods.

Slavery was a determining factor in the rise of Athens from a city state based on agriculture to a trading city and a great sea power which came to be head of an empire.

The mines at Laurion in southern Attica were particularly important in the development of the economy; it was here that the silver was extracted for the coining of money. They were run by very wealthy citizens such as Nicias, who will be discussed more fully in the chapter on economy. Fortunes were made by these men who were given contracts to exploit the mines.

The labour force in the mines consisted almost entirely of slaves who were mainly foreign and were employed in every phase of the operations: digging, extracting, washing the ore and smelting.

In the mid-fourth century B.C., when trade was particularly healthy, there were some 30,000 slave

Many craftsmen used slave labour, particularly for the working of metal. There were arms factories employing slaves in both Athens and the Piraeus. (Museo dei Conservatori, Rome).

workers in the Laurion mines. As in all mining operations, conditions of work were very hard: a shift lasted ten hours, the men digging by torchlight and extending the galleries, extracting the ore and carrying it up to the surface. The workings reached a depth of well over 300 feet and revealed an engineering technique of extraordinary accuracy. There were safety regulations covering the use of pit props and other installations in the mines. The ore was treated in workshops nearby and these also contained accommodation for the men. They have yielded interesting remains to the archaeologists.

The slaves employed in running the household clearly had a better life. They were called *oiketai* and acted as servants, handymen, maids and nurses. They could be employed on general duties or assigned to one particular member of the household. The wealthier families employed them in many different tasks such as guards, cooks, travelling companions, and so on. They were often kept as concubines. The more educated and intelligent slaves could even hold positions of some responsibility such as family doctor or children's tutor.

In addition to mining, agricultural work and household duties, another occupation was open to slaves: that of public service in which they were employed as door-keepers, town-criers, cashiers, scribes. Some functions required them to have other slaves under them. In their capacity as clerk to a tribunal or as a book-keeper they could have the right to sign documents and authenticate administrative memoranda. Their long experience of public administration was particularly useful as public officials in Athens were in office for only a year at a time. It is especially interesting to note that in the fifth century the police service developed from slave labour. It began in 476 B.C. when a force of 300 Scythians was used to keep order in the streets during public assemblies. They were later given the unpleasant duty of carrying out death sentences.

LIVING CONDITIONS

A slave, therefore, could work either for a private individual or for a public body: in either case his function was an executive one. The Greek word most commonly used for a slave was *dulos*, which meant 'servant'. Our concept of 'slave' goes back only to the Middle Ages and it is significant that in Athens the same word *dulos* was used for the day-labourer, who was a free man. A characteristic of the slave in Athens was less a deprivation of rights than a lack of individual autonomy.

Aristotle, defining the slave as 'an instrument with a soul' (*Nichomachean Ethics*, 1161 b), also said that such a person was a 'slave by nature' (*Politics*, 1254 a). This did not mean that he was by nature devoid of rights, but rather that he was destined by natural inclination to slavery. We might feel today that his status was rather more coincidental.

Remains of inscriptions on the Erechtheum on the Acropolis, Athens, show beyond doubt that slaves worked on the building together with free men and for the same wages. Slave labour, however, tended to depress the earnings of all workers, and many poor citizens would come to envy the slave who had a good master and was at least assured of food and lodging. Opposite: the knife-grinder. (Uffizi, Florence).

110

The legal status of the slave in Athens was somewhat limited by the right of his owner to dispose of him as he wished; yet he was never considered quite as an inanimate object. After he had been bought, according to the legal term, as ' human merchandise ', the slave was completely deprived of the political rights enjoyed by the free citizen. There was, however, another class of citizens who, though born free, were also without rights: these were the metics, the many foreign residents in Athens. A slave could not give evidence in a court of law, yet any crime committed against him was not only considered a crime against his master, but was also punishable as a crime against the slave as well. In this sense the slave was recognizable under law. In contrast to the free-born citizen, however, a slave could be tortured: this, according to Demosthenes, was the only difference be-

tween slaves and free citizens! The only protection the slave had against ill-treatment by his master was the right of sanctuary in certain holy places, where the priest would have to decide whether to send the slave back or sell him again to a new master. Finally a slave might be allowed to marry, but any children born to him belonged automatically to his master.

The treatment meted out to slaves and their daily living conditions depended less on their lack of rights than on the temperament of their master, the social status of the household and various local conditions.

Some master were sadists, miserly and mistrustful, who beat their slaves, left them without food or chained them up. Others on the other hand put great trust in them and treated them with considerable generosity.

Theophrastus' ' Characters ' gives us the clearest picture of the everyday life of a slave in Athens at this time: the slave sent to the market to do the shopping, the slave at the theatre offering his master a seat, the slave-girl at home inciting the jealousy of her mistress. The Attic comedies of Aristophanes and Menander show us various types of slave: the faithful, the cunning, the lazy and the scrounger.

There was no restriction on the slave's movements in public. A somewhat old-fashioned observer in or about the year 403 commented acidly on the fact that in Athens the slaves did not give way to free citizens in the streets and, moreover, since all were dressed more or less alike, it was very difficult to distinguish them. Slaves were admitted to certain religious observances, sacrificial feasts and mystery cults. Remains of epigraphs on the Erechtheum on the Acropolis record the fact that day-labourers and slave-workers toiled together on the building for the same wages. Free workers were continually up against competition from slave-labour. Citizens who had been dispossessed could rightly envy the slave whose master provided at least bed and board, as the poet Philemon recorded.

Slave-workers could keep back for themselves a part of their wages, particularly in cases where they ran a business for their master or were in charge of a workshop and had their own quarters. They had to provide for themselves and pay their master a fixed sum from the product of their labour, thus ensuring for him a return on the capital he had laid out in his purchase of them.

For many Athenians the income they thus received from slave labour enabled them to live very well. Anyone who possessed three slaves to hire out for labour had enough income to live in considerable comfort. The master was not the only one to benefit from this arrangement. The slave himself could save enough money eventually to purchase his freedom. Slavery was no doubt a form of exploitation of labour, but it was to some extent mitigated by the possibility of eventual freedom.

THE POSSIBILITIES OF RANSOM

As a rule, any slave who could offer his master an adequate sum was released. Several slaves or several free citizens could club together to raise the money needed for the ransom. A slave could be freed by his master in recompense for his faithful service, without having to pay anything, as happened in the case of the slave who acted as tutor to Themistocles. The freeing of a slave was merely a formal act before witnesses, like his purchase or his sale. There were nearly always conditions such as the slave's obligation to look after his master in his old age, to pay him rent or remain under his roof. A freed slave in Athens did not gain civil rights: his legal status was similar to that of the metics. He was, however, allowed to assume the title of citizen and no obstacle was put in his way towards his rising on the social ladder. In the fourth century a certain Pasion, a slave in the service of a banker, was enfranchised by his master, married his widow, inherited the bank and obtained citizenship. His son became a counsellor and moved in the highest circles in Athenian life. Cases occured of many slaves being enfranchised at the same time on the decision of the people because they had fought alongside free citizens as volunteers. They were not obliged to undertake military service, yet many did so, in particular at Marathon, at the naval battle of the Arginusae Islands (406 B.C.) and at Phyle (404 B.C.). After their defeat by Philip of Macedon at Chaeronea (338 B.C.) the Athenians, fearing another attack, decided to enfranchise all the slaves so that they too could take part in the defence of the city. The attack never came, however, and the decision was never carried out.

In the light of the relative liberty enjoyed by the slave in Athens, the possibilities of enfranchisement and of advancement in society, it is not surprising that there was never any serious rebellion by the slaves. It should also be remembered that they had absolutely no class consciousness and that no slave leader ever arose to put forward programmes of a political or a revolutionary nature. Except for a few modest professional or religious associations, there was no slaves' organization, which in any case would have proved impractical as they came from different peoples, spoke many different languages and worked often in isolation in households or factories. Wherever they did gather in large numbers, as in the mines, they were more closely guarded. A runaway slave was branded with a hot iron on recapture. During the war with Sparta 20,000 Athenian slaves fled from the city and gave themselves up to the Spartans, hoping to achieve their freedom, but the Spartans merely sold them to the Thebans. It was quite impossible for a slave to free himself in this way.

A slave-girl fastens her mistress's sandal. (Grave stele of Ameihokleia, National Museum, Athens).

Yet the first movements which ultimately led to the abolition of slavery started in Athens. Sophists such as Hippias and Antiphon in their critique of society taught that the difference in state between the free and the non-free was a contradiction of the principle of natural order. Alcidamantes, a follower of Gorgias of Leontini (Sicily) (*c.* 485-375), added that God had made all men free, and nature could not enslave anyone (Scol. Arist. Rhet. I 1373 b.). Euripides (480-406) and Socrates (469-399) affirmed in their turn that being a slave was not a matter of legal status but of a man's inner conviction that he was one.

Though slavery was to last for a long time, some in Athens had begun to point the way to a respect for man and for liberty which was eventually to lead to a world where slavery was unknown.

THE BANQUET, A CUSTOM OF THE AGE

The banquet was an opportunity for merriment in the evening, and the Greeks knew how to provide enjoyment for both the senses and the spirit. Conversation round a well-furnished table, far from the eyes of wives, copiously flowing wine and beautiful girls decked in ribbons and garlands were for the average Athenian the dolce vita *which few could indulge in but many envied. This was the* symposium *such as a man might offer his friends and which could include clowns, acrobats, jugglers, dancers and women flute-players, as well as succulent dishes washed down, according to strict rules, by cups of fine wine.*

For some it could be much less or much more: an evening among friends with a great deal of buffoonery and coarse joking, in the smoky light of oil lamps, wine cup in hand and troubles left behind, or, for those differently inclined, a communion of the intellect in the everlasting search after truth.

The latter was the kind of banquet which Plato defined in the first books of his Laws *as a training-ground for man's intellect: a banquet in which wine had an active part to play in both opening up men's minds to freedom of discussion and in providing a release from inhibitions. In such an atmosphere a man's judgements would be tempered, his spirit would find a new source of inspiration and ' like a piece of iron heated to incandescence, it would become malleable in the hands of those who would lead it back to what it was in the happy days of long ago '.*

The custom whereby men sat down to eat together, which gave rise in the fifth century B.C. to the banquet, or *symposium*, was as old as the Greek world itself. It dated back to the camaraderie of soldiers gathered round their chiefs as described by Homer. This was true in both the Achaean age, when the ancient heroes endeavoured to capture Troy (Mycenaean period, about 1200 B.C.) and the so-called ' dark ages ' which followed the overthrow of the Achaean civilization by the new Greek hordes, the Dorians (*c.* 1100 B.C.).

In this early age of Greek history the chief was surrounded by his men and all fought together, united by the strongest bonds of loyalty and interdependence. The men fed at the chief's table. In the fourth canto of the *Iliad* Agamemnon, speaking to the Cretan Idomeneus, recalls the bonds which unite them: ' You know how greatly I honour you amongst all our knights, in war and elsewhere, and at table when the Argive nobility mix in the bowl the full-blooded wine which is served at our feasts. For the Achaeans with the long flowing hair, the ordinary ration: for you, as for me, the full cup. Drink to your heart's desire '.

The custom was virtually the same in Sparta, where the feast brought people together as equals and where aristocratic aloofness was not favoured. All citizens had to take their evening meal together, in groups of fifteen, and even the children were obliged to do the same. This public eating *(syssitia)* was said to be due to Lycurgus and, according to Plutarch, was intended to prevent soldier-citizens ' from spending their time indoors, lounging about on costly couches, the prey of merchants and cooks, growing fat like greedy brutes and ruining not only their minds but also their bodies '.

Everyone participating in the public meal paid a monthly contribution: barley flour, wine, cheese, figs and a small amount of money towards the meat.

A favourite was the famous (and infamous) black broth of heavily seasoned pork. Anyone who could not afford to pay was automatically excluded from the category of citizen.

At these meals there were none of those indulgences which the Spartans condemned in the feasts of other Greeks. There was healthy enjoyment in eating and good company, the recitation of fine acts and heroic deeds, and children were allowed to listen in.

Spartan austerity was eventually relaxed, it is true. The public meals became less frugal and those participating came to recline on soft couches, until eventually the *syssitiae* were an anachronism, and Sparta, the city of scandalous social inequality, could hardly recognize itself as the former bastion of military customs inherited from time immemorial and of those regimental 'tables' which perpetuated the comradeship of the soldiery and forged the intrepid spirit of the peers.

In addition to these comradely gatherings there were many opportunities for friends to meet for a simple drink, and this custom was to be found in the most ancient times, whether it be in the lands of Doria, Aeolia or the more voluptuous Ionia. The elegies of Theognis of Megara (second half of sixth century B.C.) have lines in praise of wine and banquets: 'Let us now enjoy the pleasures of drinking and making noble discourse; what shall come hereafter is in the hands of the Gods'. The same sentiments are echoed in the verses of the poet Alcaeus of Lesbos (7th-6th century B.C.), for whom, as Athenaeus said eight centuries later, any occasion was an excuse for drinking: 'Let us not abandon our hearts to grief; grief will not cure us of ill, oh Bacchus! The best remedy is to send for wine and get drunk'. Even the refined poet Anacreon of Theos liked to drink in convivial company, but with moderation: 'Bring the water, boy, bring the wine, bring the garlands of flowers that I may measure my strength against that of Eros'.

We can see another kind of banquet from the fragments of the sixth-century Ionian poet and philosopher Xenophanes of Colophon, who described philosophical assemblies at which the participants discussed, in a pure atmosphere of religious solemnity and moral gravity, matters of divine import. The passage is worth quoting in full: 'Behold the floor of the room is swept, the hands are washed, the wine cups polished clean. One gives out crowns to the guests, another offers in a cup a sweet perfume. The bowl is raised on high amid exclamations of joy. The wine in the jars is ready, plentiful, sweet and perfumed; the incense fills the air with its pleasant vapours. The water is cool, sweet and pure. White bread is served, the festive board is covered with cheeses and honey. The altar in the middle is decked with flowers. The whole room rings with songs and gay laughter. Firstly the philosophers praise the gods with pure and pious words, drinking libations and asking for grace to be just. There is one thing, my friends, we are particularly careful about: we drink only what we can carry home with us unassisted, if our strength has not been diminished by age'.

FREE MEN'S AMUSEMENTS

In the fifth century the banquet became a recognized part of Athenian life and as such provided the free citizen with his principal form of relaxation.

Bust of Socrates (Uffizi, Florence).

'Alcibiades: Agathon, have me brought, if there be one, a large cup...' (Plato, Symposium). 'Socrates: When cultured persons meet to dine, they do not need the company of flute-players, dancing-girls or lute-players; they are sufficient unto themselves for their own entertainment...' (Plato, Protagoras). Banqueting-cup. (Capitoline Museums, Rome).

It was essentially an institution for men, and only 'kept' women were allowed entry.

There were important differences between the two parts of the banquet: eating and drinking. The guests ate reclining in twos and threes on couches arranged in the shape of a horse-shoe around the table containing the food. They would lie with their legs outstretched and their bodies upright, supported on cushions. The host took the position at the head of the table and invited the most honoured guest to sit at his side.

The eating ended with the drinking of libations and the singing of hymns to the Gods, as if to bring a greater sense of gravity to the drinking which was to follow. But a *symposium* was more than a banquet, more than eating and drinking at a common table. The Greeks, with their concern for law and order, distinctive characteristics of human society, considered the participants as a state in miniature, requiring the appointment of a leader and the elaboration of a constitution. In this sense, Plato's *Symposium* is very characteristic: the drinkers, tired from all the wine they had consumed on the previous day, decided to limit their conduct and to 'restrict themselves in drinking to what was only their own pleasure'. They chose Phaedros to be lord of the feast, as it was he who had made the proposal to which all had agreed: to devote a whole evening's conversation to love, in the course of which each guest would have the opportunity of praising a god who, although the father of our destinies, had not yet found his true prophet.

There could also be revolutions in the miniature state of the *symposium* as well as in the *polis*. Everyone remembers Alcibiades' appearance at Agathon's banquet in Plato's *Symposium*. He was completely drunk and wore on his head a thickly-woven crown of ivy leaves and violets hung about with ribands. He bawled at the guests and asked if he could join them at the

table. He immediately proclaimed himself lord of the feast, on the pretext that the others were too sober: 'Therefore to preside over your drinking, until such time as you can drain your cups as is befitting, I shall be the chosen one! Agathon, have them bring me a large cup of wine, if there is one...'. But the new *archon* (as he proclaimed himself) was no tyrant and deigned to enter into the proceedings arranged before his noisy and scandalous irruption. If he had to speak he would do so, and it should be a eulogy of Socrates, one which, in truth, should not stray too far from the pre-arranged theme of love.

Even such a well-regulated society ran the risk of being broken up by force. A band of noisy revellers, finding the door open, burst into the banqueting hall and banished all semblance of order (*cosmos* in Greek, the word being equally applicable to correct behaviour at a banquet and to the harmony of the universe). The guests then proceeded to drink without restraint until eventually some left and others fell asleep. Even Aristophanes and Agathon, who for a long time competed with Socrates, talking and drinking from a large cup which they passed around among themselves, finally nodded off and the banquet came to an end. Only Socrates was left and he rose, mind still clear and gait still steady, to retire, followed by his faithful Aristodemos, to the Lyceum *gymnasium* on the banks of the Ilyssus, where he loved to spend the day.

We must not forget that Plato's *Symposium* is a transposition of reality into symbolic terms. It does, however, capture the characteristic atmosphere of all Athenian banquets worthy of the name, particularly in the fixed order of its proceedings. These could obviously vary considerably, but three elements were common to all: drinking, games and convivial conversation.

THE PLEASURES OF DRINKING

Drinking was the basic feature of all *symposia*. 'I, my friends', said Socrates in Xenophon's *Symposium*, 'am fully disposed to drink, for it is perfectly true that wine, as it distils through the mind, puts care to sleep as the mandrake induces torpor in the body, and at the same time it awakens joy as oil feeds a flame'.

The Greeks knew what it meant to drink, as we realize from the conversation of the guests at the beginning of Plato's *Symposium*, when they remem-

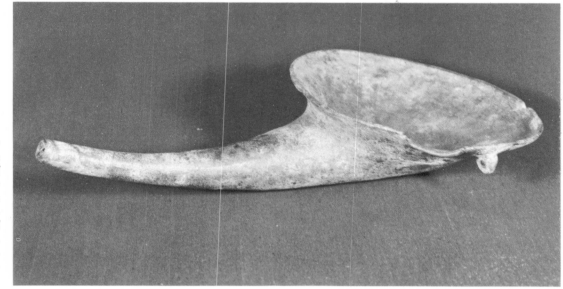

The function of dancing-girls was to bring delight to the banquet, a ritual which symbolized 'love' and friendship. This perhaps explains the use of the crocus, held to indicate 'love'. They were also required to hand round the cups and the drinking-horns. Opposite: detail from a vase. (National Museum, Ferrara). Right: drinking-horn. (Benaki Museum, Athens).

bered the libations of the previous day and the state of heaviness and malaise which resulted. Pausanias turned to the other guests and said: ' Well, my friends, how can we drink to cause least offence? For myself, I confess that I feel greatly upset after the wine we drank yesterday and I need some respite '. And what about the others who imposed their presence on the company? What about Alcibiades, completely drunk, supported by a girl flute-player and a few of his devoted followers, or the revellers who threw themselves on to the couches and incited everyone to drink freely?

The vase paintings bear out the literary texts: one of them shows a guest at a banquet supported by a flute-player, vomiting into a vase.

The excesses perpetrated by certain guests at banquets were typically satirized by Aristophanes in *The Wasps*. Old Philocleus soon let the wine get the better of him. ' After he had stuffed himself with a quantity of good things he began to dance, sing and jump about and to do even worse things, like a donkey fed on toasted barley ', then he beat the slaves hard and ' insulted his guests with coarse jokes and rambled on with unending pointless stories '. He then returned home, completely drunk, with a lighted torch in his

hand, lashing out with his stick at everyone he met. He was threatened with being brought up before the *archon* on the following day, but this did not seem to have penetrated his blissful stupor. He brought along with him, humming all the while a wedding march, one of the girl flute-players, and he filled her ears with boastful speeches: ' Come here, my little gold cockchafer... You have seen how clever I was to get you away from the other guests. So be nice to me... But you will not be nice to me; you will not even try to be; you will deceive me and have a good laugh at me... Yet, if you do not wish to be a bad woman, when my son dies I will ransom you and take you as a concubine '. Here the son Bdelycleon arrived on the scene and tried to reason with his father, ' that old imbecile, that whore-monger '. Faced by the threats of his father's victims, the son had no other recourse than to shut him up indoors, where he continued to rant and rail. A servant came to tell of his strange behaviour: ' The old man, after drinking and listening to the flute for a long time, became wildly excited and danced all night long without resting those famous dances of the olden days such as Thespis used to perform in the competitions. And he tried to prove that the tragic poets of today

Drinking in banquets was accompanied by the performance of short pieces of music. Above: a young woman brings wine to the guests. Dancing and music, for which, like the discourse among the guests, there were precise rules, were

are old men in their dotage and defied them to come and dance with him there and then'.

The consequences of drunkenness could be more serious in less civilized sectors of Athenian life. In his speech 'On the Corrupt Embassy' Demosthenes tells of a banquet held in Macedon, into which a woman from Olynthos was introduced. She was both beautiful and intelligent and had been taken prisoner during the occupation of her city. At the beginning she was offered wine and sweetmeats, then, their passions inflamed by drink, the guests ordered her to stand by the table and sing. 'As this lady, in despair, could not succeed in singing for them and finally refused, Eschines and Frynos shouted that her behaviour was insolent, and could not be tolerated in an Olynthian, that she belonged to a people who were the enemies of the Gods and sacrilegious and that she was their prisoner. Then: "Call a slave! Send for a strap!". A servant came with a leather belt, then, as those who incited him were drunk and, I think, vile, whilst she wept and cried out, the slave stripped off her tunic and thrashed her many times on the back. Distracted by her suffering and the indignity of the treatment she was receiving, she broke loose and threw herself at the feet of Hiatrocles, knocking the table over. If Hiatrocles had not protected her she

to elevate the mind to reasonableness and truth and were considered an adequate training for manhood. All this was, of course, proper to persons of culture. (National Museum, Ferrara).

16.

Greek artists decorated with inspiration and elegance the jars used for storing wine during banquets, and these were also used as decoration in the wealthier households. Above: wine-jar of the so-called 'volute' style. (National Museum, Ferrara).

refreshes the mind and makes it more docile and amenable to the voice of reason. Every banquet, therefore, should be under the authority of a president *(archon)* who should be temperate and wise and should know how to lead the gathering to its natural conclusion, which is the improvement of all participants, and to turn to the virtue of self-control what might have been disorderly self-indulgence. If this cannot be done, Plato would not hesitate to call for the total abolition of banquets.

These 'banqueting laws' as Plato called them, and the austerity which they implied, would have been difficult to impose on the Athenians, and it is well known that Plato's last great treatise was particularly severe and utopian. If in fact the men of Classical Athens were little given to temperance, it was because they had a different concept of drunkenness. For them inebriation meant honouring their greatest God, Dionysus, the protector of the vine, those who cultivated it and those who drank its produce. It meant imitating a God who was frequently shown followed by drunken companions, and recognizing his omnipotence, since Dionysus, whom the Athenians also called Eleutherios, the Liberator, freed men's minds from the golden bonds of reason.

ENTERTAINMENTS

This explains why the word orgy, which was originally a cultural manifestation with acts of unbridled violence in honour of the God of the vine, came to assume the meaning it has today. The Athenians were too reasonable and too sociable to wish to limit their feasting merely to drinking, even if this did have a religious meaning for them. Any host worthy of the name would see to it that his guests had other forms of entertainment as well.

The entertainment most guests appreciated was provided by girl flautists, lute-players and dancers, often shown in banqueting scenes on vase paintings. There is no doubt that these ancient Geisha girls were also courtesans: they show their calling not only in the clothes they wear, often reduced to a minimum, but also in their bold and provocative demeanour.

Plato, ever the strict moralist, pours scorn in his *Protagoras* on those vulgar persons who 'incapable, through lack of education, of finding within themselves the material for conversation when they drink

would have been beaten to death, for drunkenness is a vile and fearful thing'.

The fact that banquets could and often did degenerate into orgies would explain Plato's concern in his *Laws* with the control of the use and consumption of wine in *symposia*. Let us imagine, he says, a puppet moved by wires; some of these are of iron (the emotions and the passions) but one is of gold: 'the holy order of reason which is called the common law of the *polis*'. If the puppet is made to absorb great quantitites of wine its entire mechanism gets out of phase and reason cannot control the lower parts. On the contrary, a drink taken in moderation

At every banquet there were two slaves for serving the wine. One poured it undiluted into a large receptacle. The other, with his empty cylix and skyphos, mixed it with water and served it to the guests. (National Museum, Ferrara).

her to go outside and play to herself or to the women-folk, whichever she pleased.

But a very similar company in Xenophon's *Symposium* willingly interrupted its learned discourse to devote its whole attention to a cabaret show put on by a Syracusan impresario, and consisting of a young flute-player, an acrobat and a boy who could dance and play music.

'The Syracusan made an astonishing amount of money out of this show. For the pleasure of the guests the flautist played her instrument, the young boy the lyre, and both were much appreciated'. Socrates thanked Callias, the host: 'May Jove be my witness, you have treated us royally. Not content with serving us a fine meal, you have also given us what is most pleasing to the eye and ear'. This first show was put on as the guests got up from the table and was followed by various interludes. Thus, while the flautist was playing, the acrobat was juggling with twelve hoops, 'calculating the height she would have to throw them so as to catch them at the right moment', then she leapt through a hoop bristling with swords, causing great excitement among the spectators and moving Socrates to commend women's courage. As for the young lutanist, Socrates was delighted with his playing and dancing and, to the great amusement of the other guests, asked the Syracusan to let him give him dancing lessons.

These entertainments were not always interludes and it was quite common for the guests to take part themselves. A certain Philippus gave a comic imitation of the graceful dances of the ballerina and her companion and was loudly applauded. The wine cups passed round again amid great bursts of laughter and encouragement. Serious conversation was in no way impeded by these entertainments and Socrates found ample occasion to philosophize.

When the conversations took on a serious note again and the guests began to lose interest in the entertainments, the Syracusan became resentful and began to argue with Socrates. A new trick by one of the acrobats, in which he read and wrote seated on a potter's wheel, did not have much success with the company and Socrates asked them to perform living tableaux. The Syracusan agreed immediately and they performed an extraordinary spectacle: Ariadne waits for her Dionysus, who has been drinking with the Gods; he returns and the two give expression to

together, or of tuning their voices and their discourses to the common good, cause the cost of hiring a girl flute-player to rise because they pay a high price for the voice of a flute to replace their own, and thus procure for themselves the means of passing time in company. When cultured persons gather to drink together, however, you do not see them in the company of girl flute-players, dancers or lutanists; such persons are sufficient unto themselves for conversation and have no need to add to their own voices any hired senseless chatter'.

In Plato's *Symposium* Eryximachus sent away the flute-player who had come into the room and asked

their love. The miming was so good and the actors were so ardent that the guests seemed to be watching 'two lovers brought together after a long separation'. This signalled the end of the banquet: 'When the guests saw the actors leave with their arms round each other, those who were unmarried swore to wed without delay and the married ones leapt on their horses and galloped straight home to enjoy their own wives'.

PARTY GAMES

The guests did not always need professionals to entertain them. One of their games, which enjoyed great popularity, was called *kottabos* and consisted of aiming the dregs of the wine at a cup in the middle of the room and invoking at the same time the name of one's beloved. If the drops fell into the cup it was regarded as a favourable omen. On a certain base by Euphronius a beautiful courtesan reclining on a couch is throwing her wine-drops, and underneath an inscription reads: 'This throw is for you, Leagros'. The winner was the one who threw with most accuracy or elegance and he received a prize of an apple, a cup or a kiss. When Theramenes was condemned to death by Critias, one of the Thirty Tyrants, he threw down the last drops of the hemlock as in the *kottabos* game and shouted 'Good health to noble Critias!'.

The guests also liked to dance. From what we can see of these dances on the vase-paintings, they were more like vulgar contortions and juggling acts in which a full jar of wine was balanced on the stomach or an arm or leg.

The guests also sang in chorus, and this was perhaps their favourite pastime of all. 'As we all have a desire to speak', Socrates called to Xenophon, 'would it not be better if we all sang together?'. Whereupon he immediately intoned a song. Sometimes each guest in turn sang a *scolion*, a convivial song accompanied by the lyre, during which the singer held a branch of myrtle in his hand. The word means 'twisted', alluding no doubt to the irregular order in which it was taken up around the table.

The finest lyric poets of Greece like Simonides (*c.* 556 - *c.* 468 B.C.), Bacchilides (*c.* 505 - *c.* 450 B.C.) and Pindar (*c.* 520 - *c.* 440 B.C.) were pleased to write songs such as these, and they have left a very rich collection. Their themes were extremely varied. Some evoked the pleasures of drinking, such as the verses which Pindar dedicated to his friend Trasibulos: 'I send you this collection of happy songs to be sung at the clearing of the table. It may please the assembled guests and will be a stimulus to the fruit of Dionysus and the wine cups from Athens. This is a time when the burdens are lifted from a man's troubled brow and when, as on an ocean of riches and amidst an abundance of gold, we all glide to those imaginary shores where the poor become rich and our hearts

Musical instruments used at banquets: double flutes, single flutes and castanets for dancing-girls. (Kannellopoulos Collection, Athens).

125

grow kind, tamed by the bow of the vine'. Sometimes the theme was love: 'There is need to love', says Pindar, 'to yield to its call in due season: do not, oh my soul, run after dreams more becoming to an older person'. For Xenophon of Corinth, who had provided fifty sacred courtesans for the sanctuary of Aphrodite in that city, he wrote: 'Aphrodite permits you without reproach, young men, to enjoy the fruit of your tender age. When necessity demands it, all is well'.

There were also more serious subjects. Some of the songs moralized on the blessings of life, as for example the one to which Plato alludes frequently, which classifies them virtually in descending order: health, beauty, and wealth honestly gained. Others were patriotic and democratic and sang of the liberation of Athens from the tyrants. These songs had a long life. One of them recalled the town of Leipsydrion on Mount Parnes in which the patriots suffered a grave defeat at the hands of the Alcmeonidai: 'Ah, treacherous Leipsydrion. How many men have you caused to perish; they were noble and brave and showed you whose sons they were'. The best-known of all, which came to be called the 'Harmodias', evoked the courage of the men who slew the tyrant Hipparchus: 'I shall carry my sword hidden in a myrtle branch, like Harmodius and Aristogiton when they slew the tyrant and set Athens free'.

In every banquet that Aristophanes put on the stage he quoted from the 'Harmodias', a sure indication of the song's great popularity.

RIDDLES AND 'PORTRAITS'

There were many little party games, some of them quite ingenious, which were also very popular, and over fifty of them were listed by the lexicographer Pollukis. Certain riddles and 'portraits' occur in Aristophanes' *The Wasps*. At the beginning of the play two servants are talking. One of them has dreamt of an eagle which was holding a shield in its talons and let it fall; he then propounds a *gripos* (riddle): 'Guess who I mean when I say that the same animal has dropped his shield on land, in the air and on the sea'. This was a very personal allusion to a certain Cleonimus who was so cowardly in battle that he dropped his shield so that he could run away more quickly.

This passion for guessing games extended also to the table in ancient Greece, and it would be applied equally to the most venerable of ancient myths such as, for example, the famous riddles about the three ages of man which the sphinx put to Oedipus.

'Portraits' could be of the simplest kind when played in ordinary company. Philocleon and his friends indulged in the most commonplace: the starving Lysistratus calls him a 'Phrygian slave' and a 'donkey hiding away in the straw', and he in turn is called a 'grasshopper which has lost the leaves from his cloak'. In Xenophon's *Symposium* there is a very comical 'parasite' called Philippus whose speciality, much appreciated by the other guests, is making comparisons, but Socrates is not amused; he considers they are insolent and go too far and attempts to silence him.

Entertainment at banquets was provided not only by dancing-girls, flautists and lute-players, but also by acrobats and jugglers, as we know from literary sources and from vase paintings. 'One of them, standing near to the dancing-girl, handed her some rings, twelve in all. She took them, continuing the while to dance, and threw them up into the air, calculating how high she would have to throw each one so as to catch them in sequence... Then a hoop was brought with straight blades attached all round the rim. The dancing-girl ran towards it, them somersaulted right through it...' (Xenophon, Symposium). Cup showing male kordax dancers. (Kannellopoulos Collection, Athens). The kordax was a licentious, drunken dance.

Even Agathon's refined banquet has some of these. Alcibiades looks for names in the past which can be applied to the men of the day: the Spartan general Brasidas recalls Achilles, Pericles, Nestor or the Trojan philosopher Antenor. Only for Socrates can he find no comparably great name in the past. It is Alcibiades himself who composes a picture 'wholly drawn on truth and not for comic amusement'; Socrates is 'just like those *silenoi* (satyr-like companions of Bacchus) one finds all over the place in sculptors' workshops, shown in the attitude of playing a pipe or a flute, which, if cut open in the middle, are found to be full of figurines of Gods!'. Later on the young guest is moved to confess: 'I happen to have seen those figurines inside him, and they are so divine, of such exquisite substance, so beautiful, so extraordinary, that I cannot but obey Socrates' every command'.

CONVERSATION

For the Athenians, however, the greatest pleasure in being together when the wine-cups were passing round was conversation. The many speeches made at table must have been extremely varied in character according to the temperaments of the hosts and the guests and the circumstances: declamatory or gently spoken, dealing with the troubles of the moment or the great questions of all ages. It is perhaps not surprising that very little of these have come down to us except for a few anecdotes by later authors, and these are often suspect.

We do, however, have an extraordinarily interesting account of two banquets in which the level of conversation rose far above the anecdotal: the *Symposia* of Plato and Xenophon, both written in about 385. They have several features in common: a banquet held in a rich man's house in honour of the winning of a prize in some competition; Socrates takes part with friends, and instead of contenting themselves with ordinary pleasures, they devote their time to the discussion of a serious topic; each guest makes his own contribution and deals with the subject according to his own talents and his particular calling. Socrates leads the discussion and draws it towards its ontological and moral conclusion. The two works are, however, as different from each other as

their authors were; their only common bond was that they were both disciples of Socrates.

It would be sacrilege to try to reduce Plato's finest dialogue to a few lines, and it can merely be said that, beneath its apparent superficiality, it is concerned entirely with the question of love. It opens with five speeches which give, in styles ranging from the burlesque to the poetic, five different concepts of love. Socrates, in the magnificent lyrical speech which he puts into the mouth of the priestess Diotima, propounds what the philosopher considers to be the deepest meaning and the essential function of love: to lead the mind from the beauty of the body to the beauty of the spirit, thence to the beauty of conscience and finally to the knowledge of absolute beauty, which is God. Alcibiades shows that Socrates represents the purest incarnation of this love, of which the mysteries have been revealed through the mouth of Socrates by the foreign priestess from Mantineia. It is remarkable that the dialogue remains on such a high plane and is so moving and so convincing, even when it comes down (though this word does not occur) from the divine mysteries of love to the mortal Socrates.

Xenophon's *Symposium* is quite different. In the house of the rich and vain Callias, Socrates and his friends speak quite freely. The dialogue is purposely more fragmentary as the author's intention is to preserve the free speech of a true *symposium*, and, as we

have seen, the conversation is frequently interrupted by various music-hall type interludes which keep the level down to the more commonplace subjects. There is, however, a central theme, which is the *kalos kagathos* or the 'good man'. Each guest explains what gives him the greatest pride: his wealth, his poverty, his knowledge of Homer, his father, his sons, his friends or his beauty. Socrates, who mocks at the others without appearing to do so, speaks gravely of his pride in being an intermediary, or go-between, meaning evidently that he is a philosopher and therefore a 'procurer' of virtue and wisdom. The end part consists entirely of a long speech by Socrates on love, real love, that is the communion of the spirit, the only thing which allows the lover and the beloved to become truly 'good men'.

There is no doubt, in spite of appearances to the contrary, that Xenophon wrote his *Symposium* later than Plato wrote his, and that he intended even to improve on Plato. Plato's Socrates would be too sublime and too metaphysical for Xenophon's taste, and Xenophon no doubt wished to show his master in a truer light, closer to his fellow-men and concerned particularly with moral problems.

We shall probably never know, though we shall continually wonder, what the real Socrates was like. However it may be, the *Symposium* gave each author a chance to expose his own ideas about truth.

These vase paintings clearly show certain moments of the banquet which were governed by accepted rules. After Plato's time banquets were without doubt conducted according to rules which were written down by Plato himself and by Aristotle, Xenophon and Speusippus, a nephew of Plato. (Attic vase of the fifth century, B.C.).

The existence of rules for the conduct of banquets implies that there was unruly conduct of all kinds. Right: *a courtesan helps a drunken guest to get rid of his excess of wine.* Left: *a convivial scene (both details from Attic cups in the Museum, Würzburg).*

Both Plato and Xenophon have preserved for us something of the fascination that the Greeks felt for banquets of this kind: the freedom of speech, the variety of entertainment, the Attic elegance. We know nothing of the philosophical banquets of Aristotle, Speusippus (the nephew of Plato) or Epicurus (341-270 B.C.). The theme was taken up in the declining age of Hellenism by Plutarch (A.D. *c.* 46 - *c.* 120) in his *Banquet of the Seven Wise Men* and *Symposiaca*; by Athenaeus (*fl. c.* 200 B.C.) in his *Connoisseurs in Dining*, and later by Lucian (A.D. 115 - *c.* 200) in his *Banquet*; by Julian (emperor 361-3), Macrobius (*fl.* 400) and finally by the good bishop Methodius who daringly imitated Plato in his *Symposium of the Ten Virgins*. There is no lack of wit in some of these works: Lucian's is a tract of surprising violence and bitterness against philosophers, whom he considers to be dirty old men squabbling over the biggest morsels of food and ogling the flute-players or the wine-waiters. Most of the works are mere pretexts for boring speeches strung together on some flimsy thread of pedantry.

The literary banquet did not outlive the friendly *symposia* of the Athenians.

THE PLEASURES OF FRIENDSHIP

The importance to the Athenian of these banquets doubtless lay in the opportunity they provided for the satisfaction of the most varied desires. For Aristophanes, just as no doubt for the average Athenian, the *symposium* was the centre piece of the good life. We only have to read again the end of *The Archarnians* (425 B.C.) where Lamachus limps home wounded from the war and Dikaiopolis, whose personal truce with the Spartans is over, celebrates in fine style: 'Quickly, to the banquet! Set off with your basket and your barrel of oil: it is the priest of Dionysus who invites you. But make haste, you are delaying the feast. Everything is ready: tables, cushions, covers, garlands, perfumes, daintly morsels of food; there are courtesans, dancers, cakes, sweet-meats, sesame bread and the song "Beloved Harmodius". Dikaiopolis's conversation whilst he prepares his feast is mouth-watering and as for the pleasure to follow, Aristophanes makes them sound even more appetizing. Dikaiopolis comes in with two beautiful girls, whose greatest attribute was not their modesty, and proceeds to pay court to both of them.

In contrast to these elementary pleasures the banquet also contrived to uplift the soul, as in the first two books of Plato's *Laws*. Here wine brought the same benefits to the spirit as physical exercise did to the body: not only did it serve to reveal one's character, but it was the 'remedy which gave the soul modesty and the body health and vigour'. Even the dangers of the banquet could be edifying: under the leadership of a temperate and shrewd lord of the feast the guests would learn self-control and obedience to the necessary regulations: 'Their spirit, like a piece of iron heated to incandescence, would take on a new malleability and a freshness so that it would become responsive in the hands of those who would shape it, as in the days of its youth'.

Utopian? Not necessarily. Moreover if these communal festivities did not always have such noble results at least they provided an opportunity for the pleasures of friendship which the Greeks considered the noblest pleasures of all. 'Stay for wise discussion over the cups of wine, my friends', said the old poet Theognis (second half sixth century B.C.) 'and see to it that, banishing all discord from your gathering, a general conversation shall be profitable to each and every one; thus it is that a banquet remains a gathering of friends'.

THE COUNTLESS GODS OF OLYMPUS

The rise and development of religion in Ancient Greece is a complex story. Two elements can be clearly discerned: an early, official and aristocratic religion, the Olympic-Homeric, and a naturalistic religion, accepted particularly by the less wealthy, the Dionysiac. The coming of democracy after bitter struggles brought the two strands together to form the Apollo-Dionysiac. This form of religion was born from the needs of the humble people to find a true, eternal life beyond the confines of their wretched earthly existence, and it was founded on the figure of the god Dionysus, originally the god of the fertility of nature (birth, death and rebirth of everything). It subsequently developed into the forms of the Mysteries, which were initiations into eternity.

This allowed a vision of a single and orderly whole into which could be fitted the ancient pantheon of the countless Immortals (Hesiod claimed that there were thirty thousand) from whom everything devolved. Over and above all, above Zeus himself, the source of life, over gods and men, hung the eternal law of destiny which controlling and transcending everything, was the raison d'être *of the Universe and, through order (in Greek* cosmos) *brought the balance and moderation which is beauty. Evil, therefore, lay in disorder and immoderation, in the affirmation of self, in arrogance.*

Like other Aryan peoples, the Greeks originally worshipped celestial, luminous deities. As they gradually settled down to agriculture and their lives became more closely bound to the land, there was a corresponding change in their religious concepts and in the character of their gods. New deities arose, some co-existing with the old, others replacing them. The gods of the Mycenaean period had distinctly terrestrial characteristics and they gave place to the more celestial deities of the Homeric period, in which, it should be noted, the representation of the gods was strongly influenced by their description in the poems.

The gods' return to heaven from earth was mainly due to the effects of the Greek colonization of Asia Minor, where there were none of those local barriers which had tended in the mother country to favour the cult of parochial divinities. It was thus possible to have a unified religion with pan-Hellenic deities.

Thus arose the system of the Greater Gods (whose canonical number was fixed at twelve) on whose separate origins the Greeks were vague until the eighth century, lumping them all together in 'one sacred stock of the Immortals' as Hesiod called them.

In the Homeric age these gods were given human attributes, even though they were of higher status than the other gods, together with the privilege of immortality, eternal youth and everlasting joy. Like men, however, they were considered subject to the passions of love and hatred, and this concept was reinforced by the family ties with which the imagination of the ancient poets had endowed them, not to mention the close interest which the gods were supposed to take in man's daily life. All this could cause altercation and even open conflict between the gods without, however, seriously ruffling their Olympian calm.

The greatest deity, king of both gods and men, was Zeus (the Roman Jupiter). He was Lord of the

Heavens, sent the good and the bad weather, piled up the clouds, showered down the rain, commanded the thunder and the lightning and hurled the fearsome thunderbolts. The brothers of Zeus, Poseidon (Neptune) and Hades (Pluto) reigned respectively over the sea and the underworld, where the souls of the departed were gathered. Zeus was honoured by the great Olympic games first held in 776 B.C., and Poseidon by the Isthmian games. The wife of Zeus was Hera (Juno), protectress of marriage and maternity, and of their union were born Ares (Mars), the god of war, Hephaestus (Vulcan), god of fire, a skilled smith and protector of metal-workers, and finally Hebe, the goddess of youth.

Hephaestus was depicted as ugly and lame, yet he had as a wife the most beautiful of goddesses, Aphrodite (Venus), born of the sea-foam and goddess of beauty and love.

Another goddess greatly venerated by all Greeks, and especially by the Athenians, as she was the patroness of their city, was Athena (Minerva) the goddess of wisdom and intellectual powers, said to have sprung from the head of Zeus himself.

Of the union of Zeus and Leto (Latona) were born two of the greatest deities: Apollo (Phoebus) and Artemis (Diana). Apollo was the god of light and the sun, who sent epidemics and restored health; he invented the arts and was the inspirer of prophecies and oracles. He was always accompanied by nine maidens, called the Muses, each one of which watched over one of the arts. Artemis was the goddess of moonlight, the woods and mountains, of hunting and wild animals.

The god of trade, the art of eloquence and of gymnastics was Hermes (Mercury). The goddess of the home and family sanctity was Hestia (Vesta) and the god of the vine, wine and banquets was Dionysus (Bacchus).

The goddess of agriculture and cereals was Demeter (Ceres), whose daughter Persephone (Proserpine) was said to have been carried off by Hades to the underworld. Demeter's despair moved Zeus to order Hades to allow Persephone to return to earth in the spring and stay until autumn, thus remaining with him only during the winter. The two goddesses, Demeter and Persephone, were therefore regarded as the ones who could ensure for the souls of the departed a happier resting place in the underworld.

The centre of their cult was Eleusis in Attica, where the so-called Eleusinian Mysteries were celebrated each year.

Prosperity or misfortune, victory or defeat, health, sickness or death, the Greek knew that everything depended on his gods, whether they be major or minor deities, and his fate was also subject to a host of spirits such as the Sirens, the Graces, the Harpies, the Satyrs, the Sileni, the Centaurs, and so on, who almost always acted on impulse, and could be well or ill disposed over a mere trifle. He also knew that even the actions of the gods were subject to some control, exercised by the will of Zeus and the acts of an immutable destiny which was fixed for each man from the day of his birth to that of his death, and could never be changed even by the gods.

It seemed nevertheless prudent to submit to the will of the gods and to propitiate them. Hence the growth of a cult of rites and formulae for prayers and the placation of the deities, and of a body of experts, the priests, who knew best how to perform the rites, and undertook to intercede on behalf of all in the appropriate places set apart at altars (in the Mycenaean period) or inside the temples (in the Doric period and afterwards) built for this purpose.

As time went by some of these temples became more important than others, especially those to which the gods came down to give answers and advice to the assembled mortals. Such were, for example, the oracles at Dodona (sacred to Zeus), at Delphi, Delos, Miletos (for Apollo) and Epidauros (for Asclepius).

Two elements of the post-Mycenaean period were new: the temple and the image of the god. There was, however, a remarkable continuity between the Mycenaean and successive periods: many of the places which became famous sanctuaries had Mycenaean origins, and so also had much of Greek mythology in general, as the principal centres of Mycenaean civilization became also the centres of the most important cycles of Greek mythology. The Greek custom of honouring the gods with games and festivals at the place of the most important sanctuaries was also inherited from Mycenae.

The same was true of the cult of the dead, not as powerful beings to be propitiated, but as wretched shades, tenuous souls (*psyche* was the breath, the spirit leaving the body at death) condemned to a pale, sad existence. By means of sacrifices and libations it was

The Hephaesteum, or the temple dedicated to Hephaestus and better known as the Theseum, overlooked the Agora from a little hill covered with well-kept vegetation. It is perhaps the best preserved temple of classical antiquity.

hoped to give the shades of the departed some joy and vitality. In the post-Homeric period the cult of the dead became the cult of heroes, created from the epic poems by the degradation of secondary deities into mortals worshipped throughout Greece. As the Greeks became familiar with their epics they came to consider their ancient deities as men who had really lived and so was created a new race of demi-gods or heroes.

The pattern of Greek religion in the Doric-Ionic period was further fixed by the creation of a large number of 'polias' gods, protectors of towns and cities, to which they gave their name. These were nearly all chosen from among the major Olympic deities. A first attempt to give an account of the genealogy of the Greek gods was made by Hesiod (eighth century B.C.), who also wrote a long poem about country life called 'Works and Days'. The peasants described by Hesiod, however, cared little for the religion of the rich and powerful citizens of

Attica, and took very little part in its observance. Their religion was the practice of the mysteries *(orgia)* surrounding the cult of Demeter and Dionysus, the god of vegetable growth, neither of whom were in the Homeric or the Olympic family. From the religion of Demeter there spread throughout Attica the Eleusinian Mysteries, a cult designed to bring to the initiated a better life beyond the grave. The orgiastic religion of Dionysus, a cult partly exotic (from Thrace) and partly pre-Greek (Mycenaean), was also soon to flourish all over Greece. This was the religion of the ordinary people in the towns or the countryside, but the cult eventually spread to all classes, becoming more refined and civilized as it moved into the city, where its ritual developed into the earliest drama.

A further development in religion in the Classical period was the growth of Orphism, a set of rituals stemming from the Dionysus cult (Orpheus was a prophet of Dionysus) and aiming to uplift the soul with a hope of salvation founded on religious and moral concepts. This was in contradiction of the spirit of traditional Olympic religion, and although it attracted some thinkers of the time, it never grew into a movement of any importance.

The victory of a city over the barbarian invader favoured the development of the cult of local gods who had watched over the safety of the inhabitants and led to victory the army of hoplites. This brought about a considerable development of the figurative arts, especially sculpture, in the creation of images, soon to become stereotyped, of the various deities.

Religion became democratic: the Olympus of the *polis* was opened to the plebeians who infused it with a new spirit, a spirit at once more fervid, more enthusiastic, but also more superstitious. These same traditional religious beliefs were also questioned by the philosophers as a wave of free, unprejudiced ideas flowed into Attica from virtually everywhere in the Greek world and from certain areas of Asia.

In the fourth century B.C. there was a distinct movement towards anthropomorphism. The gods took on a more distinctive human shape in the sculptures of Praxiteles and Lysippus, and preference was given in the various cults to those deities considered to have more human characteristics, such as Asclepius, the god of medicine. The cult of the dead grew hand in hand with that of the heroes. There was even a kind of personality cult of the living: Lysander (d. 395 B.C.), the Spartan naval commander, received honours fit for a god at Samos, as also did Agesilaus (444-361 B.C.), king of Sparta, at Thasos. The religion of Dionysus flourished with the growth of the mysteries and the absorption of exotic superstitions, and here and there, notably in Boeotia and Magna Grecia (the Greek cities of the Gulf of Taranto in the south of Italy), there was an upsurge of Orphism.

Meanwhile, as the *polis* began to decline, the religion of the city state declined with it. A new universal and supranational body politic arose under the great Philip of Macedon, and this produced a new religion in which East and West, Greek and Barbarian were united: the cult of the sovereign, the man-god, which continued until it was inherited by the Roman Emperors. They then united this religion and the popular beliefs of the many subject peoples into a powerful barrier against the advancing tides of Christianity.

ATHENA AND HER CITY

Athena, the virgin daughter of Zeus, is indissolubly linked by her name to the city of which she was the goddess and patron. The fact remains, however, that her more ancient name was not Athena, but Pallas Athene, as she was called by Homer and Hesiod. There is no certain explanation of either of the goddess's two names: the first is thought to refer to the strength in a quivering spear as it strikes, or to youth or to virginity, and the second may contain the idea of youth in flower *(anthos)* or may refer to the goddess's miraculous birth. It will be remembered that she was held to have sprung, adult, from the head of her father Zeus and thus had no breastfeeding or childhood. The root *the* from *thenion* meant 'milk' and the prefix 'a' meant 'deprived of'. The city took the second of these names and became *Athenaia* or *Athena*. It is also claimed that the city goddess Athene, called 'the Athenian' *(Athenaia)*, gave her name to the cities of the Cyclades (a group of islands in the southern Aegean) and of Ionia. There she was worshipped under this name, to which would be added the name of the locality. Wherever the truth may lie in these many theories, it is certain that her cult lasted longer in Athens than in any other part of Greece, though she was always one of the more important and more widely venerated of the pan-Hellenic deities.

Athena was a celestial divinity, and the place she occupied in the heavenly mansions is shown by the saga of her birth and by the things she did. According to one myth, she was born of the Ocean and the Night: it will be recalled that in Homer almost everything and every deity was born of the Ocean. For this reason we frequently find the goddess worshipped on the banks of lakes and rivers especially in Boeotia, where her cult flourished on the slopes above Lake Copaidis; in Arcadia, on the banks of the river Alpheus; in Elis on the shores of the Laryssos; in Laconia near the river Nedon, and near Cnossus in Crete.

The other myth connected with the birth of Athena is better known. According to this she sprang from the head of Zeus. In the *Iliad* she was said to be the god's favourite daughter: the 'mighty daughter of a mighty father' whom he alone conceived and to whom he confided his intentions and gave the most

Athena in battle, a fifth-century bronze in the National Museum, Athens. Athena, to whom the city was consecrated, had given Attica an olive tree as her own solemn gift. A symbol of her wisdom was the owl, often seen on the reverse of Athenian coins which have the goddess on the obverse.

18.

Model of the Parthenon (Agora Museum, Athens) and a hypothetical restoration of the eastern pediment of the temple (Acropolis Museum, Athens). The pediment tells the story

difficult tasks. The myth appeared in its first complete form in the Homeric hymn to Athena and in Hesiod's 'Theogony'. Zeus' first wife was Metis, daughter of the Ocean and the personification of reason and intelligence. Fearing that she might give birth to a son more powerful than himself, Zeus swallowed her. She had conceived and her child, Athena, was born through her father's head which Hephaestus had opened with an axe.

Athena was closely associated with Hephaestus in another connection. The goddess Hera and Zeus were supposed to have quarrelled, and as a result Zeus produced Athena unaided and Hera gave birth to Hephaestus. The meaning of the myth would seem to be clear: Athena the goddess was born of strife in heaven, amidst the flashes of lightning and the claps of thunder which tear apart the curtains of the clouds. She was the radiant goddess who calmed the divine storms and brought back light and sweetness to the heavens. She was thus a warrior goddess, born amid strife and bearing arms: she sprang out of the head of Zeus carrying a spear and a shield. The spear represented the lightning which rends the clouds and over which, like Zeus, she was all-powerful; her shield, called the *aegis* (given to her by her father and another link with him) symbolized the stormy sky rent by flashes of lightning. In the middle of the shield was the Gorgoneion, the horrible head of the Gorgon Medusa. Originally the Gorgon probably symbolized

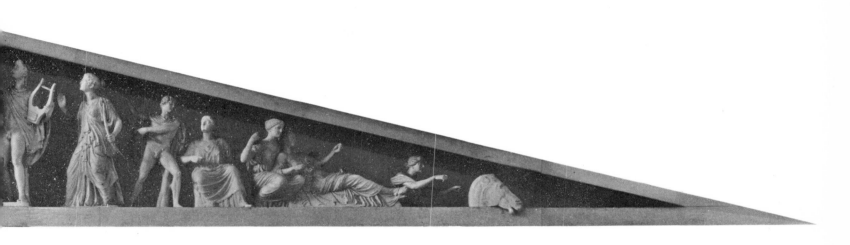

of the birth of the goddess and shows the greatest gods of Olympus. In the centre Zeus on his throne, with winged Victory by his side, looks at his daughter, born armed with lance, shield and helmet. On the left as we look at it, Hera with her sceptre and Mercury. On Athena's left Hephaestus and Poseidon with his trident; after Poseidon, Apollo with his lyre.

Those taking part in the many processions connected with the frequent festivals held in the city wore their ceremonial clothes and put crowns on their heads. Detail from vase paintings in the National Museum, Ferrara. The proces-

night, with moonlight, or storm clouds. In a later form of the Gorgon myths, Medusa, a young girl with very beautiful hair, was loved by Poseidon, and because of this she aroused the jealousy of Athena who changed her hair into snakes and made her face so horrible that anyone who looked at it was turned to stone. At the command of the goddess the monster was slain by Perseus and the terrifying head, fixed to the centre of her shield, brought death to anyone who gazed on it. Athena was sometimes called ' the goddess who slew the Gorgon ' or the ' goddess with the look of the Gorgon '.

The myths also tell of Athena's warlike pursuits and of the prominent part she played in the struggles against the Titans. More important than the deeds themselves was the cult to which they gave rise, and

it is as a goddess armed with helmet, spear and shield that Athena is most commonly represented.

She also symbolized virtue, in the widest ethical meaning of the word, as she was also the daughter of Zeus and Metis and could be held to be the personification of wisdom and prudence, inherited from the father of the gods. She was also held to have taught men to ride and to sail boats; in this her cult was closely associated with that of Poseidon.

As the goddess of intelligence, Athena naturally protected all works of peace, and above all, as a woman, she watched over the arts and the labours of her sex which were often called the ' labours of Athena '. As the protectress of women, she gave them fertility in marriage and watched over the birth and

sions often ended with the sacrificing of animals or the offering of fruits of the earth to the divinity. Sacrificial altar. (National Museum, Athens).

the growth of their offspring. Her protection also extended to all those activities of men connected with agriculture and industry: from her, Attica learned to cultivate the olive, and the same tradition was preserved at Rhodes. She was also the protectress of the fine arts and the handicrafts of both men and women; she invented music and dancing, and in Boeotia was held to have invented the flute (though elsewhere this is often credited to the satyr Marsyas); she also invented trumpet playing and warrior dances. Finally from Athena, the pure virgin who personified the clear light of heaven, came the light of understanding, prudence, common-sense and astuteness. From her were derived the depth and range of the intellect which led to philosophy and the discovery of new truths. She was regarded as the natural protectress

of philosophers and scientists in the golden age of Athenian culture.

The concept of Athena as a goddess of peace rather than of war came eventually to prevail in Athens, and she was regarded as the tutelary genius of the state, the goddess of the city *(Polias)* and as such honoured everywhere. She protected the city, purifying the air and maintaining public health, warding off diseases and infirmity and, like Zeus, fostering the growth and the perpetuity of the people and their families. Together with the father of the gods, she watched over the city's good governance, protected her laws and her constitution and guaranteed her alliances freely entered into.

She was, therefore, a pan-Hellenic deity, present and at work everywhere where human intelligence and activity were manifest. But Attica was the goddess's favourite abode and Athens the city where she lavished her favours and her gifts. To gain possession of this territory, according to the myth, she had had to win a contest against Poseidon set up by Zeus, according to whom the land would belong to the deity who donated the move useful gift. Poseidon had given the horse, but Athena the olive tree.

In the cult of Athena both aspects of the deity are reflected: the more ancient, naturalistic of the goddess of celestial phenomena, and the more recent of the goddess of warrior virtue and works of peace, the inventor and protectress of the arts and industry. She was worshipped in both these guises in two sanctuaries dedicated to her by the Athenians on the Acropolis. In the first, the Erechtheum, which was restored during the Peloponnesian War,

The Sanctuary of Apollo at Delphi with its celebrated oracle, consulted alike by private individuals and public bodies, was the greatest religious centre of ancient Greece. The sanctuary was reached by the Sacred Way, a road dignified by monuments, imposing buildings and votive offerings made by the faithful from all parts of Hellas; these included sixteen bronze statues by Phidias. The Athenians built their own 'Treasure House' (opposite, below), a little temple in which their offerings were kept. They also built the so-called Athenian Portico after the battle of Salamis. Below: *the Castalia spring where pilgrims on their way to consult the oracle had to purify themselves*. Opposite above: *the 'Omphalos', a stone regarded as the central point of the earth, which was kept in the sanctuary*. Right: *the valley leading up to Delphi with, in the background, Mount Parnassus and Mount Helicon*.

143

there was a statue of the goddess which was said to have fallen from heaven. Here also was the sacred olive tree given by Athena to the city, and here she was worshipped as Polias, that is the protectress of the Acropolis, together with other divinities closely connected with her cult and her myth such as Erechteus, Aglaurus and Pandrosus, all of them chthonic, and with Poseidon himself. In the second, the Parthenon, rebuilt also in the time of Pericles, she was worshipped as the pure goddess of all human intellectual activity and as a national and political deity. Between and in front of the two buildings stood the colossal statue of Athena Promachos (the 'Defender'), erected to commemorate the victory, aided by the goddess, over the Persians. In the various suburbs of the city there were local cults and traditions connected with the protection by the goddess of the land of Attica and with her good will towards its people.

The little temple of Athena Nike on the Acropolis. It was consecrated to Athena 'the bringer of victory'.

THE PRIESTS AND THE CULT

Unlike Rome, where the priesthood was a public office and individual priests were grouped in colleges, with their own hierarchy, Greece had no hierarchical priesthood invested with any particular rights or authority. There were, in fact, no religious truths to be revealed or propagated, there was no religious instruction to be given to the people. The priestly function was simply to administer the cult in the temple or the sacred precinct to which he was attached, where he worked in the name of the whole community.

In Greece (and here there is a similarity with Rome) there were two faces to religion: the public and the private. Public religion, which involved the whole community, was a state function and some of the most solemn religious ceremonies were the responsibility of the magistrates in office. These magistrates themselves were often learned in the *mantica*, or the science of interpreting the wishes of the gods by means of various signs. Private religion was the concern of the head of the family, and he saw to its observance within the walls of his house. The functions of the priest, therefore, were restricted to the temples in which they practised.

Some priesthoods were handed down through members of certain families who from time to time would have to elect a new priest. Most of the priests, however, were publicly elected from a list of candidates by choice or the drawing of lots. Only the family-elected priests held office for life; the others held their posts for a fixed period of time, usually for one year, though sometimes for two, three or four years according to the frequency of the feasts of the god in whose temple they served.

Certain conditions were required for the exercise of the priesthood: a person should be free from any physical defect and have an unimpeachable character, a knowledge of the specific ritual of the temple to which he was to be attached, full rights of citizenship and a regular family status. It was also required sometimes that the supplicant should be of the same sex as the deity of the temple and take vows of chastity, either for short periods or for perpetuity, and abstain from certain food and drink. Priests were required to be adult, except for certain temples which specified young persons who had not yet attained puberty: in these cases the term of office expired when the age

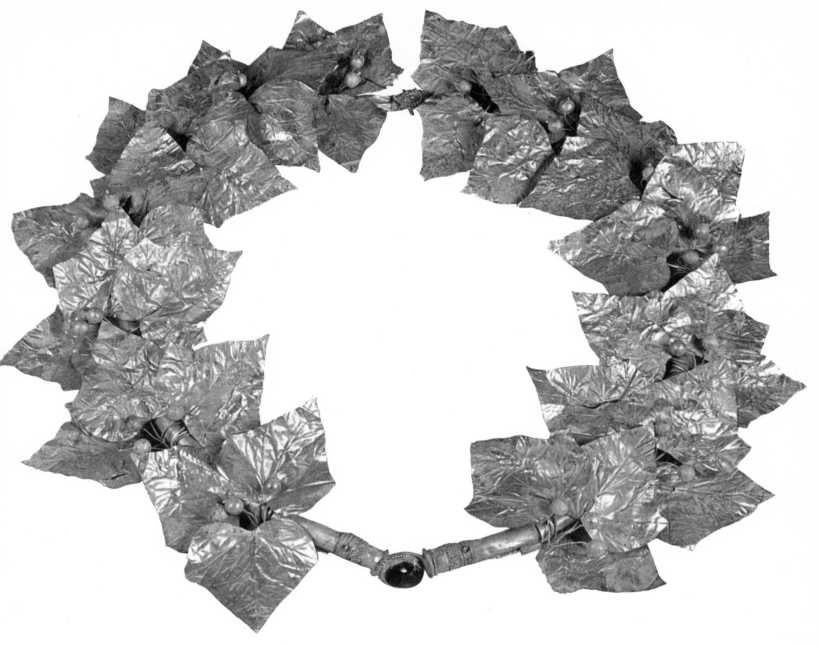

Gold crown (Benaki Museum, Athens). Crowns of myrtle, laurel or olive were worn by priests in processions and during the performance of rituals. Sometimes the crowns were made of precious metals.

of puberty was reached. Priests wore a long white tunic, allowed their hair to grow long and, when they were officiating, put on a crown of olive or myrtle leaves. We know, however, from Aristophanes that the priest of the Dionysiac cult in Athens wore a crocus yellow tunic.

A priest's emoluments were rather poor: in addition to some part, which he could generally choose, of the sacrificial animal, he received gifts of cakes, fruit, wine and often money; he had the right to use certain parts of the temple for his private rooms and even some of the possessions of the temple, and he was exempt from all taxes. All this was just about enough to cover his expenses, which could be con-

siderable when, as was frequently the case, the cult required costly vestments for the celebration of certain feasts, processions, banquets, gymnastic and musical contests. Certain priesthoods could therefore be filled only by the wealthy and attracted those eager to acquire honours and social privileges such as the *proedria* (a position of honour in the theatre, games and assemblies) which were some of the perquisites of their office.

The most important ceremony which the priest had to perform was the sacrifice. The victim, an animal offered as a gift to the deity, had to be physically perfect. Before the sacrifice it was adorned in various ways with garlands and sprinkled with holy water.

After the sacrifice parts of the animal were roasted and eaten by those present sitting at a communal table. Sacrifices were well attended, as they were thought to be the best means of influencing the deity and getting a hearing for one's requests. There was also a form of prayer, a simple religious act which consisted in the priests putting his hand to his mouth and then raising it on high to plead for favour or protection against some calamity.

Another function of the priest was the performance of purification rites. These were enacted every time there was communication with the deity: before entering the temple, before the sacrifice or before any religious ceremony, and before prayer or the taking of a vow. The ceremony was also applied to the area in and around the temple where the cult took place and to all sacrificial victims. It was done by sprinkling pure or salted water with a twig.

Private religious practices were centred on the home and on Hestia, the goddess of the hearth. They were presided over by the head of the family who collected together all its members on the occasions of family celebration such as birth, marriage and adoption. At the birth celebration the new-born child was carried round the hearth and ten days later given its name at a ritual family feast. Weddings were held at the bridegroom's home where the couple ate together the traditional cake, the ceremony being presided over by the bridegroom's father.

Altar for divination (The Louvre, Paris).

DIVINATION AND MYSTERY: THE ORACLES

One important aspect of ancient religions, especially those of Greece and Rome, was the exercise of the art of divination, or the practices by which one could come to know the will of the gods through its various manifestations, for the near or distant future, and its likely effect on the course of human destiny. Knowledge of this art and the means of applying it were therefore sacred and in Greece the interpreter of omens *(mantis)* was held in higher esteem than the priest himself. Here too considerable differences are apparent between the practices of Greece and Rome: divination in Rome was the province of two priestly colleges — of *Auguri* and *Aruspici* — regularly appointed and functioning in accordance with a precise procedure within the framework of the republican

constitution. In Greece, however, divination was virtually a private profession and was handed down from father to son. Anyone could go to a diviner for advice in connection with his private affairs; magistrates also sought guidance in matters of public interest if they felt incapable of interpreting the will of the gods themselves.

The will of the gods could be revealed spontaneously through various signs which the *mantis* had no difficulty in interpreting, such as thunder and lightning, eclipses of the sun or moon, and casual everyday events such as the people one met in the street, the words one overheard, a sneeze on the right or the left and so on. There were also signs which the diviner had to read more subtly, such as those inferred from the entrails of a sacrificed animal or the study of the flight of birds from special locations.

Other forms of prophesy eventually became more important than divination. These were the Oracles, regularly organized and officially recognized in all Hellenic cities, both throughout Greece and in her colonies, as the places where the gods made themselves manifest. They were especially concerned with Apollo, the god of prophesy *par excellence*. They were consulted both by private individuals and officials, not only for prophesies but also for suggestions and advice on the most widely differing affairs: before issuing laws or declaring war, before changing the government or entering into a peace treaty.

The oldest oracle, known even to Homer, was that at Dodona in Epirus, where Zeus made known his will by rustling the leaves of an oak, the tree sacred to the god because it was often struck by lightning. The most famous and the most venerated oracle was that at Delphi in Phocis. This was the shrine of Apollo, whose will was made known through a priestess called the *Pythia*. From the seventh century B.C. the Delphic oracle had begun to assume some importance in the political as well as the religious world, and every city sent special ambassadors called *theoriai* to question the god on the outcome of their plans for the future and on the likely success or failure of their present affairs. Thus, before deciding upon the settlement of a colony they would consult the oracle, whose priests, through their extensive and continuous contact with all the Greek peoples, and even with many barbarian nations from the Mediterranean area, were in a good position to provide useful information. Apparently the oracle was almost continuously under the political influence of one or other of the Greek cities, thus giving its answers in accordance with that city's interests.

The agency of the Delphic oracle intervened in two notable events in the political life of Athens. The first was in 513 B.C. after the failure of the conspiracy of Harmodius and Aristogiton against Hippias, the eldest son of Pisistratus, and his brother Hipparchus. The Alcmeonids, a noble Athenian family, took up the conspiracy with the help of the oracle which had been gained to their cause as the family had spared no expense in the reconstruction of the temple after a disastrous fire in 548. The *Pythia* proclaimed that the god willed that the Spartans should put their

Cup with symbols against the evil eye (Kannellopoulos Collection, Athens).

armies at the service of the democratic cause under the leadership of the Alcmeonids to drive the tyrant Hippias out of Athens (Hipparchus meanwhile having been killed). This oracular pronouncement coincided closely with Sparta's policy of always opposing tyrannous regimes.

The second notable occasion was thirty years later. The terrible threat of a Persian invasion hung over the whole of Greece and, unable to agree on a common defence policy, the Greek leaders consulted the oracle at Delphi. Its reply indicated support for the plan of the Peloponnese and the Spartans, the latter in particular having a powerful influence at Delphi. The advice was that only the isthmus of Corinth could be defended against such superiority of numbers.

147

When the Athenians interrogated the oracle they were told that they would be unable to resist the tide of invasion within the boundaries of their city, and that Athens could be defended only by her fleet.

It would be impossible to enumerate the thousands of oracles which sprang up all over Greece; most of them were of purely local interest. Attica had one oracle worthy of note, the fame of which spread throughout the land. This was a 'healing' oracle to which the sick and infirm had recourse to ask for a cure and alleviation of their suffering. Almost all these oracles were under the protection of Asclepius, the god of medicine, but the one in Attica enjoyed the patronage of another deity, the Argive-Theban hero Amphiarus whose will was made known through dreams to his suppliants as they slept. The shrine was erected at Oropus on the Attic-Boeotian border.

When the suppliants arrived, they paid their fee, lay down to sleep on the skin of the sacrificial animal, and awaited their dream. Men and women lay down separately, the former on the west side and the latter on the east side of the altar.

Another method of entering into communication with the deity was through magic formulae and rituals. One of these was the *ordalia*, or 'judgement of God'. Anyone who did not feel capable of defending himself or standing up for his own rights could call the gods to witness by submitting himself to painful and difficult tasks such as touching red-hot iron, immersion in boiling water and so on. If he came through these tests successfully he had proved the truth of his affirmations. Similar to the *ordalia* but more 'civilized' was the oath pronounced to invoke a god as guarantor; in Attica the god was always Zeus.

The sacrifice of animals was considered the most meaningful act of the cult, men and gods taking part symbolically at a common banquet. The parts of the animals offered to the deity and set aside for the consumption of the participants could not under any circumstances be taken out of the sacred precincts, as they were held to be holy and endowed with special properties. Below: a votive bull in bronze. (Kannellopoulos Collection, Athens). Opposite: basin for holy water (Museum of Ancient Inscriptions, Athens) and the 'Moscophorus' or Calf-bearer (Acropolis Museum, Athens).

It was also a practice to invoke a curse on anyone guilty of a crime which human justice had not seen fit to punish him for; he was thus handed over to the vengeance of the gods. A similar method of vengeance was that of writing the name of the offender on a lead tablet *(katadesmos)* to be thrown down some hole thought to communicate with the underworld.

THE CULT OF THE DEAD AND THE ELEUSINIAN MYSTERIES

It is not possible here to give a full account of the Greeks' ideas of death and the world beyond the grave, or of the changes in those ideas throughout the centuries. They were reflected in the rites which accompanied or followed death and were performed during funeral ceremonies. The dying person was entrusted to Hermes, called the *psuchopompos* or 'conductor of souls'. At the moment of death a great din was set up by beating pots and pans with sticks to drive off evil spirits which might try to steal the soul away from Hermes and lead it astray. The corpse's eyes and mouth were closed and the face was veiled; it was then washed in warm water, anointed and dressed in a white tunic, garlanded with flowers and laid in the entrance hall of the house with its feet towards the door. Dirges were sung as the sad procession accompanied the corpse to its last resting place, which might be a tumulus or a funeral pyre. Cremation was the later method of disposing of the dead, and in this case the ashes were collected in an urn and placed in a tomb outside the city. After the

death of an illustrious citizen there were occasionally funeral games, but every funeral was followed by a feast and the drinking of libations to the dead person; these could include the use of blood, water, wine, milk and honey and the sacrifice of sterile black sheep or heifers.

All this, however, was not enough for those cultured and refined intellects who desired to penetrate the mysteries of the world beyond. From the early sixth century B.C. there is increasing evidence of forms of mysticism which seek a solution of the great enigma of life beyond death. They were at first connected with the worship of Dionysus, to which were added exotic and orgiastic ceremonies in honour of other deities: these eventually led to quite a different doctrine, that of Orphism, which was more religions and speculative. This brings us back to Athens, as it was in the literary and artistic circles protected by the court of the Pisistratids (sixth century B.C.) that the new developments in the cult of Dionysus took place and were performed through the great Eleusinian Mysteries.

The Eleusinian Mysteries may be defined as the Attic offshoot of Orphism. The two doctrines are so similar in all their essential elements that they may, however, have developed one from the other and the Eleusinian have been influenced by the Orphic, or they may have a common source which some scholars have traced to the Egyptian cult of Isis. The Eleusinian Mysteries were originally local to Eleusis in Attica and were later adopted in Athens where the ceremonies were presided over by the King Archon.

Superintendence of the Mysteries was entrusted to two Attic families of Thracian origin, the Heumolpides and the Cherices. The former supplied the chief priest, the *hierophantis*. The faithful were classified, according to their degree of initiation, into *mystai* and *epoptai*.

The Mysteries were dedicated to Demeter, the 'Earth Mother', originally worshipped as the goddess of the harvests, and to Kore, the maiden goddess, symbolizing the seed which sleeps for a part of the year in the womb of the earth, her mother. The later Orphic development of the cult identified Kore with Persephone, the wife of Hades, and made the 'Two Goddesses' the deities to which departed souls would implore for admission to the kingdom of the blessed. This, therefore, was the principal object of the initiation into the Eleusinian Mysteries: to learn while still alive the formulae and rites necessary for the soul to enter a promised and long-awaited paradise.

The initiatory rites took place during two periods: the first, or 'lesser' mysteries took place in the month of Anthesterion (February-March) and were preparatory only; the second, or 'great' Mysteries were held in Boedromion (September-October) and completed the instruction — the initiates, or *mystai*, then becoming *epoptai*.

The initiates purified themselves in sea-water and then took part in the great procession in which the Thracian-Dionysiac deity Iacchos was carried from Athens along the Sacred Way to Eleusis. Here they went into the sacred precinct of the Thelesterium, or great hall, where all strangers were strictly forbidden to enter. Any unauthorized witnesses could be put to death. Here the initiation proper took place, during which the *mystai* learnt the way they would have to take in Hades, saw the sacred objects and drank a beverage of flour and water.

The ceremony over, a mystery play was held by torchlight, showing Kore being carried off by Hades, her mother Demeter weeping and Kore's subsequent return. After this the *epoptai* were free to leave, serenely happy that the life beyond the grave was now no longer a mystery and that the way of the blessed was open to them. Woe betide anyone who dared to reveal what he had seen inside the sanctum of the Thelesterium!

The Eleusinian cult of Demeter and Kore, with its widely celebrated Mysteries, its doctrines and its moral dogma, was one of those which suffered least in the vast levelling out of all creeds and religions throughout the Mediterranean lands with the coming of the Roman Empire. The Eleusinian religion renounced both the advantages and the disadvantages which this development from Rome brought with it: on the one hand it did not see its mysteries grow outside the sacred Thelesterium, overlooking the sea of Salamis, or its *hierophantoi* multiplied in the magnificent Hellenistic cities or the great Latin metropolis; on the other hand, in compensation it preserved intact its ordinances and its doctrines, the prerogatives of its privileged families and, like the Roman Vestals, it did not decay, but survived intact with the remaining vestiges of paganism just as it had been in the times of the Pisistratids.

THE TWILIGHT OF THE GODS

When Greek religion came into contact with the cults of the Eastern Mediterranean, and especially with Egypt after the conquests of Philip of Macedon, it had reached a stage of crisis and weakness which inevitably accelerated its decline. With the dwindling of local cults, the traditional religion was further debilitated by the humanistic doctrines of the Epicureans and the Sceptics and by the theories of Everemus, who represented the gods as ancient sovereigns and the benefactors of mankind. It is not surprising that the cults and the spirit of Eastern religion itself should so thoroughly permeate the Greek world, or that in the reverse direction the influence of Greece on the East was limited to such superficialities as the giving of Greek names to barbarian gods, who nevertheless retained their old identities, be they Anatolian, Syrian, Phoenician, Persian or Egyptian.

In the religious systems of the East the Greeks found satisfaction for the demands which their local religion could not meet. Thus more and more of them turned to those mystery cults which reserved the satisfaction of their teachings, their comfort and their promises to those who had shown themselves worthy by undergoing some process of initiation: such were the religions of Attis, Osiris and Mithras. All these gave a new impetus to the ancient Greek mystery religions such as the Eleusinian, and especially in the third and second centuries to the worship of the Cabiri (gods of fertility) in Samothrace, gods to whom the courts of Macedon and Egypt were particularly devoted.

New deities such as the goddesses of Fortune or Chance (Tyche) and Necessity (Ananke) arose to satisfy restless longings which could not be met by a state religion which glorified the King and, with its

151

official pomp and circumstance, gradually extended its deific privileges to all members of the dynasty, including eventually those still alive. One consequence of this apotheosis was the showing of the King's image on coins in place of the patron deity of the city or the state.

Two salient features of Hellenistic religion were the rise of religious societies and the spread of belief in magic, the latter due in particular to the extraordinary development of Babylonian astrology in the third century, according to which every man born under a good or a bad star was for the whole of his life a slave to the destiny he had inherited at the moment of his birth. What could he do to escape from it? This is where he had recourse to magic, a practice which taught him how to rule the gods themselves, to disarm them and force them to withdraw the sentence they had pronounced against him, innocent, unfortunate wretch that he was. It was not, however, given to everyone to succeed in these dif-

ficult rites, and therefore help was sought from those who claimed to possess occult power capable of working miracles and effecting startling cures. Such, in Roman times, were Apollonius of Tyana (b. *c.* 4 B.C.) and Alexander of Abonuticus.

This coition of Eastern cults and Greek national religion formed the basis for new systems of thought: Eastern science and Greek religion gave rise to astrology; this early religion and philosophy fathered the doctrines of Aristotle and his contemporaries, Epicureanism and Stoicism, and, some centuries later, neo-Platonism. Like the religious creeds of the Hellenic world, all these doctrines responded to the desire of men, deprived of all the ideals they had worshipped in their local gods, to find a little consolation and some peace of mind. This desire caused them to inquire into the nature of their gods and the influence they had on their lives and man's destiny, and into the kind of relationship there should be between men and gods.

THE ATTIC CALENDAR

The Attic year had twelve lunar months of 30 and 29 days alternately, giving a total of 354 days. The first day of the month, which followed the night of the new moon, was called the 'new month'; the last was called the 'day of the old moon and of the moon already new'. The year, which began at different times in Greece according to the religious practices of the various cities, began in Attica with the first new moon after the summer solstice, and was given the name of the first of the nine archons (in Sparta it was the name of the first ephor and in Argos that of the first priestess of Hera).

From the third century it became current practice to date the year with reference to the Olympiads, beginning from the traditional 776 B.C. This had the particular merit of giving the whole Hellenic world a common chronology. As the games took place only every four years it was customary to refer to the first, second, third or fourth year of such and such an Olympiad.

There is a simple method of converting an Olympiad date to our system: multiply the Olympic number by four and subtract from 780. The 195th Olympiad, for example, was the first year A.D.

To maintain correspondence with the solar year, from which the Greek lunar year differed by eleven days and six hours, an additional month of thirty days was intercalated from time to time. The need to fix this intercalation led to considerations of longer divisions of the time into 'cycles' of years of twelve and thirteen months.

The best known of these cycles were:

a) The Octaeteric cycle, equal to five ordinary years and three years of thirteen months, that is 99 months with a total of 2,922 days. This was adopted in Athens in the time of Solon (*c.* 640 - *c.* 558 B.C.)

b) The Metonic cycle of nineteen years, instituted by Meton in 432 B.C. This had twelve ordinary years and seven leap years, that is 235 months with a total of 6,940 days.

Model of Olympia (Olympia Museum). The Olympia Festival, held every four years, became a reference point for the dating of events throughout the Greek world. It was used by, amongst others, Hippis of Regium and Thucydides and became accepted practice by the fourth century, B.C.

HECATOMBAION (July-August)	**12** *Kronia:* in honour of Kronos and Rhea.	**16** *Synoikia:* in honour of Athena and in memory of the work of Theseus.	**24 28** *Panathenaia:* in honour of Athena, held the third year of each Olympiad.	**?** *Nemaia:* Pan-Hellenic games held at the beginning of the second and fourth years of each Olympiad in the valley of Nemea.
METAGEITNION (August-September)	**11 16** *Olympiad:* in honour of Zeus Olympus. Pan-Hellenic games held every four years at Olympia.	**?** *Pythia:* in honour of Apollo. Pan-Hellenic games held at Delphi every four years.		
BOEDROMION (September-October)	**3** *Eleuteria:* in celebration of the victory over the Persians.	**5** *Genesia:* in memory of the dead. **6** *Marathonia:* in celebration of the victory of Marathon.	**7** *Boedromia:* in honour of Apollo Boedromios (the Saviour). **12** *Caristeria:* in memory of the liberation from the thirty tyrants.	**16 25** *Great Eleusinian:* celebration of the Eleusinian Mysteries.
PYANOPSION (October-November)	**7** *Pyanopsia:* in honour of Apollo. **8** *Theseia:* in memory of Theseus.	**9 13** *Thesmophoria:* in honour of Demeter and Persephone. Only for married women.	**?** *Oschophoria:* in honour of Dionysus and Athena for the grape and olive harvests.	**19 21** (?) *Apaturia:* the feast of the phratriai dedicated to Zeus Phratrios and Athena Phratria. **29** *Calcheia:* in honour of Hephaestus and Athene Ergane.
MAIMACTERION (November-December)				
POSEIDAION (December-January)	**?** *Haloa:* in honour of Poseidon, Demeter and Kore. For women only.	**?** *Rustic Dionysia:* in honour of Dionysus.		
GAMELION (January-February)	**12** *Lenaea (Dionysic):* in honour of Dionysus with Eleusinian priests.			
ANTHESTERION (February-March)	**11 13** *Anthesteria:* in honour of Dionysus. Festival of the new wine.	**19 21** *Lesser Eleusinian:* celebration of the Eleusinian Mysteries.	**23** *Diasia:* in honour of Zeus in Athens.	**?** *Procaristeria:* in honour of Athena, Demeter and Kore.
ELAPHEBOLION (March-April)	**9 13** *Urban or Greater Dionysia:* in honour of Dionysus, with theatrical festival.			
MUNYCHION (April-May)	**?** *Delphinia:* in honour of Apollo of Delphi.	**16** *Munychia:* in honour of Artemis.	**25** The sacred bath of Athena Polias.	**?** *Isthmia:* in honour of Poseidon. Pan-Hellenic games held in the second and fourth years of each Olympiad in Corinth.
THARGELION (May-June)	**6 7** *Thargelia:* in honour of the sun for the ripening of the harvest.	**19 25** *Callinteria and Plinteria:* dedicated to the cult of Athena.		
SKIROPHORION (June-July)	**12** *Skirophoria.* **14** *Arretophoria:* both in honour of the city's divine patroness. For women.	**?** *Diipolia:* in honour of Zeus Polieos.		

Calendar of Attic religious festivals and Pan-Hellenic games.

MEDICINE IN ANCIENT GREECE

The primitive, popular, magic medicine of the Greeks (a medicine which has no recorded history) developed away from superstition towards faith-healing practices. The faith of the sick and the psychological experience of the priests attached to the great sanctuaries were of considerable therapeutic value in the context of primitive religiosity. Proof of this is seen in the recording of miraculous cures on the marble steles of Epidaurus and Lebena. These cures were effected after the patient had fallen into a deep sleep, a state thought to be ideal for entering into communion with the gods, especially with those gods whose habitat was in the depths of the earth. That certain healing practices took place in the sanctuaries of the appropriate gods, based first on observation, then on reflection and study, is shown by the fact that some of the great medical schools sprang up close to the temples and that their founders came from priestly families.

But the more specifically scientific medicine, closely connected in origin with the speculative thought of the schools of philosophy, also showed a clear evolution in methods and an improvement in results. The greatest name in ancient medicine was the Greek Hippocrates. Born about 460 B.C. on the island of Cos, he was a contemporary of Sophocles. His brilliant intuitions, his experimental method and his sense of the professional dignity and responsibility of the doctor was an entirely original development.

Practices of popular magic and occult prescriptions, the legacy of all primitive 'medicine', entered very little into the formation and development of Greek medical science. There were two factors which brought medicine out of the narrow confines of magical practices: faith in the healing power of the gods (especially after the assimilation and humanizing of local deities into the figure of Apollo Olympus) and the experience of priestly colleges in psychology, which was a valuable aid to traditional therapeutic methods. Theological doctrine and sacred ritual obviously stood only on the fringes of science, but the crowds of sick people who flocked to the great temples and the variety of their ailments must have stimulated the priests to observe them. The records of miraculous cures, though fragmentary, imprecise, and dedicated to the glory of the relevant deity and the confusion of the unbeliever, offered a fruitful field of investigation to minds more inclined to reflection. In the sanctuaries where the gods of healing were worshipped there arose the major schools which, from the sixth century, transformed magical practices and pragmatic therapy in Greece, substantially similar to those in the Middle East, into truly scientific inquiry. As this was incompatible with blind faith in the thaumaturgy of the tutelar deities and the practices they demanded, the medical schools quickly broke away from the sanctuaries where they had originated. Tradition died hard in Greece, however, and the schools maintained formal links with certain cults and sanctuaries, though there was little reciprocal influence either of 'temple medicine' on scientific activity and development, or of medical schools on religious beliefs and practices.

Magical practices only enter into the history of medicine in Greece indirectly in giving rise to the rudimentary descriptions of illnesses, symptoms and remedies in the accounts of 'cures' *(iamata)* carved on the marble steles in the temples of Asclepius at Epidaurus in Argolis or at Lebena on the southern coast of Crete. The cures appear to have been effected by the god while the patients, some of whom had certainly doubted his miraculous power, lay in a deep sleep.

This faith healing thus took place in conditions thought specially appropriate for communion with the gods, in particular with those whose habitat was supposed to be the depths of the earth: sleep (*enkoimesis* in Greek, *incubatio* in Latin) in the temple. This allowed the god to manifest himself to the patient and make known his wishes or his replies, as happened at the oracles, and even to give tangible proof of his kind intervention. This 'incubation' technique, practised at shrines dedicated to Asclepius, from Epidaurus to Tricca, from Cos to Pergamum and from Lebena to Rome, sustained the association of the god with the underworld.

'Cure effected by Apollo and Asclepius. Ambrosia of Athens, blind in one eye. She came with supplications to the god, and as she walked round the temple she smiled at the accounts of some of the cures which she found incredible and impossible, accounts which related how the lame and the blind had been cured by a vision which came to them in a dream. She fell asleep and had a vision. The god appeared before her, telling her that she would be cured and that she had to dedicate in the sanctuary a pig made of silver as a token of her ignorance. Having said this he cut out the bad eye and immersed it in a medicine. She awoke at dawn, cured.

'A man with an ulcer in his stomach. While he slept he had a dream. The god appeared to him and ordered his assistants to hold him so that the god could cut out the affected part. The man tried to escape but he was seized and fastened to a door. Asclepius then opened up his stomach, cut out the ulcer, sewed him up again and finally released him. The man awoke cured, but the floor of the *abaton* was covered with blood.

'Gorgias, son of Heraclitus, had a suppurating wound. He had been pierced in the lung by an arrow in battle and for eighteen months the suppuration had been so bad that he had produced sixty-seven basinfuls of pus. When he had fallen asleep he had a vision. The god appeared to him and took out the point of the spear. When day broke he walked away cured, carrying the tip of the spear in his hand.

'Climene, an Argive, was paralysed in his body. He came to the *abaton*, fell asleep and had a vision. The god appeared to him, tied a thread of red wool round his body and led him to bathe in a small lake near the temple, the waters of which were extraordinarily cold. As Climene was afraid, Asclepius said that he did not cure cowards, but only those who approached him in the temple trusting that the god would do them no harm but send them away healed. Climene awoke, washed himself and went away cured' (Inscriptiones Graecae).

In most of the cases described here, the cure is presented as a *thauma*, or miracle, but the crude surgical techniques used by the god in some of the visions, notably the *iamata*, seems to indicate that the priests working in the temples visited by the sick had acquired at least some medical experience. Magical practices seem also to have included some elementary pharmacology, as is evident from the prescriptions dictated by the god during the *incubatio* and recorded in votive epitaphs in the temple of Asclepius at Lebena. These refer, amongst other things, to preparations based in medicinal herbs, the use of the ashes of sacrificed animals, and 'holy water'. There was the case of the epileptic cured in the temple of Asclepius at Pergamum by a miraculous substitution of quartan fever for the epilepsy. This was quoted by the Pergamum doctor Oribasius in his 'Collection of medical experiments' (XLV 30, 10-14). Oribasius was physician to the Roman Emperor Julian (A.D. 361-3), and he wished to confirm the efficacy of this ancient cure. Proof of the existence of some medical practice in the sanctuaries of the healing gods is afforded by the fact that at least some of the notable Greek medical schools sprang up around these very sanctuaries, and their founders came from families whose members were priests or otherwise closely connected with the cults. Thus in Caria the Asclepiads of Cos and Cnidos promoted two rival medical schools which achieved great fame. In Ionia another *genos*, devoted to Apollo Ulios, gave rise to a school which had its centre in a city founded by Asian Ionians at Velia in Lucania.

SCIENTIFIC MEDICINE

Like the cult of its major patron Apollo, Greek scientific medicine was born in Asia Minor and was

An entire family entreats Asclepius (bas relief in the National Museum, Athens).

closely linked with the development of the early schools of philosophy. Individual schools of medicine developed differently according to the varying directions taken by philosophical thought, and these differences were reflected in the diversity of their clinical experience and standards of diagnosis and treatment. The technique of the early *iateres*, who in the former age had appeared, like *demiurgoi*, similar to specialized craftsmen, such as metallurgists and potters, and to prophets or sages, gradually evolved into physiological and clinical theory. Conversely the philosophical schools found much to clarify and elaborate their own doctrines in the experience of the doctors.

Some importance was given to the study of medicine in the schools of philosophy which sprang up around Pythagoras (b. *c.* 580 B.C. in Samos). It is possible that a medical school already existed in Croton (Magna Graecia) when Pythagoras arrived there from Samos in about 530 B.C., or perhaps the philosopher and his followers founded a school themselves. This school was soon considered the most authoritative, even in Asia Minor, the birth place of scientific medicine. Herodotus in his *History* (Book II 125-38) tells the adventures of Democedes, a doctor from Croton who, having served in Aegina and in Athens, had entered the service of Polycrates, the tyrant of Samos. Here he was captured by the satrap of Sardis in 522 and reduced to servitude by the Persian King Darius. At the latter's court in Susa, Democedes, ' skilled in the art of medicine more than any of his contemporaries ', gave of his singular ability by curing the king of a painful fracture. This had been beyond the powers of the Egyptian doctors at the court, though they were ' reputed to be the first in the art of medicine '. He then cured the queen, Atossa, of a more serious illness. ' It was mainly on his account that doctors from Croton acquired such fame: in his time they were considered the best in Greece, and next came those from Cyrene '. A tradition unknown to Herodotus connected Democedes with the Asclepiads from Anatolia, making his father Calliphontis a priest of the Asclepius temple on Cos. This may be pure invention, but it is significant that it should have been thought necessary to find a link between the medical school at Croton and the cult of Asclepius. The most ancient of the surviving documents concerning Greek medicine, the epigraph on the marble *kouros* indicating the tomb of 'Sombrotidas, doctor, son of Mandrocles' at Megara Iblea (Sicily), shows that this man's family also came originally from Asia Minor, as the name Mandrocles is derived from that of a pre-Hellenic god of Anatolia, Mandros.

In the history of medical science the first great name is also that of a man from Croton, Alcmaeon, a contemporary of Pythagoras, who first established that scientific investigation should be based on the examination of concrete data, and opposed the abstractions of the *physiologoi* who were concerned mainly with the discovery of the principles behind the creation and the governing of the cosmos. But to the study of the human organism he added, like his co-disciples of Pythagoras, the study of the *ethos*, and in both the central point of the inquiry was man, the reasoning and the sentient being. The doctrine of the *isonomia*, or the balance of opposites, in contrast to the *monarchia*, or the predominance of one quality over another, was as valid for the well-being of the animal organism as it was for the mind and for human society.

This demand for harmony in all forms of life explains why the followers of Pythagoras called medicine 'the wisest of their arts'. The 'medical' study of man could not therefore be divorced from the philosophy of this school which was careful to distinguish, inspired by the oracles at Delphi, between the human and the divine spheres of activity. The school was equally careful not to bring over into scientific inquiry and *techne* the dogmatism common to all 'physiologists' from the Milesii to Empedocles (born first quarter of the fifth century B.C.), who raised experimental data into principles *(archai)*, and the Eleatic school of philosophers who, though exposing the illogicality of these theories, nevertheless substituted for them an ontology which verified experimentation. A famous saying of Alcmaeon epitomizes the attitude of a disciple of Pythagoras to the problems of nature: 'Of the invisible and the mortal the gods have certain knowledge: man is given to conjecture'.

Asclepius and his daughter Hygeia (fifth-century votive relief, National Museum, Athens).

HIPPOCRATES AND HIS SCHOOL

Whereas the medical schools of Magna Graecia and Sicily followed the 'physiological' method, the method of inquiry and synthesis practised by Alcmaeon and the school of Pythagoras was taken up and perfected by the genius of an Asclepiad from the island of Cos, Hippocrates (*c.* 460-370 B.C.), who was a contemporary of Socrates and founded the most famous medical school of antiquity. There is reason to believe that the school had its first centre in Astipalaia, the ancient capital of Cos, near a temple dedicated to Asclepius. It seems, however, to have been independent of the temple, and when in 366 the newly constituted separate state of Cos made Asclepius its principal deity and dedicated a great sanctuary to him at the gates of the new city of Cos, the medical school was held to be exempt from all magical practices. It is quite likely that the great prestige of the Hippocratic school influenced the temple to Asclepius at Cos, where there is no record of any miraculous *iamata*, to adopt a different kind of cult to that commonly held in other similar temples. This divergence in the Coan cult would seem to be borne out also by the devotion of Hippocrates and the Asclepiads of Cos and Cnidos

to the Pythian Apollo, a devotion which secured for them particular privileges at Delphi, and which links their school with that at Croton inspired by Pythagoras. Following the line taken by Alcmaeon, Hippocrates inveighed against certain doctors and philosophers (' Concerning ancient medicine ', 20), Empedocles amongst them, from Ionia, Italy and Sicily, who had ' written concerning nature, discussing the principle: who is man and what is his origin and of what elements is he constituted ? '. Similarly, the Coan school had a fierce argument with the school of Cnidos which had been satisfied with a descriptive diagnosis and a pragmatic and improvised therapy.

Certain well-founded doubts have been raised, as a result of recent historical and philological research, about the authenticity of much of the available biographical data concerning Hippocrates and about the attribution to him of the so-called ' Corpus Hippocraticum ', a body of medical writings which go under his name. It is, however, recognized that his doctrines were distinctive and original and that they determined the direction which medical thought was to take for all succeeding ages. The criterion, the method and the critical yet impartial attitude taken by Hippocrates against the philosophers and doctors who had preceded him are all to be seen clearly in his book ' On ancient medicine ', in which he says: ' I do not say that the ancient art *(techne)* of medicine should be rejected as if it were not a *techne*, or had not been properly inquired into because it has not achieved precision in all things; I rather hold that because it is pervaded with ignorance, what it has discovered must be regarded with admiration, as this is proof of some good and true inquiry ' (Ch. 12), and ' Some doctors and philosophers *(sophistai)* say that no one can know medicine who does not know what man is and that those who would cure men well must first learn this. But their speech inclines towards philosophy in the manner of Empedocles and others... I maintain on the other hand that what has been said on the nature of man by philosophers and doctors belongs less to the art of medicine than to literature. I also believe that a science of nature can have no other source than that of medicine, and can only be achieved when this art has been properly understood. But it seems to me that this is still a long way off, I mean when we shall know precisely what man is, what were his origins and other questions of similar nature. There-fore it seems necessary to me that as far as nature is concerned the doctor should know, and make every effort to learn, if he wishes to fulfil any of his duties, the answers to these questions: What is the relation of man to what he eats and drinks and to his mode of life, and the reaction of the individual to each agent ? ' (Ch. 20).

The superiority of the Coan over the Cnidian school is exemplified in one of the more authentic parts of the ' Corpus Hippocraticum ' called the *Prognosticum*, which inspired authors outside the field of medicine such as the historian Thucydides (*c.* 460 - *c.* 400 B.C.) and thinkers such as Socrates and Plato. Plato, in his dialogue *Laches* (198 D) said: ' It seems to me and to Laches that in every range of studies there is not one science *(episteme)* which is different according to whether it seeks to know the past, to know how it came about, or the present, to know how it is, or the future, to discover how best things might be and how what has not yet been will come about, but rather that there is one and the same science for all these things. As far as health is concerned, for instance, medicine, which is not diverse, but one, observes the past, the present and the future '.

In the opening words of the *Prognosticum* Hippocrates set down his conception of prognosis as the necessary development from a diagnosis based on the record of the past *(anamnesis)* and on the observation of the present: ' I hold it to be an excellent thing that the doctor should practise foresight *(pronoia)*: therefore when he shall recognize and declare to his patients by his science alone, their present, past and future condition, revealing all that they have omitted to tell him, he shall be the better held capable of knowing these cases of his patients, and men shall not be afraid to trust in their doctor. And the doctor, knowing in advance what shall be the outcome of their suffering, shall be better able to prescribe for their cure '.

The high level of scientific thinking attained by Greek medicine in the classical age was matched by the sense of dignity and professional responsibility of the doctor as expressed in the so-called ' Hippocratic Oath ': ' I swear by Apollo the physician and by Asclepius and Hygieia and Panacea and all the gods and goddesses to be my witnesses that I will fulfil this Oath and this covenant to the best of my ability and my judgement. I will consider him who has taught me in this art as equal to my parents...: I will impart the doctrine, both oral and written, and all other teaching to my sons and to the sons of him who has taught me and to pupils bound by covenant to observe the rules and by their pronouncement of the oath of the physicians and to no other... I will not give to anyone, even though it be asked of me, any deadly drug, nor any advice to such a purpose; and likewise I will not give any woman a pessary to procure abortion. I will keep my art and my life pure and holy...' One paragraph of the Oath which states 'I will not operate on any person suffering from gallstones but yield in this case to the experts (in surgery)' contradicts other texts of the 'Corpus Hippocraticum' which state that in the Coan school, as also in others, surgery was not neglected, but developed *pari passu* with anatomy and physiology. But the commonly-held opinion that in surgery it was the operating technique which counted more than the discipline of method must have induced some well-qualified physicians to leave operating, at least in some sectors, to others whose training had been mainly practical. The apparent underestimation of surgery in the Hippocratic Oath can be virtually discounted as a considerable number of scientific treatises on surgery, bother general and particular, were written at this time, some of them, in fact, in the 'Corpus'.

The figure of Hippocrates dominates the whole development of classical medicine. Outside the Coan school progress was also made in the so-called Sicilian school inspired by Empedocles and connected with the school at Cnidos. Hippocrates' doctrines were taken up by his most famous successor Diocles of Carystos, a contemporary of Aristotle. The efficacy of Hippocratic teaching was reflected in the medical school at Alexandria, which achieved fame through the eminent physiologist Erasistratus of Chios and Herophilus, a pioneer in the study of the nervous system, both of whom flourished in the first half of the third century B.C. In the field of polemics one of the oldest schools was that of the so-called Empiricists (founded in the third century B.C.), which thought that the basis of all medical science should be experience — one's own and that of others *(historia)* — and analogy.

During the period of Augustus and his successor in Imperial Rome there was an echo of the old polemics. The medical school at Velia was recalled, probably by the Emperor Claudius' doctor, Stertinius Xenophontis, who was an Asclepiad from Cos. This was to bring in Parmenides Uliades, a *physikos* and therefore a person of distinction, with the *iatroi* from the *ghenos* of Apollo Ulios who had provided a succession of directors *(phylarchoi)* of the medical college which they had organized on the model of the Pythagorian community. This throwback to ancient history, however, would seem to indicate that medicine in Imperial Rome did not in fact find itself hampered by polemics. In the second century A.D. the doctrines and the history of the Hippocratic school were studied, explained and coordinated by the Platonist Galen. It is mainly due to him that the tradition of Greek medicine survived until beyond the Middle Ages in Europe and the Islamic East.

ATHENIAN GAMES AND FESTIVALS

On the long frieze of the 'Little Metropolis' of Athens the chisel of an unknown sculptor represented symbolically the most famous festivals in Attica. The most famous only because, in the words of Pericles, 'games and festivals follow each other from one year's end to the next and these games and these festivals, day after day, banish melancholy'.

The festival, which has always had a religious connotation, served to lift the burden of living from man's shoulders and to open up for him, beyond his individual life, the hope of a communal life beyond the grave. The solemn ceremonies, therefore, were not in Athens a sign of idleness or inertia, but rather occasions of collective joy and of mass participation in the folk-lore of the rituals, in the games and contests.

The festivals held in the shadow of the Acropolis were rarely conventional or merely commemorative: they celebrated not only the events of the past but also the achievements of the present, they were political as well as religious and their evocation of the vision of the eternal repetition of life through fertile nature demanded also propitiatory acts of magic.

Everyone took part in these games and festivals, young and old, men and women, free men and slaves. The young honoured life, celebrating, through their contests, strength, beauty and fertility, but the real protagonist was always Athens, the whole of Athens, its city and its countryside.

'As a respite from our labours we have procured numerous diversions and entertainments for the spirit in games and festivals which succeed one another throughout the year and, in our domestic lives, those games which, day after day, banish melancholy'. These were the words of Pericles in his speech honouring the first men to fall in the Peloponnesian War, a speech which is also the finest tribute to Athenian civilization. No other city in the ancient world had such a full religious calendar. Two thirds of the year were said be spent in festivals. This would appear to contradict the reputation that Classical Athens has always had for hard work, but it must be remembered that these festivals provided employment, as the faith and the myths which they served required temples, stadia, theatres and statues and the performance of tragedy, comedy and song.

There were very few purely conventional or commemorative festivals. The commemoration of Marathon on the sixth day of Boedromion and of Salamis on the sixteenth of Munychion meant not only honouring the heroes of the battles but also thanking the deity who had favoured the victory. There were many festivals connected with nature and rooted in very ancient magical rituals to ensure the fertility of flocks and fields. There were also many festivals for the anthropomorphic deities of classical Olympus who after existing alongside them took over from the fertility gods. The festivals of Periclean Athens, which were both religious and political, enjoyed a heritage of two thousand years of nature worship and mythology and the continuous exercise of religious practices and creative fantasy. In spite of the speculation of the Sophists and, later, of the great schools of philosophy of the fourth century, which attempted to undermine it, the festival, or *panegyris*, remained fundamental to life in the city. Its tradition may even have survived the coming of Christianity with its completely new festivals, and remains alive today.

Each festival had its own *raison d'être*, its meaning and its character, but there were some ritual acts common to all: the procession *(pompe)*, the sacrifice *(thysia)*, or the offering, and the contest *(agon)*. The first two acts were openly religious and are, in fact, common to all the religions of the world. The contests, or games, however, might appear to have been mere diversions for the masses who poured into Athens from the surrounding demes in the Attic countryside. So they were, in fact, in the later stages, although they always had an element of the worship of beauty and strength. Originally they must have been purely religious acts of ritual. This was particularly true of the dramatic contests in the great Dionysiac festivals, as was known to those who participated. The religious motive behind gymnastic contests is not always clear, though there is a general reference to it in Homer when he speaks of the games Achilles put on for the funeral of Patroclus (*Iliad*, XXIII) and those games mentioned in the *Odyssey* (VIII and XXI).

One of the most important contests in the Panathenaic games was the torch race *(lampadedromia)*. The winner was the one who reached the end first with the torch alight in his hand. The contest was included in the Panathenaic games in imitation of the festivals held in honour of Prometheus, the ancient Attic god of fire. The purpose of this festival was to rekindle the fires which burned in the hearths of private houses and on the public altar in the Prytaneum from a torch lit on the altar of the god. The sacred flame was carried by runners so that it should not be polluted by the atmosphere through which it passed. Only the flame which did not go out could be guaranteed the best. And what was the religious significance of the country-fair type of contest held on the first two days of Anthesterion to find out who had the greatest capacity for wine, or of the balancing contest on two inflated greasy bladders in the rural Dionysiac festivals?

One other factor, less constant but just as important, stands out in these festivals, even before we begin to turn the pages of the Attic religious calendar. This is the performance of some mystery rite. In the Anthesteria, the festival of Dionysus as the God of Wine, there was a sacred ritual marriage; in the Thesmophoria and the Arretophoria there was a basket containing sacred objects; there was the ritualistic trial of a sacrifical axe in the Diipolia; in the Thargelia two men, supposedly carrying the guilt of all, were driven through the streets; the celebrations of the Lenaea were magic and mystery rites from very ancient times when man's life was rooted in the countryside and not in the city. These rites, which were mostly episodic in Athens, were to become the centre of the great Mysteries at Eleusis.

THE SUMMER FESTIVALS

There were many festivals in the Athenian liturgical calendar. It will be sufficient for our purpose to single out the more important ones as the unknown sculptor did on the frieze which runs along the front of the Little Metropolis in Athens. The civic and the religious years began in high summer the month of Hecatombaion (July-August). The first festival of the year fell on the twelfth of the month and honoured Kronos and Rhea. It was a popular festival which took place mostly within the family and brought to the same festive board both masters and their slaves. On the sixteenth Theseus was honoured for having united Attica in the name of Athena and ensured her power and her glory. It was, however, the end of the month which brought the festival intended to stir the heart and pride of every Athenian citizen: the Panathenaia, a great celebration in honour of the city's goddess and patroness. This festival normally lasted for two days, but every fourth year it was celebrated for longer and with some solemnity. As a Pan-Hellenic festival it dated back to 566-565 B.C., when the athletic contests were introduced. The prizes were simple amphoras of oil decorated, as they were in the olden days, with black figures and showing a menacing Athena in battle on one side and on the other a picture of the contest for which it had been awarded. The highlight of the festival was that caught forever by Phidias' chisel on the frieze of the Parthenon: the procession which, at dawn on the 28th, carried into the Acropolis the sacred offerings, including the most precious one of all, the robe specially woven for the goddess. The whole of the preceding night there had been activity throughout the city. Young men and girls sang and wove intricate dances, the *epheboi* had run their torch-races, and in the lower part of the city, near the Ceramicus, there had been

The solemn entry of the Panathenaic procession into the Acropolis in the August sunshine. It has passed through the Propylaea and is coming into view of the Parthenon (detail from a model in the Royal Ontario Museum, Toronto).

feverish preparations marshalling the procession into position. These were the last preparations, because nine months previously during the festivals of Athena Ergane, patroness of work, the *ergastinai* had already begun to make the robe. The procession had a fixed ceremonial: first came the offerings: virgins carrying baskets, cups, jars and incense-burners; four oxen, four rams and innumerable heifers intended for sacrifice

on the great altar. It was this mass slaughter which gave the month its name of Hecatombaion. The sacrificial animals were followed by the *scaphephorie*, dressed in red chitons and bearing offerings of sweets and honey in silver cups; then came the water-carriers and the musicians. So that the robe could be seen with all the splendour of its embroidery which told the story of the goddess's victory over the giants, it was hung up for display on the mast of a cart made to represent a ship, according to a custom which properly belonged to the festivals of Dionysus who came from the sea. The procession was completed by priests, magistrates and the mass of citizens, escorted by the imposing *epheboi* on horseback. After passing through the Agora, the procession wound its way up the slopes of the Acropolis and here, in the splendour of the morning sunlight glittering on her marble temples, Athena received the homage of her city, her demes and her colonies. In the evening, down in the city, the people feasted on the flesh of the sacrificed animals, forgetting, or perhaps not knowing, that to eat the meat of a sacrificial victim meant banqueting with the gods.

THE AUTUMN FESTIVALS

Boedromion (September-October) was a particularly sacred month. Its name came from the festival in honour of Apollo the Saviour (from the perils of battle: Apollo Boedromios). In fact it was a month of battle commemorations: the 3rd was the anniversary of the victory at Plataia over the Persians (479 B.C.) and the 6th that of Marathon. A few days later such events which concerned man as a social animal were to be forgotten when man faced his destiny as an individual being in the celebrations of the Great Eleusinian Mysteries. These began in the middle of the month. ' Happy is he amongst men who possesses the vision of these mysteries. But he who has not been initiated into the sacred rites shall have a different fate when he goes after death into the dark underworld '. These words occur in the Homeric hymn to Demeter, the sorrowing mother in search of her daughter Kore, a hymn to the seed which dies in the earth and is reborn to become an ear of corn, and to the man who can return to earth and question in his anguish the mysterious future, seeking salvation. This is what we can see dimly through the veil which the ancients drew over the most sacred mysteries of their faith in the great hall of the Thelesterium at Eleusis. Let us also respect this secrecy and follow the initiates *(mystai)* only in their outward preparations. The 15th was a day of watching. The candidates, who had become initiates a year previously at the festival of the Lesser Mysteries at Agrae on the Ilys-

Dancing was a traditional feature of many Athenian festivals, particularly those celebrating Dionysus such as

sus, met in Athens. Here the sacred objects, contained in a casket *(cista)*, had been brought some days previously and deposited in the Eleusinium. On the 16th they went down to the sea and, when the priests cried ' To the sea, Mystai ' they plunged into the water, each carrying a sucking-pig destined for the sacrifice. After this purification ceremony two further days were spent in Athens. On the 19th the solemn procession set out singing hymns and following the sacred casket. It stopped at several sanctuaries along the Sacred Way and at the bridge over the river Cephisus to indulge in traditional horseplay. It arrived at Eleusis at sundown. The whole night was spent in vigil with singing and dancing and the following day in fasting with new offerings and purification rites. The 21st, 22nd, and 23rd were the days of the Mystery rites, and when these were over the crowds stayed on for another three days for the gymnastic and theatrical contests. This must have been the Attic festival which attracted most people, as the only ones debarred from attending would be those who did not speak Greek or who were stigmatized by some public guilt.

the Anthesteria, the Dionysia and the Oschophoria. Above: satyrs and bacchantes dancing as they follow the god (Detail from an Attic vase, National Museum, Ferrara).

The month of Pyanopsion (October-November) had more festivals than any other. To the secular eye the most picturesque of these was the celebration of the Pyanopsia in honour of Apollo, one of the most typical of the propitiatory rites. The god was offered a plate of beans and a plate of vegetables made into a paste with cornflour. A youth, whose parents had both to be still living, carried the *eiresion* in procession. This was a branch of laurel or olive adorned with strips of red and white wool and strung with first fruits. To the accompaniment of singing from the youths, the fruit was hung near the door of Apollo's temple. Similar branches were carried through the city and hung at the doors of houses, where they were left until the next festival. The Oschophoria, a festival in honour of Dionysus, was somewhat similar. Two youths dressed as women and holding vine branches laden with grapes led a procession from Athens to Phalerum Bay. Here sacrifices were made and libations drunk to the god of wine, to the accompaniment of ecstatic shouts. The festival ended up in the meadows where the *deipnophorai* handed round the food and the company was entertained by dancing, the recital of mythical tales, athletics and races.

These two were clearly harvest festivals. The last festival of the agricultural year, the Thesmophoria, celebrated the new cycle of life in the fields with the sowing of seed. Sacred ploughing ceremonies were performed so that the land should be blessed and prepared for the new growth, and the Thesmophoria was a ritual in honour of Demeter and Kore which would ensure that the seed fell into the furrow with good promise of fertility and abundance. Only married women took part, as they alone live through the mysteries of conception. They lived segregated in the sacred hall of the Thesmophorium for three days. They brought out from underground recesses the *thesmoi*, remains of sacred objects buried four months previously, and mixed the seed with them to give it potency. They then fasted and wept for the departure of Kore to the dark labyrinth of Hades. On the third day they rejoiced in the exalted atmosphere of the sacrifices and other fertility rites. This ritual and that performed in the two days of fasting, part of which took place on the sea, had one thing in common with certain other festivals: the uttering of obscene gibes, showing a faith in the magical power of words, designed to bring a greater fertility to the fields.

The Arretophoria, held in the month of Skirophorion, had a similar purpose and ritual, but was in honour of Athena, the protectress of vegetation and human fertility. Her priestesses were the *arrephoroi*, two ten year old girls, whose innocence would guarantee the successful outcome of the ritual. Their function was to deposit in and to take out of underground recesses the mysterious caskets of unmentionable things *(arrheta)* as well as to help in the weaving of the tunic to be offered to Athena, which began at the end of the month with the festival of the Chalkeia.

There were still three days of festival to come in the warm Attic autumn: the Apaturia, during which youths and girls were enrolled on the lists of the phratries and sacrificed lambs and goats to the gods who protected the continuation of the family lineage.

But the end of autumn often saw storm clouds gather over the peaks of Mounts Hymettus and Parnes,

and the month of Maimacterion was generally poor in festivities, though the Greeks did not fail to honour Zeus at this time so that he would keep the storms away from the newly sown fields.

THE WINTER FESTIVALS

The month following Maimacterion saw the beginning of the winter festivals, the rowdiest and the wildest of them all. Almost all of them were devoted to Dionysus, who was honoured in the various aspects of his exuberant and mysterious nature, and some were concerned with the making of wine and in praise of its potency. The fate of the seeds sown in the furrow some months previously was not, however, forgotten. The feast of the Haloa (derived from the threshing-floor and the ploughed field) was intended to protect the young grain. It was dedicated both to Poseidon as a chthonian deity and as the god who gave his name to the month, and to Demeter and Kore. Only women, and this included courtesans, could take part. The symbol of fecundity was the protagonist of the feast, just as it was also in the Rustic Dionysia held

In March and April the purificatory rites of spring and the sacred marriage of Dionysus were celebrated in various ways. It was a very ancient tradition that young girls should take part in these festivals and three-year-old little children were given floral crowns. The early Attic spring formed a background of bright colours to the dances, processions and games (Bas-relief, The Louvre, Paris).

in the same month. The aim was the consecration of the countryside in the numerous Attic demes, in an atmosphere of unconfined joy. The greatest moment was the procession, which we can see through the *Acharnians* of Aristophanes. The joyful company was led by a young girl carrying a basket overflowing with country gifts and followed by two slaves bearing symbols; finally came the crowd, personified by Di-kaiopolis, singing a hymn to fertility. The singing continued outside the procession in the *komoi*, which were the origin of comedy and, although improvised, were performed in a spirit of keen competition. Roars of laughter would break out at the sights of half-drunk peasants trying to keep their balance on greasy inflated wineskins for a prize of wine.

The real wine festival flooded the streets of Athens with gaiety two months later. This was the celebration of the Anthesteria, when the new jars were opened. Before this, however, there was the feast of the Lenaea on the twelfth of the month of Gamelion. Held in an enclosed area near the Agora, it was a Bacchanalian feast with wild dancing, a procession led by the King Archon and dramatic contests held before the restricted public of Athens only, in contrast to those of the Greater Dionysia which attracted an audience from all over Attica.

The Anthesteria lasted for three days (11-13 of Anthesterion) of which only the first two were devoted to Dionysus. The third day, known as the Chytroi, was in honour of the dead and took its name from the earthenware pots *(chytroi)* in which a compost of vegetables and seeds was boiled to make an offering to Hermes, the conductor of souls, with prayers for their well-being. This is the first recorded prayer for the dead in Western civilization and it is not surprising that it is found in Athens, where there were other festivals in honour of the departed (the Genesia, the Nemesia, the Epitaphia). On the same day it was not unusual to see in the gardens of Athens young girls swinging on ropes: this was not a game, but a very ancient ritual of purification connected with the spring. This took place on the day devoted to the dead because the act of making one's peace with them was in itself purifying and conferred a blessing on the coming new season. There were similar propitiatory rites during the first two days of the festival, such as the sacred marriage between the Basilinna, or Queen, and Dionysus, impersonated by the King

Archon, and the crowning with flowers of three-year-old children. Let us, however, follow the ceremonials of the feast. On the first day the jars of new wine were opened and libations were drunk. The second day saw the feast of the wine-pitchers, and this included drinking competitions with yet more wine as prizes. The contest, which was also a ritual, took place amidst the silence of the onlookers, and it was a question of who could gulp down his pitcherful of wine the fastest. On the same day there was a carnival-like procession through the streets of Athens accompanying Dionysus on a boat-shaped float, and the consummation of the sacred marriage took place in the *Bukoleion*. In the evening bands of drunken men went to pour the last of the wine on the altar of Dionysus, and the revelling continued all night until the morning of the day devoted to the dead.

The Great Dionysia, second only to the Panathenaia in solemnity and in the number of foreigners it attracted, was the most recent of the festivals of Attica. Instituted by Pisistratus in honour of Dionysus Eleutherius, it passed on the highlights of its ceremonial to the Rustic Dionysia, from which it took and developed the drama festival, which eventually became one of the finest theatrical 'seasons' in the world. It was held from the 8th to the 13th of Elaphebolion (March-April). On the evening of the 8th a torchlight procession, recalling the god's first entry into Athens from rocky Eleutherium, brought the ancient wooden statue of Dionysus from the Academy district to its sanctuary under the southern slopes of the Acropolis. During the morning of the 9th there was a second solemn procession, then songs and dithyrambs sung by youths and men. On the 10th there were performances of comedies and on the 11th and 12th of tragedies, all of them beginning early in the morning and lasting until sundown. Like the athletic contests, these had a politico-religious significance and always began with a purification ceremony using the blood of a sucking-pig, while a chorus danced around the altar of the god.

Other festivals followed in the last three months of the year. On the 16th of Munychion (April-May) offerings were made to Artemis in the shape of cakes surrounded by illuminated candles. On the 25th of the same month the old wooden statue of Athena Polias was carried to Phalerum Bay and there immersed in the water for a sacred bath. On the 6th and 7th of the following month were held the purification rites of the Thargelia under the protection of Apollo. On the first day the *pharmakoi* were beaten with sticks and driven outside the walls of the city. These were two men who were held to bear all the evils and misfortunes of Athens and were treated as scapegoats. On the second day the god was offered as a first-fruit of the coming harvest a sack of cereals. Finally in the month of Skirophorion (June-July) there were further festivals for Demeter and Kore, Athena and Poseidon and, on the Acropolis, a very ancient ritual in honour of Zeus. In the latter barley cakes were laid on the altar, bullocks were brought up and the first animal to eat one was sacrificed. There was then a ritual trial at which the sacrificial axe was condemned and cast into the sea.

PUBLIC GAMES

There were many other festivals, both public and private, scattered throughout the calendar and observed in Athens and the demes. These were the high moments of an intense religious life, in which nature was always present, and experiences from the remote past were preserved by history and tradition.

Public games formed an integral part of these festivals and were an essential element in the education of youth. We have already mentioned some of these games and there will be others in the context of the Pan-Hellenic festivals. They were basically very different from the games held in the circuses or arenas of Imperial Rome, and we shall see this difference if we stop for a while inside a gymnasium or beside a running track in a stadium. *Paides*, youths of twelve to fifteen years of age and *neanskoi*, youths between fifteen and eighteen, execute their movements under the watchful eye of a trainer *(paidotribes)* and to the accompaniment of a flute which gives the rhythm. They are naked, and bronzed, their limbs covered with oil and sand. Their contests are not exhibitions of brute strength, nor is the athlete compelled to face up to any wild and savage beast. Their show of strength is part of the training of their bodies to attain a dignified bearing and to withstand fatigue; it is also a training and an education in beauty. The characteristics of their training are balance and control as seen in the throwing of the discus, with its great parabola, which calls for the elegant coordination of the whole

Model of the Bouleuterion at Olympia, the city's Council Chamber. On the right the temple of Zeus. The Pan-Hellenic games at Olympia, dedicated to Zeus, were reserved to Greek contestants who had to show that they were not guilty of any crimes against the state. During the days on which the games were held, all military action was suspended. Women were banned from the stadium and its vicinity, though they were allowea to watch equestrian events. (Olympia Museum).

body, and the rapid, agile hurling of the javelin. The only contests in which there may be said to have been some violence were boxing and wrestling, but even here there was a sense of control and a respect for the defeated opponent who could raise his hand as a sign of surrender or to ward off the blows from the victor's bound fists. The atmosphere of these games has been perpetuated in statues, bas-reliefs, vase paintings and in the songs of poets, all of which reveal to us the varied incidents and the moments of glory in Hellenic athletics.

The most varied and complete of the contests was the pentathlon, in which the youths attempted successively wrestling, racing, jumping, and throwing the discus and javelin. There were several categories of race: one length of the stadium, two lengths *(diaulos)*, four lengths and occasionally long-distance races of twenty-four lengths. Sometimes races were run with the competitors wearing the heavy uniform of a hoplite or carrying lighted torches. The jumping was for length, and the athletes clutched a dumb-bell in each hand to assist the balancing motion of the arms when they fell. The discus was of bronze and weighed from two to nine pounds according to the age of the athlete. The javelin was a smaller version of the war spear and was thrown either for the longest distance or to make it fall within a given target area.

In addition to the pentathlon were boxing matches in which the fists were bound with leather thongs, the contest taking place in an open area without any time limit. Wrestling also combined an element of boxing, all blows being permitted until blood was drawn. There were also equestrian events in the hippodrome which included races with two and four-horse chariots. Here too one of the most characteristic contests was performed in battle dress and included a leap from the chariot near the finishing post. There were other kinds of contest which have received less notice, such as games with balls and hoops, regattas on the waters of the Piraeus and off Cape Sunium, as well as those connected with rituals which enlivened the crowds at festivals throughout Attica.

THE ATHENIANS AND THE PAN-HELLENIC GAMES

The Athenians entered wholeheartedly into the games connected with their local festivals, but it should also be remembered that they attended also the great Pan-Hellenic festivals. Olympus, Delphi, Isthmia and Nemea all saw many an Athenian athlete compete with others from all over the Greek world for his personal honour and the glory of his city. As in Athens, the games held at these well-known

sanctuaries were a fundamental part of the religious celebrations held every four years (at Olympus and Delphi) or every two (at Isthmia and Nemea). They were essentially religious in origin.

The Olympic games started as funeral games at the tomb of Pelops, or, according to tradition, were instituted by the divine Zeus himself, and, after a long and mysterious period of gestation, are first known to have been held in 776 B.C. They recurred every four years and gave a common chronology to the varied calendars of the numerous Greek city states until A.D. 394, when they were abolished by Theodosius. For seven days, at the time of the summer full moon, Olympus was the scene of religious, sporting and literary activities. Writers took delight in reading their finest works to a public which had come from all over the Hellenic world; concerts and recitals alternated with the athletic contests which took place during the middle five days. The first day was devoted especially to religious observances, sacrifices on the great altar of Zeus and libations poured over the tomb of Pelos. Then there followed five days of contests: all the athletic and equestrian specialities for youths and adults. The games ended with the proclamation of the victors before an exulting, cosmopolitan crowd and with the procession of the athletes, crowned with wild olive branches.

Instituted by Apollo as funeral games after his victory over the serpent Python, the Delphic games were originally musical contests in which the song of Apollo's defeat of the Python had to be performed to the accompaniment of a lyre. Later there were competitions with the flute *(aulos)* but the hollow melancholy sound of this instrument seemed out of keeping with the praising of the god of Olympic harmony, and so these contests were soon dropped. The games were reorganized in 596-585 B.C. and from then on were held every four years. On the model of the Olympic games, athletic and equestrian events were added and, later, dramatic contests.

The Isthmian games took place on the Isthmus of Corinth. They were said to have originated in honour of Melicertes but according to another tradition were reorganized by Theseus on his way to Athens after the destruction of the brigand Sciron. This made the games particularly dear to Athenians, as Theseus was their legendary hero, and they had the right of precedence *(proedria)* as well as the award of 100 drachmae to each victor in the contests.

The Nemean festival, where the games resembled those at Olympus, was held in the valley of Nemea (Argos) at the shrine of Zeus. It was said to have originated in commemoration of the death of the infant Opheltes, son of the King of Nemea, during

The Olympic games consisted of running, wrestling, boxing, the pancration (a mixture of boxing and wrestling), the pentathlon, throwing the discus, throwing the javelin and horse racing. Opposite: a bronze discus, with an inscription dedicating it to the Corinthians, used in the Olympic games (Olympia Museum). Below: two strigils, used for scraping the oil from the skin (Kannellopoulos Collection, Athens).

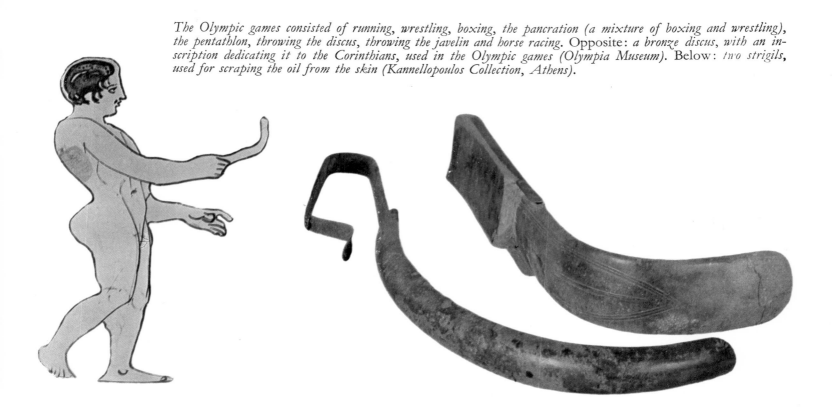

In the Pan-Hellenic games, at both Delphi and Olympia, Athenians were often to the forefront, being particularly successful in equestrian events. The four- and two-horse chariot races and races in which the charioteer wore his armour and leapt down to the ground at the finishing-post were all very spectacular and greatly attracted the crowds.

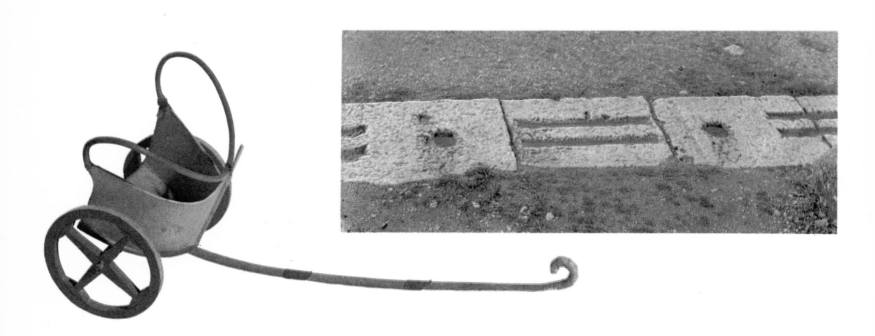

Five pictures of the Pan-Hellenic games: a cup commemorating chariot-racing; a leap from a chariot by an armed contestant (bas-relief, Agora Museum, Athens); reconstruction of a two-horse chariot (Museum of Science and Technology, Milan); the starting-line at the Delphi stadium; the so-called Delphi Charioteer from the Delphi Museum.

the expedition of the Seven against Thebes. Here again the cult of the local hero was submerged in the ritual honours to Zeus, but traces of it remained in the victory prizes, which were crowns of celery, a symbol of grief and bereavement. The same kind of crown, though there was also another of pine-wood, was awarded at the Isthmian games; at Delphi the crowns were of laurel, grown in the valley of Tempe, and at Olympus of wild olive. In addition to this religious and symbolic honour, in addition to the acclamation of the crowds in the stadium, the hippodrome and the theatre and to the distinction of a hero's welcome when he returned triumphant to his native city, the victor at these games had his name glorified by the songs of the poets and might be commemorated in statues by great artists.

The records of these festivals and the lists of the winners show more names from Athens than from any other major centre. Our examples are confined to the Olympics.

The first Athenian winner was in the 21st Olympic Games (696 B.C.). His name was Pantakles and he was a runner in the *stadion* event (about 200 yards). His name comes up again in the next games with a double victory in the *stadion* and the *diaulos* (about 400 yards). Some decades later in the 27th Olympiad, the winner of the *stadion* event was another Athenian, Eurybates. From then on there were many Athenian successes at each of the games, some of historical importance. A detailed list would be very long and we shall recall only the most outstanding ones. The 91st Olympiad was a very good year. Alcibiades, the son of Kleinias, won the four-horse chariot event: he had seven teams competing and obtained a first, a second and a fourth. The feat was recorded by many contemporary writers. Flushed by victory, Alcibiades offered a banquet to all present. The Athenians decreed that he should be provided with food free for the rest of his life. The painter Aristophontes showed him being crowned by personifications of the Pythian and the Olympic games and, in another painting, resting in the lap of a personification of Nemea. These paintings also alluded to his numerous victories in other fields. Over his triumphs, however, hung the shadow of a long trial for corruption and intrigue, as he was accused of having purchased one of his teams from the Argos army. To show how things really change very little in this world, there was a similar event in the 112th Olympiad in 332 B.C. Kallippos of Athens had won the pentathlon, but it was a victory by arrangement with his opponents. He was fined heavily, in spite of a plea by the distinguished orator Hyperides (b. 389 B.C.). The Athenians refused to pay his fine for him and they were all excluded from any further participation in the games. It took a warning from the Delphic oracle to persuade them to pay up.

In the Hellenistic period Athenian victories in the games became less frequent as there was competition not only from the traditional Greek centres but from the new realms of the Diadochi (Alexander's successors) and, later, from Imperial Rome. With the loss of her liberty and her democracy, Athens also lost the strength which lay at the root of her civilization. There remained only the glory and the memories.

THE THEATRE: FROM RITES TO PLAYS

A chorus of men dressed as goats used to celebrate the rites of Dionysus in ancient times. The rites were rhythmic dances and songs and made up a sacred performance. From this dancing and singing, through stages of evolution unknown to us, the theatre was born. As religion permeated every activity of public life, the theatre also retained its sacred origin, although the action on the stage eventually lost its ritual meaning and came to tell the stories of the myths, the dramas or the intrigues of satirical comedy. Before the performances, which took the form of contests between authors in honour of the god, the priest killed a sucking-pig as a rite of purification, and the statue of Dionysus was brought in and placed in its position in the orchestra. The priest, the city authorities and those whom Athens wished to honour particularly, watched the performances from the front row. Everything was official and governed by ritual: in the orchestra the chorus repeated the ancient dance-steps.

Theatrical performances in Athens were an authentic popular festival. From dawn to dusk, without interruption, the crowds watched the plays, approving or disapproving according to their mood, the circumstances and party passions. They took part themselves, like a second chorus, alongside the actors in cloak and mask.

In Greek, as also in Latin, one did not say 'to recite' a tragedy, but 'to teach' it. This mode of expression, so different from ours, had its particular significance and goes back to the earliest known performances and perhaps even further. The earliest poetry, from which the plays arose, had a didactic purpose, as is revealed in the myths, which were allegories with a moral content. The play as we now know it would probably never have developed had it not been for certain historical events which made it necessary and almost inevitable.

The first of these was the struggle by the poor and ordinary people of Athens, the potters, the cobblers, the artisans, the peasants, against the few rich families who held all the power and the wealth, for equality of rights, for a democracy. Tragedy took its first uncertain steps towards the end of this period, the mid-sixth century B.C., when Pisistratus, brought to power by the peasants, saw that it would be a

means of educating the citizens of Athens and of leading them towards self-government. He organized the Dionysia, festivals of the god of vegetation, which were held at the most important times of the year: when nature dies, or goes to sleep, in December, and when it re-awakes in March. These celebrations brought into the city satyr-like dramas of dancing and singing from a country folk ever conscious of the cycles of nature. They were probably performed by various tribes in competition with each other. New dramas were created for successive festivals and thus through the intervention of a far-seeing tyrant, Pisistratus, the theatrical contest, or *agon*, was created.

Other events and other experiences, such as the hard war against the Persians, combined to give the Greek theatre its definite characteristics and, as Pisistratus had foreseen, the dramatic and comic poets made a positive contribution to the education of the people, making them ever more conscious of their rights and duties, and especially of their dignity and their liberty.

THE THEATRE OF DIONYSUS

Aristotle's account of the origins of tragedy, together with an examination of the shape of the better-preserved ruins of theatres which have survived in Greece, Magna Graecia and Asia Minor, provide the most direct and interesting explanation of the origin of theatre buildings.

Greek tragedy arose, as has been said, out of the rustic singing and dancing at the altar of Dionysus. The chorus of performers was surrounded by crowds of people, of whom the first row could see everything, the second row a little less and the other rows little or nothing at all. How could the performance be made visible to all? There were two ways: to put the actors on a raised platform or to raise the spectators. The second was more rational, though more costly.

A suitable hillside was found and its slope adapted to form a semi-circle on which wooden seating was arranged in terraces behind the chorus. During one performance in a theatrical competition which took place some time between 500 and 496 B.C., and which included Aeschylus amongst the competitors, a wooden platform collapsed, killing some of the spectators. It was then decided to build in stone to avoid similar disasters: thus was born the idea of the theatre of Dionysus Eleuterius, erected on the side of the Acropolis, which was probably the model for all the theatres of the world. By good fortune most of it has been preserved and its architectural development can be studied.

The *cavea*, or theatre in the strict sense of the word, as described by, amongst others, Vitruvius in his treatise *De architectura* (late first century B.C.), consisted of a number of rows of seats arranged in a semi-circle with their backs to a slope, divided into sectors by steps running (as in modern theatres) from top to bottom and with wide gangways running round the rows.

There were high-backed chairs on the lowest row reserved for dignitaries, each chair inscribed on the back with the occupant's office. On many chairs found among the ruins of the theatre in Athens we can still

Masks were a very important feature of the Greek theatre, as they portrayed immediately the personality of the characters which were rather limited and conventional, and as such easily recognisable. Below: a woman lyre-player and a man with a double flute. The double-flute player usually accompanied the chorus and walked with it. (Agora Museum, Athens).

176

The Theatre of Dionysus, Athens. Situated at the foot of the Acropolis, the theatre uses the natural slope of the rock for the terracing for the spectators. The seating and other parts of the building were all later additions, the first theatrical performances being mystery ceremonies in which only the chorus took part. In the course of time one member of the chorus took on a solo part, becoming an actor, called the hypocrites, or ' the one who answers '. Subsequently there were two, three and even four actors. Yet it was above all the necessity (probably more ritual than theatrical) of allowing the increasing number of spectators to see the movements of the chorus which gave rise to theatres of this kind.

177

read the names of the magistrates for whom they were reserved. In many theatres the public were admitted only to the higher rows of seats; in some the spectators seem to have had to go in via the gangway by the stage and reach their seats by crossing the orchestra and going up the various rows of steps.

The *orchestra* ('dancing place') was where the chorus performed. It was slightly raised, but lower than the *skene* (stage) which stood behind it, and was divided from it by a space which allowed latecomers to reach their seats without disturbing the performers. The seats and the orchestra were completely open to the sky. The two entrances *(paradoi)* to the orchestra, one on the left and the other on the right of the terraces, could also be used by the public. Some authorities have suggested that the front part of the stage *(proskenion)* communicated with the orchestra by means of a wooden ladder.

The back part of the stage *(skene)* was a stone erection which became more profusely decorated as the years went by. It contained a number of doors, as required by the action of the play. A tragedy gen-

erally took place in front of a palace or a temple, for which one door was sufficient. A comedy was often set in two or three nearby houses, each one of which would require its own exit. At Tecmessos a stage was discovered with seven doors, the central one being the largest and the others diminishing in size on each side.

The background changed sometimes during the performance, as in Sophocles' *Ajax*, which takes place partly in a military camp, partly by the shores of the sea. Changes of scenery were effected by a complicated system of movable arms which lowered into place during the performance the various detachable elements as required. These fitted into holes in the ground in front of the stage and when not in use remained suspended aloft. Behind the *skene* was an area known as the *skenoteka* where actors could store their clothing and equipment.

The action of the plays by all the great writers of the time, whether of tragedy (Aeschylus, Sophocles, Euripides) or comedy (Aristophanes, Menander) set problems of staging which scholars have submitted

to patient and minute investigation in an attempt to establish how the scene-setting was managed. In the successive phases of the theatre of Dionysus, such as we have reconstructed hypothetically, they have tried to equate the needs of the performance with the available physical arrangements as revealed in the ruins of the various parts of the theatre (orchestra, front and back stage and so on). Each play has been analysed from the point of view of the actual physical space it would require to stage, of the scenery, including buildings, and the scene changes, of the intervention of the supernatural and of the devices used to produce extra light and sound, for thunder and lightning for example, which could not properly be done in broad daylight in the open air with the limited means at their disposal. Certain mechanical contrivances were used which gave, if not a complete illusion, at least some semblance of plausibility to the action. When in Aeschylus' *Agamemnon* (458 B.C.) Clytemnestra killed Agamemnon and Cassandra she did it off stage. After the murder the two bodies were brought forward out of the palace on a mobile

platform (called an *ekkuklema*) pushed from behind the stage. This was a device to show to the audience what had been happening behind the scenes.

In Aeschylus' *The Persians* (472) the ghost of the old King Darius was evoked by the chorus to admonish the spectators. He came up on to the stage from below by a hidden ladder or through a trap door.

Characters such as Medea, who had to fly or go up to heaven, were hoisted up on a plank by rope and pulley.

There was also a kind of mobile platform which could be raised or lowered from the stage ceiling. It was called a *theologeion* and on it an actor, representing a god, would descend to pronounce the solution of an hitherto intractable situation. This the Romans were later to call the *deus ex machina*.

Thunder was represented by rolling a barrel full of stones *(bronteion)* over a flat sheet of metal.

Athens also had covered theatres used specially for musical or choral performances. They were called *odeioi* (from *ode*, a song) and the oldest was that built by Pericles in about 442 B.C. near the theatre. This was a square-shaped building with a dome-like roof and a central stage. It had a double order of columns with a propylaeum and its domed roof was made out of the masts of Persian ships. It was covered by a huge tent in the shape of a pavilion and is said to have resembled the tent of Xerxes.

THE DRAMA

The heroic-religious origins of drama (action represented on the stage) are highly controversial. When we approach Attic tragedy and see the many elements of which it is composed, the constituent parts are so interlocked and arranged within a set scheme that we cannot trace their separate development. Furthermore, music and dancing cannot be omitted from any consideration of drama, as they were an integral part of it.

Tragedy *(tragodia)* means 'song of the goat', but the connection between the two is not certain. The word was usually taken to mean 'song concerning a goat', the animal presumably having been sacrificed or donated for the theatrical contest. But it would seem rather to have implied 'song sung by goats', that is by actors dressed as such, a primitive satyresque composition performed as a fourth element after the trilogy of tragic plays. This is Aristotle's explanation, and it is supported by the *silenoi* (satyr-like companions of Dionysus) and goats shown on vase paintings and by the fact that in Attica the ancient chorus of Peloponnesian satyrs was made to include *silenoi*, though they were still called goats *(tragoi)*. There would therefore seem to be a connection between the goat and the satyr-like reveller. Finally tragedy came to have a chorus of men.

A recent theory, somewhat less plausible than this, sees the origin of theatre in the primitive funeral dances performed in honour of heroes and overlaid successively with elements of the Dionysiac cult, especially by the satyresque drama. This would seem to be borne out by the circular area, later to become the *orchestra* of the theatre, on which could have stood the altar of the god. Ritual dances were performed in a circle round the altar, and all those participating in the cult would take part. There is no doubt that Attic tragedy was connected with dithyrambic choruses. The dithyramb was a choral lyric, said to have been first used by the semi-mythical poet Arion and developed into dialogue form by Bacchylides (*c.* 505 - *c.* 450 B.C.). Arion is said to have had the performers, who sang in a circular chorus, dress as satyrs, and this would have made the dithyramb a Dionysiac song. In the Great Dionysus festivals in Athens tragedy reached its final perfect form in the fifth century B.C. only after a period of successive modifications which we are unable to retrace today.

The theatre of Epidaurus, showing the stage area, the round 'orchestra' where the chorus performed and, at the two sides, the 'paradoi' or entrances for both the chorus and the spectators in the lower seats. Only a few stones of the stage remain.

Attic tragedy consisted of different elements distinguished from each other by the metre of their verse: a *prologos* which preceded the entrance of the chorus and formerly introduced the action itself; a *parados*, a song sung by the chorus as it proceeded to its allotted place, the orchestra, along one of the two passageways left free between the orchestra and the stage and hence called the *parodoi*; one or more *epeisodia*, or scenes recited by the actors and interspersed with short choral songs or lyric dialogues between chorus and actors known as *kommoi*; a *stasimon* sung by the chorus while it stood in one place (i.e. as opposed to the *parodos* which was sung when the chorus was entering), having a subject more or less related to the episode; and finally an *exodos*, or conclusion of the action and exit of the chorus.

181

THE TRAGIC POETS

The above was the arrangement followed by the great tragic poets. What elementary organization had existed in the presentation of drama before the Classical age was said to be the work of the semi-legendary poet Thespis (*fl.* second half of sixth century B.C.). Tradition has it that he travelled throughout Greece with his famous wagon on which his plays were performed. He arrived in Athens during the rule of Pisistratus and certainly took part in the contests of 535. He was followed by Choerilus (*fl.* first half of fifth century) and Pratinas (*fl.* early fifth century). Phrynichus of Athens (*c.* 512-476) brought historical subjects on to the stage with his *Capture of Miletus* and *The Phienissae*.

Of much greater interest are writers such as Aeschylus, Sophocles and Euripides who brought tragic form to its perfection. Aeschylus (525-456) was born at Eleusis, near Athens, and he was present at both Marathon and Salamis. Not all his plays have sur-

vived, but we have sufficient to judge his great dramatic technique and his undoubted genius for linking his subject matter with morality. In the context of the political situation at the beginning of the fifth century, Aeschylus was a man of action and a thinker. While he took part in the Graeco-Persian war he nevertheless gave his dramatic attention to the human side of a long struggle between two violently opposed worlds.

His *Prometheus Bound* is an expression of his religious spirit, which was almost monotheistic and void of Herodotus' 'envy of the gods'. His concept of divinity was much higher and purer: a divinity punishes not the happy, but the sinner, and if disaster often strikes the fortunate, it is because they are more inclined than others to pride (Agamemnon) and therefore to sin. In human affairs Aeschylus saw a mysterious force, an inexorable justice which seeks out the guilty man and punishes him, either in himself or in his next generation.

The tragedies of Sophocles (496-406) are representative of one particular phenomenon in Athenian life. The city was rich and at the apex of its power; Pericles seemed to be leading it to even greater glories and there was a need for this to be reflected in the theatre. The audiences who lived in the shadow of this greatness wished to see also on the stage characters worthy of their admiration. Sophocles was particularly suited to supply this need. He was himself typical of the high-born Athenian: clever, of great charm, equable of character, persuasive and witty, he was a sculptor, a minister in the Treasury, a military leader, an admiral and a friend of Pericles. Attica, the land 'of fine horses and a beautiful sea, of the purple grape' with its 'gay rows of olive trees' was not only his native land, but also formed the magical background of his tragedies.

The works of Sophocles bring a new element of grace to Greek tragedy. Whatever the intricacies of the action, the protagonist emerges as a person gigantic in concept and in suffering; it is in him that the public watches the interplay of passion, or religious feeling and the awareness of an inexorable fate, and it shares in the struggle with sympathy and understanding. It is the protagonist, whose bitter experiences reflect on the minor characters, who comes to terms, often lyrically, in peace and resignation, with his tragic destiny.

Sophocles had faith in man and admired him. 'There are many wondrous things', he said, 'but nothing is more wondrous than man'. Yet he could be bitter, and to a certain extent he foreshadowed Euripides in his tragic sense of life, as, for instance, in the chorus of *Oedipus at Colonus* in which the ninety-year-old poet's meditations were summed up by ' not to have been born were perhaps the best, and to return whence one came the second best '. For him, man's adventure ended with the truth: born in darkness, man returns to darkness.

Euripides (*c.* 480-406) has been called an atheist, a negator and a cynic, but in this, critics have been excessive. The truth is that his rationalism was aimed against current mythology and its attendant religious fables. He argued on the grounds of morality in an attempt to establish a more reasonable and a more human ethic. Euripides did not, it is true, attain the higher, truer, burning faith of Aeschylus or the solemn, glowing creed of Sophocles. As a critic and an observer of life with noble ideals, but disillusioned, he yearned for a betterment of man's lot and a more just legal and ethical code. All he was left with was

doubt and a vague hope. His great virtue is not that he believed but that he understood.

He expressed his vision of a society gone wrong and in need of guidance in a fictitious world of characters whom he wished to show as real people from ordinary life. The setting of his plays was not the glowing world of the heroes of Aeschylus or the fatalistic background of the idealized characters of Sophocles. His characters were generally nothing more than men and women. There is no doubt that their diminished stature and their commonplace surroundings did much to encourage comedy, which showed particular concern for the average man.

Euripides' tragedy *Medea* (431) has a subject of eternal interest: the relationship between a civilized man and a barbarian woman; the struggle between two races, the conquering and the conquered. The heroine of the play, who amongst all the women of the Greek theatre commits the most monstrous crime, is, if not justified, at least investigated with sympathy and understanding, so that all her ' reasons ' are understood.

Euripides, by a curious twist of innocence and compassion, gives his Electra a simple peasant for a

Opposite: sacrificing the goat. Actors in the most ancient tragedy, which had not then attained the form in which we now know it, were chorus members dressed as goats, clearly in connection with certain fertility rites. The sacrifice of the goat can be related to the killing of the scapegoat in the Hebrew religion which, through Egypt, shared in the magic and mystery rites of the Mediterranean countries. Right: the killing of Clytemnestra. Tragedy was based on myth and poetic tradition, which it often transformed and adapted to popular taste, to the culture of the period and to current morals, with a declared didactic and formative aim (National Museum, Ferrara).

husband, who, however, respects her and never dares to touch her. She is still a heroine, and a heroine of Euripides. She incites Orestes to the tremendous act of vengeance against their mother, but is haunted by the horror of the deed.

Euripides' Electra is different from that of Aeschylus or of Sophocles: the character is pitched in a lower tone and is more human.

THE ORIGINS AND THE NATURE OF COMEDY

Two possible derivations have been suggested for *komodia*, the Greek word for comedy: from *komos*, revelling after a banquet, with a procession of dancers and singers; or from *kome*, village, because the actors wandered through the villages to perform as they were looked down upon in the towns. According to Aristotle the first is the correct one.

One fundamental element of Attic comedy was the *parabasis*, during which the chorus spoke to the audience in a series of passages divided by an interval in the middle which had originally been for the *phallophoria*, a procession in which the phallus, the symbol of fertility, was carried in a rite of propitiation.

Another essential element was the recitation by the actors, who bore different names in the various regions of Greece, Magna Graecia and Sicily, of comic or farcical scenes. Corinthian and Apulian vase paintings have shown us the kind of clothes worn by these players, especially by those known as the *phlyakoi*, from a Spartan colony in Taranto. It is significant that they are shown carrying the phallic symbol, and that Dionysus appears in the same painting. Their name shows a connection with the fertility of the crops.

While the chorus from its beginning was an Attic creation, the players and their traditional costumes came from Doria. The farce, as known to the *phlyakoi* and the Megarese and having only a chorus as actors, shows how Attic comedy was a fusion of Attic and Dorian. The Megarese, both from Megara Nisea in Greece and Megara Iblea in Sicily, boasted that they were the creators of comedy. The *phlyakoi* variety was later (fourth century B.C.) elevated into a literary genre by Rinton of Siracuse (called the 'Tarantine'), author of pieces known as the Rinton fables.

THE AUTHORS OF COMEDY

The first names handed down by tradition as authors of pre-Attic comedy are those of Epicharmus, a Sicilian who lived in Syracuse in the late sixth century, and Phormis (or Phorm[i]o), also a Syracusan. We have, however, evidence only of the former, in hundreds of fragments and many titles.

Attic comedy reached its peak in the second half of the fifth century, but of some forty authors and hundreds of titles only a few fragments have come down to us.

One of the more important early writers was Cratinus (*c.* 520-423), who was praised by Aristophanes and won several contests from 453 B.C., one

notably in 423 with *The Bottle* against Aristophanes'
The Clouds. Crates, another early fifth century author,
was somewhat younger than Cratinus and wrote seven
comedies full of subtle humour. Sophron of Syracuse
(fifth century) wrote mimes in Doric and was admired
by Plato.

Comedy was not officially admitted to the theatrical contests in Athens until 486, but it had been
performed in Attica for a century before this, firstly
at the festival of the Lenaea and then at the Great
Dionysia.

Little is know of the life of Aristophanes. He was
born in Athens in about 445 B.C. and wrote his first
play *The Banqueters* in 427. Others followed and in
424 he won first prize with *The Knights*, the first play

to be entered under his own name. He wrote over
forty comedies in all, but only eleven have survived.
He died in about 385.

The structure of comedy had certain similarities
with that of tragedy and had *prologos*, *parados*, *epeisodia*,
stasimoi and *exodos*. One permanent feature was the
agon, or violent dispute between two players. The
chorus was larger, reaching twenty-four members,
and there was the characteristic *parabasis* (sometimes
there were two) after the *agon*.

According to most people, Aristophanes was a
conservative, a traditionalist and an anti-democratic
enemy of all social, political, artistic or philosophical
change. Many have therefore praised the clearsight-
edness and solid common sense which led him to

condemn the moral and political decadence of the world in which he lived. Others have throught him narrow-minded and reactionary.

Aristophanes seemed to follow popular pacifist opinion and to be hostile to governments. A good example is to be seen in *The Acharnians*. This play has a number of scenes about the misfortunes of war, to which Dikaiopolis, an upright citizen, finds his own remedy by making a separate peace with the Spartans and having a good time drinking and whoring, while Lamachus is wounded in battle. The contrast between the benefits of peace and the evils of war is well drawn.

Aristophanes' aim was to create a poetic, scenic art and his greatest gift is generally considered to be the satirical moralizing spirit which imbues his whole production with absolute sincerity. All his characters were created out of an inexhaustible fantasy to serve the artistic ends of the plays; thus they are rarely very close to reality, though at times they express themselves with a crude realism.

Much of the value of the plays is lost to us because we cannot fully enter into the atmosphere of late fifth-century Athens, and can only imagine the effect of these comedies on an audience which would be well capable of picking up every reference, openly audacious or otherwise, to contemporary persons and situations.

His contemporaries must have enjoyed particularly, as we do today, the verve and the comic power of *The Birds* (414). Here he succeeds in bringing inanimate things to life and in creating choruses of animals and clouds with extraordinary ability and a wonderful comic effect, transporting us continually from the fantastic to the real, and showing us all the time his own sentiments as a man who aspires to a simple life of peace, a life which he is unable to find in the city.

THE MIDDLE COMEDY

Between the ancient comedy and the new there was an intermediate genre known as the middle comedy which flourished from between 400 and 385 to 330 B.C.

There were about sixty authors, of whom very little is known. The principal representatives were Antiphanes and Alexis. Of the 800 or more plays comprising this genre, nothing survives except a few fragments. The favourite subjects seem to have been parodies of the myths and scenes of the good life, with banqueting, feasting, courtesans and parasites. The latter were made popular by Epicharmus and Alexis, and were of two types: one more noble and associated with high-born persons, the other uncouth and boorish. Both of these types show that there was a general relaxation in the tenor of life and a striving for a peaceful, bourgeois existence as opposed to the ideals of grandeur and glory which permeated the preceding century.

We cannot, therefore, know very much about the middle comedy because no single complete work has survived. The transformation from one type to another was so slow that not even the ancients themselves seem to have been aware of the movement from the ancient to the middle or from the middle to the new comedy.

THE NEW COMEDY

The new comedy is much better known to us from the adaptations it received at the hands of the Latin playwrights. It virtually banned the chorus by restricting its performances to intervals in the play, and much of the pungency of the masked characters was lost. The plot was usually based on some love intrigue which ended happily. The characters and the plot have their antecedents in the tragedy of Euripides.

After Menander its principal exponents were considered to be Philemon (*c.* 360-263) and Diphilus (*c.* 360-280). Philemon was the oldest of the three. He wrote twenty-seven plays, which survived only in fragments but were used by Plautus, the great Roman playwright (254-184). It is known, however, that he was highly appreciated for his naturalistic situations. Diphilus wrote parodies of mythology and history.

The most prolific of the writers of the new comedy was Menander (*c.* 342-292) who is known to have turned out 105 plays at least. He did not, however, enjoy much favour with the Athenian public during his lifetime and won only eight contests. Philemon seems to have been preferred. After his death his reputation grew and he is considered now the greatest of the writers of the new comedy. He was greatly imitated by the Latin authors: Plautus' *Aulularia, Bacchides, Cistellaria* and *Poenulus* and Terence's *Andria,*

Chorus master with members of the chorus. Helped by the author (unless he were the author also), the chorus master, who was both producer and choreographer, taught the chorus their movements, diction and scansion (the metre varying according to the action). He remained subordinate, however, to the choregos, the wealthy private citizen responsible for the whole show (Capitoline Museums, Rome).

Eunuchus and *Adelphoe* were all refurbishings of plays by Menander, whose influence on the modern theatre has therefore been considerable.

The plot of his *Arbitrations*, perhaps his masterpiece, is a perfect example of the new comedy, with its story of the abandoned child subsequently found again and recognized by its parents. Menander's art in this play goes beyond the simplicity of the plot and reveals itself in the delicate characterization, a profound humanity and a straightforward dialogue. His realism lies not in the naturalness of the presentation or the probability of the plot, but in his humanity, at once both strong and compassionate, which gives a high poetic value to his characters. Menander's whole world of poetry is to be found in love; there is no room in it for evil. None of his characters are

ignoble, and in this lies no doubt a good deal of his so-called naturalism.

In 1959 the lucky find of a papyrus brought to light an entire play written in his youth, *The Cantankerous One* (*Dyskolos*), and much of another, *The Citizen of Sicyon* (*Sicyonius*) has recently been reconstructed from fragments of papyri and other pieces of literary information.

MIME

Mime, a later form of dramatic performance (though not all mimes were intended to be staged), came into Athens from Sicily in the time of Plato. The earliest composer of mimes was Sophron (fifth century) who wrote in a rhythmic prose in Dorian dialect. Fragments have survived on papyrus.

The mime was performed in rural and religious festivals, the actor wearing costumes typical of the lower classes, with a great number of folds. It had speech, both monologue and dialogue, then small scenes and dances, and the subject matter was scarcely ever serious and mostly burlesque. There were male mimes (fishermen and peasants for example) and female ones (sewing-women and sorceresses). They were played without masks, even by women, and this type of comedy greatly developed in the Hellenistic period.

THE POETIC CONTESTS

Before the drama reached its final stage of perfection, action on the stage had been portrayed by the chorus in dancing and singing. The whole complex of singers and dancers was of great importance to the subsequent evolution of both tragedy and comedy. This was true even after the beginning of the fourth century, when the part the chorus played on the stage had become least important, and for a long time when a poet 'asked for the chorus' it meant asking for permission to stage his play.

In the centre of the orchestra was an altar dedicated to Dionysus on which a sucking-pig was sacrificed at the beginning of the poetic contest (Athens).

Putting on the contests was a complicated business. As plays were only staged during the Dionysiac festivals, the author had to ask the archon for a chorus some considerable time in advance, and for their part the archons also had to organize the performances into contests a good time ahead. Since the Leneae took place in January, the Great Dionysia in March and the Rustic Dionysia in December, for a large part of the year one of the highest magistrates in Athens (the eponymous archon for the Dionysia and the King Archon for the Leneae) must have been almost wholly occupied with preparations for the performances, reading through the plays and choosing the *choregos* (the private citizen who had to provide the chorus).

The archon was allowed very wide powers in his choice and judgement and could decide whether a poet's work should be accepted or rejected. In spite of his full authority he was, however, responsible to an assembly which met in the theatre two days after the end of the festival and which could praise or censure his efforts.

THE *CHOREGIA*

When the works to be performed had been chosen, the archon designated the *choregoi*, or the individual citizens who were to be responsible for the costs of staging the plays of each poet and choosing the men of the chorus *(choreutai)*. They would have all the burdens and responsibilities of production, but they would also have the honour of any prize which might be won.

The *choregia* was a *liturgia*, that is a public service, which the wealthier citizens were required to perform. Another one, for example, was the fitting out of a ship of war. The State, in fact, divided out among the rich the expenses of public works which it would not, or could not, pay out of its own funds. It was a special form of taxation which, however, was considered not only a duty but also an honour, as the popularity of those on whom the burden fell increased enormously. The *choregos* put all his efforts into winning the contest, and then if he was successful he would not hesitate to undertake further expense in consecrating to Dionysus a monument (like that of Lysicrates which has been preserved) that would ensure that the citizens did not forget too easily the play with which 'his' poet had triumphed.

Finally the archon designated the principal actor, the *protagonistes*, who in his turn chose those who were to play the second and third roles: the *deuteragonistes* and the *tritagonistes*.

When the lists of *choregoi*, poets and actors had been drawn up, the archon then sorted them out into groups composed of one of each. To avoid any possibility of favouritism, this delicate operation was left, at least in part, to selection by lot and the draw was held during a session of the Assembly in which all the citizens could take part. The names of the *choregoi* designate were drawn from an urn, and according to the order in which the names came out, each one then selected his own poet. In 472 the young Pericles was appointed *choregos* and chose Aeschylus, who presented the trilogy of which *The Persians* formed one part. The *protagonistai* were chosen by lot similarly; later, in that spirit of impartiality which characterized Athenian public life, each *protagonistes* was required to perform one play for each poet so that the adjudicators' verdict would not be influenced by one play having an oustandingly good or bad interpreter.

Amongst the honours which fell to the *choregos*, one was particularly important, and in a sense pertinent and useful: he was considered a magistrate and as such sacred and beyond the law. Anyone who dared to insult or strike him, as happened to Demosthenes when he was a *choregos* and was slapped in the face in the middle of the theatre by a certain Midias, was severely punished. The *choregos* was, in fact, performing a public service: even in later periods, theatrical performances still had a religious character and therefore concerned the whole community, and the public was always conscious of the part the *choregos* had played.

THE CHORUS

The *choregos* recruited the *choreutai* (twelve, fifteen or more, sometimes divided into two semi-choruses) from among the youths of his own tribe and from that which he had drawn in the lottery. The functions of the *choreutai* must have been in some sense obligatory, as the *choregos* had the power to fine recalcitrants and to restrain them by force. Thus he sometimes became unpopular, or, as we read in the sixth Oration of Antiphon (c. 480-411), even hated by some chorus

members. The duties were, however, generally well accepted and fathers willingly sent their young sons to the schools which the *choregoi* ran in their own houses.

Not everyone chosen to join in the chorus had an aptitude for dancing and singing, and it must be remembered that amongst all the poets, actors and chorus members there were no professionals. They were all amateurs and their talents varied considerably. The chorus master's job, which was to train the men for a good performance, was very important. He sometimes found it almost impossible to achieve success, notwithstanding bribes of all kinds such as wine in plenty so that the chorus, half drunk, would perform with greater dash, or the promise, not always backed up by the *choregos*, of a fine feast after the show. The poets, therefore, had to be content with what they could get. Some of them were very demanding, like Cinesias (late fifth century) who came to be dubbed a ' killer of choruses ' as he subjected the men to a very severe, almost military discipline.

The chorus did, in fact, move about like a squad of soldiers. It marched on from the spectators' right and sometimes moved to the orchestra at the double. There were two possible formations. A chorus of fifteen (the normal chorus for a tragedy) moved in

Kneeling silenos (companion of Bacchus) in the position of Atlas holding up the world. The silenoi were often identified with satyrs in both appearance and characteristics (Athens).

The theatre at Delphi. Theatrical performances, connected with a kind of drama competition called an argon, went on without interruption from morning till sunset for several days.

three ranks of five or five ranks of three. The other possibility was a chorus of twenty-four (usual for comedy) and these came on in four ranks of six or six ranks of four. They were preceded by the flautist playing his double flute *(aulos)*, while the chorus leader was the third in the rank nearest the audience and the leaders of the semi-choruses were the second and the fourth. We do not know how the chorus was arranged during the performance, or what movements they executed to accompany the several parts of the play. We only know that in tragedies they stood with their faces to the back of the stage and their backs to the audience, and that they danced the strophes moving from left to right and the antistrophes from right to left.

Normally the author in collaboration with the *protagonistes* undertook the instruction of the chorus

190

and the other actors, attended all the rehearsals and, even up to the day before the performance, modified and brought the text up to date. This was particularly important in comedy, which would be required to reflect the most recent events.

The author's approach to politics was critical, not to say polemical, and he therefore ran the risk of prosecution. Only rarely, and in exceptional circumstances (as during the rebellion of Samos in 440), was the poet's freedom of speech restricted; normally he was able to express openly, in a society of free men such as Athens contained, his views and thoughts on anyone and anything.

Aristophanes was charged with defamation of the State, an action brought by Cleon on the grounds that the defamation was held to have been uttered in the presence of foreigners. In other words, if the dirty washing had been done in private no one would have complained. Moreover Aristophanes fully vindicated himself. The following year, in *The Acharnians*, he found a way of saying, and of repeating 'I don't speak of the State', and the following year, in *The Knights*, he attacked Cleon himself with greater violence. Cleon was undoubtedly in the theatre, and in the front row at that, having just defeated the Spartans at Sphacteria and obtained the *proedria*.

The *choregos* thus played no specific part in the training of the chorus or the stage production. He was concerned with his own affairs and handed over to others the task of collaborating with the producer and handling both the artistic and the financial side. One of his men had a function somewhere between that of a steward and a wardrobe manager and had to make all the necessary purchases and keep the accounts. Naturally the *choregos* paid, just as he also paid the *choreutai* and the flautist *(auletes)* who provided the musical accompaniment.

Later, around 307 B.C., the duties of the *choregos* passed to his clan and were undertaken by an *agonoteta* on behalf of the State.

THE PERFORMANCE

The rehearsing of the chorus and all the preliminaries for the show came to an end with the *proagon*, which took place in the *odeion* near to the theatre. This was the equivalent of putting up playbills and gave the poet the opportunity of presenting himself to the public, telling them the title and subject of his play and the names of the *choregos* and the actors.

Meanwhile the time of the festival was approaching and the dithyrambs, the comedies and the tragedies were now prepared.

Towards evening on the first day the procession *(komos)* assembled. This was to bring the statue

of Dionysus from the Academy garden to the theatre.

Then, in the theatre, the priest of Dionysus sacrificed a sucking-pig on the altar which stood in the middle of the orchestra. After the purification ceremony, performed with the blood of the victim, the priest took his seat in the centre of the front row before the altar. The performance then began.

As it was a contest *(agon)* and no favouritism could be shown to any one author, the order of showing the plays was obtained by drawing lots. The ten adjudicators, one from each of the ten tribes, were also chosen by lot from persons appointed by the Boule (City Council) and the *choregoi*, who took an oath to judge the plays only according to their merits.

The second day was devoted entirely to lyrical poetry, the dithyrambs; the third day was allotted to comedies, at first three, then later five, each by a different author; the three days after that were devoted to tragedies by the three authors chosen by the archon, one day being allotted to each author who would present a trilogy or a tetralogy or a trilogy followed by a satyr-drama.

The performances began early in the morning, shortly after sunrise and were heralded by the shrill notes of the herald's trumpet. They continued without interruption, save for a brief interval between one work and the next, during which there was dancing and singing, until sundown. The audience did not leave their seats and during the intervals they would consume the meagre ration of food they had brought with them or the sweets, dried fruit and wine which the more generous *choregoi* would have distributed amongst them. This did not mean that they did not move about. They were, in fact, noisy and demonstrative and, despite the religious basis of the performances, they never lost the opportunity of showing their approval or otherwise by clapping, whistling and stamping their feet. They had a perfect right to do this as they had paid their two obols (a third of a drachma) to get in, and if they were too poor the State paid for them out of a special fund for festivals known as the *theoricon*.

No special places were reserved for the audience except for the magistrates and for persons (Athenians or foreigners) who had been granted the so-called right of *proedria*, that is of precedence, because of some worthy action they had performed for the State.

All others sat on the terraces even if they were senators *(bouleutai)*. Certain sectors of the terrace were reserved for *epheboi* and *metics*. The women would appear to have sat on the topmost tiers, though information on this is uncertain.

The men sat in the sector reserved for their tribe. This must have been an old tradition which was maintained out of prudence. Even so, there were often disputes and brawls in which the theatre police, armed with staves (they were called *rhabdouchoi*, or staff-bearers) would have to intervene.

When the series of performances was over and the contest had come to an end, the adjudicators would give their verdict by vote. This was no simple matter, however: to avoid mistakes or favouritism a further draw took place which eliminated five out of the ten votes, leaving only the remaining five valid.

The lots were drawn in a peculiar way. Beside the urn containing the tablets recording the judges' votes stood another urn containing ten dice, five white and five black. One tablet and one dice were drawn from the two urns simultaneously: if the dice was white it meant that the vote on the tablet was valid, if black the vote was invalid and was eliminated.

When the voting was over, the next procedure was the nomination of the winners and the awarding of the prizes. There were three prizes in each category, tragedy and comedy, and prizes for the *choregos*, the author and the protagonist. The prizes were purely symbolic and consisted of a wreath of ivy, one of the plants sacred to Dionysus, for the winners of the plays and, apparently, a tripod for the winners of the dithyrambic contest. The poets and actors received fees proportionate to the class awarded to the play.

THE ACTORS

Dramatic action began, as has been said, in the mid-sixth century when one character answered the chorus himself. He was the *hypokrites*, or 'he who replies' and his function was, in effect, to speak to the chorus and then to turn to the audience and complete the narration of the facts sung by the chorus. Originally the author himself was the actor; later another actor was introduced to answer the first. The two-part play is found in Aeschylus. Later, in the time of Sophocles, a third actor was added and the

Satyrs, mythological beings half men and half goats, were commonly linked with Dionysus and were therefore to be found at the beginning of the Greek theatre (Capitoline Museums, Rome).

author himself no longer took any part in the action. The principal actor was nominated by the archon and then chose the other two subordinate players.

In the fifth century three principal actors performed between them in one day all the plays entered by one author in the contest (the trilogy and the satyr-drama), which must have represented an enormous effort. By the fourth century we find them acting only one of the plays by each author. If the *choregos* so desired, a fourth actor could be introduced but only to take a non-speaking part. This applied only to tragedy; for comedy the number of players was unlimited.

The actors had to play their parts more by gesture and bodily movement than by any other means of expression, as their faces were completely covered by masks. They had naturally to be masters of diction, singing and declamation. Their singing and recitation, like those of the chorus, were accompanied by the flute, rarely by the lyre. The actor was required above all to have correct enunciation and a clear voice which he could adapt as needed to the several male and female parts. In certain cases he was required to dance and take up aesthetic poses.

The best actors received great honours and protection, especially in the fourth century, when their contribution to the success of the plays, whether tragic or comic, had become greater than ever.

MASKS

In the Hellenistic period the actors played more parts of ordinary human beings in the new comedy. This was shown by the masks they wore.

Masks were generally made of linen covered with stucco and painted, though they could also be of cork or wood. They were made so as to give an unmistakable representation of the character concerned. They were the most important part of the make-up and, as they were looked upon virtually as sacred, they were dedicated in the sanctuary of Dionysus.

They remained in use throughout the whole period of ancient Greece, and numerous reliefs and statuettes which have survived show the great variety of expression which could be put on the traditional types. Thus the masks representing the father would sometimes be made to show a severe frown. There were four principal types of female masks, some severe-looking, others kindly, those of courtesans being the commonest. Others represented the youth, the little boy, the soldier, the parasite, the cook, the peasant, the slave, the latter deriving from a type already existing in ancient comedy, recognizable by the rolled-up hair. They had very varied expressions which showed their individual character.

Julius Pollux, a Greek lexicographer (*fl.* A.D. 180) drew up a list of 44 different comedy masks of which there were 9 of old men, 11 of youths, 7 of slaves and 17 of women. The hair suited their ages and varied in style and colour, the beards were different as also were the shape of the eyebrows and other facial characteristics.

The children's expressions were less composed than their fathers', and those of the slaves the least so, while the range of expression amongst the women was extremely varied.

THEATRICAL COSTUME

Recent studies have shown that many later accounts of Greek theatrical costume have wrongly attributed certain usages to the fifth century B.C. It must not be assumed that styles did not vary, but there was considerably less latitude in the early theatre for changes in the shape of the dress or the ornaments which could be worn. The same holds good for the hair, the masks and the footwear; the *kothurnoi*, or thick-soled half-boots worn in tragedy, were not originally very high, nor is it true, as was originally believed, that they were worn to increase the acoustic effect. In any case theatrical costume had to be modelled on that of everyday life, with the possible addition of features which would enable the audience to understand immediately the character represented, as well as by the information implicit in the mask. Although such information as we have, particularly that which refers to the Periclean age, is not very reliable, it is known that in tragedy the kings and queens wore the long tunic with sleeves *(chiton)* and that it came down to the feet. Happy characters wore tunics adorned with strips of brightly coloured material; fugitives and unhappy characters in general wore yellow, green or blues tunics; persons grievously

afflicted wore black; women's tunics sometimes had a train; a kind of shawl was worn over the *chiton*, and could have been brightly coloured. Theatrical costume, therefore, was ordinary and decorous, so much so that when Euripides dared to introduce characters dressed in tattered cloaks he was criticized for what was considered to be an unseemly innovation.

Gods were distinguished from mortals by their insignia. Minerva carried a shield, Mercury a caduceus (a wand with two serpents twisted round it), Neptune a trident. Soothsayers such as Tiresias wore a knitted woollen garment over their tunics; hunters carried a purple sash over their left arms. Other characters had similarly distinctive ways of dressing. It is not known for certain if the chorus wore masks, but they all wore the same type of clothing, which was usually a *chiton* somewhat shorter than those worn by actors, and it had an *imation* thrown over the shoulder.

The costume worn in comedy was also similar to that in everyday use, except that it was made to look ridiculous by the addition of stuffing which puffed out the chests and the stomachs of the actors or, on the contrary, was so close-fitting that they looked practically naked. Sometimes it had sleeves, sometimes not, or one sleeve only. It could be covered with an *imation*, or a coarse, roughly woven cape, or a goatskin. Slaves wore a kind of leather jacket *(spolas)* and very narrow breeches *(anaxurides)*.

Members of the chorus in comedies were dressed differently according to the part they played. In Aristophanes' *The Birds* it would seem that they wore bird masks and wings; in *The Wasps* insect stings and in *The Clouds* great billowing tunics.

At the beginning of the second century B.C. the actors formed an association known as the ' Union of artists dedicated to Dionysus '. It was a religious body and its president, from among their members, became for the time a priest of the god. They continued to present the tragedies, comedies and satyr-dramas of the previous ages and also new epic, dramatic and lyrical plays as well as simple declamations accompanied by music. Exempted from taxes and military service, they could move freely about Greece and beyond, taking Athenian productions into territories far distant from the land of their origin, especially into Southern Italy (Magna Graecia) and Sicily.

EDUCATION IN THE CITY STATE

At the height of the Persian invasion, whilst the fleet was massing in the waters of Salamis and exiles from Athens were watching on the horizon the glow from the fires of their burning city, a decree was published in Troezen to provide for the education of refugee Athenian children.

This sensitivity to the need for primary education in such a remote age is one of the finest features of Hellenic civilization and one of the principal reasons for its flowering. Before the age of Pericles, however, education in Athens was restricted to the children of the rich and it was entirely non-vocational. Under Pericles further education began to be more specialized and provided a specific training for the offices and the magistracies of the State, or for certain paid functions in the State service. With the Sophists, and later in opposition to their philosophy which tended towards empty rhetoric, the school became the cornerstone of a man's training for life as a citizen in the city-state.

This idea of training an individual for a profession as a politician and a bureaucrat in the civil service was welcomed and put into practice not only by the schoolmasters but also by the State in its dealings with adolescents. The organization of the ephebia *(full-time training for youths of eighteen to twenty) shows how conscious the Athenian Republic was of its duty to provide free compulsory education for all its citizens at the time of conscription.*

Hippocrates of Apollodorus, the young son of a well-to-do Athenian family, knocked late at night on Socrates' door to tell him that Protagoras had arrived and wanted an introduction with a view to becoming Socrates' pupil. This scene from the early pages of the best-known of Plato's youthful dialogues the *Protagoras*, is symbolic of the educational provision in Classical Athens, at a moment between the older Hellenic education and that of the classical and post-classical period. It was Periclean Athens' greatest contribution to the future of mankind.

A century-old tradition stood behind Hippocrates. He had accepted and absorbed all that the educational practice of his country and his social class could do to train an aristocratic gentlemen on the point of attaining the status and function of citizen of a maritime, democratic republic. But he felt that the traditional type of education praised by Aristophanes, especially in *The Clouds*, no longer adequately met the needs of a new Athens or of that same aristocracy which no longer disdained to serve the State, but was determined to put itself on the same level as the *polis*, to stay there and participate to the full in city life.

Hippocrates, as befitted the scion of an illustrious house, had also had successively his three masters, of letters, music and gymnastics. He grew up for the first six years of his life according to the usages and the rites of the *genos*, from the *amphidromia*, a kind of baptism at the family hearth, to the lessons from his private tutor *(paidagogos)*. He had been cared for by a nurse, and perhaps fed by a wet-nurse or, as was the commoner custom, by his mother. He had gradually been freed from his swaddling clothes and his leading strings.

Then, as soon as he ceased to be under the care of the women of the house, he was entrusted to the company of the so-called 'slave-attendant' or *paida-*

195

gogos who accompanied him to the school of the masters of grammar, music and gymnastics.

In *The Clouds* Aristophanes imagines the children in Athens marching to their master's house without a cloak (though he says more vigourously 'naked'), even through thick snow, coming from all quarters of the city to learn, in addition to gymnastics, music and poetry, reading, writing and arithmetic. The teaching was more by word of mouth than from the written page, just as classic Greek poetry, from Homer to the decline of tragedy, was spoken by the masters and listened to by the scholars rather than written down and read. The greater and the better part of the teaching material was doubtless the myths, the epic poems, the stories of the heroes and the animal fables. The little ones, who began their 'scholastic' apprenticeship at the age of six, had perhaps already heard some of these stories at their mother's knee or from their *paidagogos*. Not only that, but they would have learned the famous names already, and perhaps even have 'seen' the famous deeds carved on the pediments of the temples or painted on the porticos. They would have heard the hymns to the heroes being sung in the festivals and the solemn processions by the choirs, and would be familiar with the feats of Achilles, Hector and Odysseus, constantly recurring motifs on the vases used in every home.

This type of education and this instruction was given in Sparta to both boys and girls, both in mixed groups and separately, but in Athens by tradition it was probably reserved to boys alone. Ancient Athenian society, in fact, as seen on the stage in Aristophanes and described by the retired soldier Xenophon, not only distinguished sharply between the sexes, but excluded women from civil life and relegated them to the *gynaikeion*. The educational reforms of Plato were looked upon as something of a revolutionary protest, therefore, when he recommended in *The Republic*, a daringly utopian tract which he tempered down later, that an education which included gymnastics and physical and military training should be given also to girls, so that women, in spite of the diversity, or even non-existence, of their effective political rights, could take their part as active citizens and armed defenders of the *polis*.

It is true that Xenophon makes Ischomachus keep quiet about the merits and the culture of the fifteen year old whom he brought as wife into his house,

The little Athenian boy was taken whilst still quite young (probably about six) to school to be taught music, grammar, arithmetic, poetry and gymnastics. For most of the Classical period instruction was mainly oral. The children were collected together at the master's house or under porticoes. Lessons lasted the whole day. Below: relief showing a teacher of the lyre. Opposite: relief symbolizing poetry (above) and music (below). (Capitoline Museums, Rome.)

but it is also true that in general there could not have been a great deal of ignorance or illiteracy, even amongst the women, in Periclean Athens. The women may not have gone to the theatrical contests and seen either tragedy or comedy, and they are even less likely to have read the plays, but they did take part in the civic funeral celebrations for the fallen, and would certainly have been educated enough to understand the public orator. There is also the famous occasion on which Athenian women are said to have applauded Pericles and showered him with flowers and wreaths in their enthusiasm and emotion at his words of consolation.

Aristophanes built many scenes and the entire plot of *The Frogs* on a comparative criticism between two poets (Aeschylus and Euripides), all of which presupposes taste, intelligence and a good memory on the part of the audience. The public of Athens was indeed far from illiterate, as its power as a political electorate could not be exercised without a sound knowledge of reading and writing. Six thousand citizens, a high proportion of those having full civic rights, were necessary for a quorum to set in motion the machinery for ostracism. There was indeed one illiterate citizen who approached Aristides (a democratic leader, d. *c.* 468 B.C.) and asked him to record his vote in favour of Aristides' ostracism because he was tired of hearing him called 'the Just', but this was exceptional and there was in fact an ordinance forbidding members to enter the assembly without writing materials (tablets and a stylus). It would seem, therefore, that everyone capable of voting was required to be able to read and write.

The years of Aristides' ostracism are the years which by tradition, and also by the accounts of a near contemporary, Herodotus, saw the schools in full

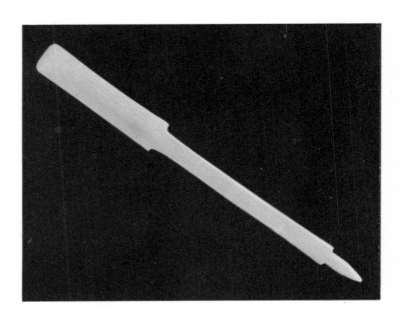

There were three stages of education in Athens: maternal, primary (beginning at six and giving the rudiments of instruction to help the child find its way in society) and higher education which could be either the learning of a trade or the highest form of preparation for life. Left: a youth studying. Right: a stylus used for writing on wax tablets. Papyrus came into Greece only at the beginning of the Hellenistic age. (Museum of the Greek Abbey of Grottaferrata and the Kannellopoulos Collection, Athens.)

198

Gymnastics and athletic contests played an important part in the training of Athenian youth. Above: youth practising with a form of dumb-bell used to give greater impetus in the long jump (from an ancient drinking-cup). Right: a dumb-bell (Agora Museum, Athens).

activity and witnessed the decree passed by the people of Troezen during the battle of Salamis to ensure that refugee children from Athens received a proper schooling. An organized system of education, directed and financed by the State, is thought to have begun in Athens in the summer of 480 B.C. This date is given by the Greek biographer Plutarch (c. A.D. 46 - c. 120) and he and his sources could possibly be mistaken, but there is some confirmation in Herodotus that organized schooling was going on in Ionia in the early years of the fifth century, and it was a regular thing, though not State controlled, in Periclean Athens.

As democracy developed in Athens, teaching and education, which were imparted in the same way to the children of noble families and to children of rural middle-class stock, gradually took a different path, leading to different ends.

In his dialogue with Hippocrates, Socrates said, or implied: 'You go to school to learn literature, gymnastics and music with no vocation or profession in view. You go to acquire knowledge and such things as will help you to be yourself, to be worthy of those who are older than you and to be equal to your contemporaries, to the sons of famous and wealthy families whose tradition it is to serve the State as soldiers, particularly in the cavalry, to administer it and to govern it as politicians'. It is true that until the generation immediately following the Persian Wars, Athenian politicians were not exactly men of thought and culture, but rather men of action, inclined to sport,

to contests, fencing or musical and choral festivals. They thus had no professional training, either cultural or political, and would be very much against it.

The contemporaries of Hippocrates, however, wanted this professional training as a means to a livelihood. They were inferior socially to him and consequently less wealthy. The young Hippocrates studied 'not for a trade but, on the contrary... for education'. In this he differed from the professionals of music and gymnastics, and also from the artists, who were also professionals with a job, be it painting, architecture or sculpture. This was true even of the great Phidias.

SOPHISTRY

Until the age of Pericles, therefore, education in Athens was non-vocational, and this was true for the men of culture themselves, the 'professionals' of poetry and letters. The writers of tragedy in the fifth century B.C. certainly did not write for gain, and the oldest of them, Aeschylus, the veteran of Marathon, would not mention his work as a poet in the epitaph he wrote for his own tombstone at Gela in Sicily. Sophocles, who came from a well-to-do family of artisans, considered himself only as a citizen, and a politician who had been a *strategos* (military commander) with Pericles. Euripides, who was one of the first men in Athens to build up his own library, was derided by Aristophanes for his modest social origins (his mother was a greengrocer). Culture may have spread through the masses in Athens in the sense that virtually everyone could read and write and received sufficient elementary education to know something at least of music, gymnastics and poetry and to be able to practise a trade, but it was never taught specifically to lead to a career in politics or civil affairs. It was not what the Greeks called a *paideia*, a culture designed to equip the leading classes for an active part in public life. This, however, was what the young Hippocrates of the *Protagoras* was looking for from the school of the Sophists: the *paideia*, the education with a professional end in view, the practical and political evaluation of culture. The Sophists said of themselves: ' I acknowledge being a Sophist and educating men ' with the avowed aim of ' making men into good citizens '.

Until the democratic revolution which took its name from Pericles, the ' good citizens ' were Hippocrates' forebears and contemporaries who had the right, through family or religious connections, to direct the affairs of the State. This was alright so long as the State was only the little *polis* with its family cliques, its religious traditions, its rural middle class and its army. The coming of the democracy, with its maritime and mercantile entrepreneurs and the need for a

drastic modernization of the economic, industrial and social structure, made it necessary to orientate education towards professionalism and to create a managerial class in politics, administration, the economy and the army. The Sophists were at one and the same time cause and effect of this development and they have gone down into history as the initiators of a revolutionary movement capable of bringing about decisive changes.

Sophistry was not therefore a new system of education, but an awareness of the vocational possibilities of education and its application to political ends. It was not an apanage or a programme of any party, nor was it an ideology. It did, however, provide the common ground, both inside and outside Athens, for all the reformers, the revolutionaries and the very destroyers of democracy, from Pericles to the conservative Aristophanes, from Alcibiades to Socrates, to the *jeunesse dorée* of the reformation and the counter-reformation of Trent, and the restored democracy which followed the Thirty Tyrants and proclaimed both the amnesty and the condemnation of Socrates. Until such time as the educational theories of Socrates and the philosophy of Plato combined to reform the State and to allow it both to foster and to utilize the energies, the enthusiasm and the activ-

Three of the commonest games amongst the youth of Athens: the long jump, wrestling and throwing the javelin. (Agora Museum, Athens and National Museum, Ferrara.)

ities of all the citizens, the two great thinkers were content to agree with the Sophists on the aims of State education. Education and service to the State were a privilege formerly restricted to a few families. Now everyone had an equal right, irrespective of his origin, background or traditions, to serve the State with his own special skill in the way in which he was best trained.

The ideal of an organic, closely-knit democracy would have been unattainable if the Sophists and their successors had not provided the age following that of Pericles with a sound educational basis.

They provided schools in particular, turning elementary institutions, where rote-learning and rudimentary craftwork were taught by masters of grammar, music and gymnastics, into places worthy of the dignity of Academies. Isocrates (436-338 B.C.) was teaching similar subjects in virtually identical institutions at this time, and, from the point of view of class, wealth or vocational aim, his pupils were very little different form those of Plato. The Academy did, however, at the same time encourage speculative mathematics and created a model for all successive institutions of scientific and philosophical research.

But the young aristocrats who went to the schools of Plato and Isocrates or had cultural connections

At eighteen the youth was presented by his father to the assembly of the demos, and after passing an appropriate examination he became a citizen and was enrolled with the epheboi. The ephebia was a two-year period of military training and, in fact, completed the instruction of the young citizen. State-appointed instructors taught him literature and music, in addition to gymnastics and the arts of war. His hair, previously allowed to grow quite long, was now subjected to a 'basin' cut.

with them, did not go in for science. Their aim was the practice of government and political action, and for this they asked of their masters a theoretical education and a justification by ideals of their future as statesmen. The school of Plato (and later the peripatetic school of Aristotle) and that of Isocrates followed, developed and carried out, therefore, the programme of Protagoras and the Sophists. They began a new period in the history of education in that with them the school and the teacher became recognized institutions with all the technical and practical aids which this implied. The teacher needed a stipendium to be able to live and, to ensure success, had to undertake active publicity to make known his merits, his methods, his objects and the method of his teaching, in competition with his colleagues.

There thus arose in the early years of the fourth century B.C. a whole literature of practical and political pedagogy, which included all the great speeches of Isocrates down to his 'On the Antidosis' (*c.* 354), a defence of himself and his methods.

At the same time there arose the figure of the new teacher, no longer a family retainer, a mystic, a saint or a slave, no longer the domestic pedagogue, no longer a Socrates. He was a professional man who taught grammar, literature, literary criticism and historiography, the theory and practice of style, the foundations of public and private law, of court pleading, and so on. The men who left his school were professionally qualified, men determined to exercise their skills in what were coming to be known as the liberal arts: teaching, advocacy, politics, and the like. They were the men who contributed to the making of the 'bookish' society and civilization of the Hellenistic East and the Romanized West, of the pagan and Christian *humanitas*, European man's inheritance.

One essential task of the school in fourth-century Greece remained therefore the safeguarding and the handing down of tradition. For Demosthenes and Aristotle the writers and artists of the previous age already had the value and the educative function of 'classics' to be studied, collected, commented upon

Above: *a glass receptacle for the oil and sand used on the limbs when performing physical exercises. The sand was used to remove the oil which was the scraped off with a strigil. (Kannellopoulos Collection, Athens).* Right: *a youth prepares for an armed race (Capitoline Museums, Rome).*

and imitated. Lycurgus, the anti-Macedonian orator, an expert in education, finance and politics, who grew up in the atmosphere of the schools and amidst wars conducted for the defence of the State, made provision during the time he was in charge of the finances of Athens for the preparation and preservation of the 'official' texts of the tragedies of Aeschylus, Sophocles and Euripides. Aristotle and his pupils studied institutions, compiled lists of winners at the Olympic and the Delphic games, studied stage directions and treatises on politics, rhetoric and aesthetics, all the material necessary for a history of literature and the basis of a profitable humanistic education.

The school thus acquired, and was always to keep, its informative, encyclopaedic quality, and freed itself from the ramifications as well as the specialisms of the competitive military training which had been the basis of all former education. This training was now to be undertaken also by professionals, and a new phenomenon arose: the military academies and institutes which turned out professionals expert in the

various branches of warfare, resolved to put their skills at the service of Macedon and of the Diadochi (the successors of Alexander the Great).

There was the danger that to meet the threat of national armies trained and equipped particularly by Philip of Macedon Athens should herself have a professional army within her walls rather than a citizen militia. There was another equally great danger in the dichotomy within the Republic, in the government of the State and the control of public opinion, because the politicians, that is the orators skilled in dialectic and eloquence, were now more than ever indifferent to matters of warfare. Thus, whilst men of the fifth century could be, and often were, both politicians and militarists, those of the fourth, such as Demosthenes and Hyperides, could not, and did not want to be anything other than politicians and advocates; they were only too willing to leave the conduct of wars to professional soldiers such as Iphicrates, Caridemus and Caretes, irrespective of whether the armies they commanded were professionals or mercenaries.

At the same time, however, at least at the end of the Alexandrine age, and during the last armed resistance against Macedonian supremacy, philosophers and politicians did contrive not to separate political and literary education from technical and military training. The two did have in common the aim of preserving or restoring ancient traditions and of safeguarding the moral and civic values of the *polis* of Athens, which were struggling hard to survive in a time of decadence and servitude. In the last, and in a sense the most concrete and realistic of his writings, *The Laws*, Plato vindicated the need to give both youths and girls a military education, even though he considered this to be inferior to philosophy, to the *paideia* (education) of those who really govern the State, and who do so precisely because of *paideia*. The structure of the Athenian institution of the *ephebia* (the compulsory two-year military training of youths aged eighteen to twenty) which we know of particulary through Aristotle's treatise ' On the Constitution of the Athenians ', discovered in the nineteenth century, was so similar to Plato's ideas of educational institutions as described in his *Laws* that it is easy to imagine a connection between the two, though in fact there was none.

It is now known, through literary evidence and recently discovered epigraphs, that the institution of the *ephebia* almost certainly preceded Plato and was functioning in its essential parts as early as the first decades of the fourth century B.C. An inscription found at Acharnai shows that when the young man took their oath it was to archaic gods. It would seem, therefore, that what Aristotle described as something new and very up-to-date did in fact date back some considerable time, and had been modernized to meet the needs of an Athens fast developing in both the civil and military spheres.

On reaching the age of eighteen and having had his birthdate and legitimacy proved by documentary evidence, the young would-be citizen was entrusted, according to his tribe, to a *sophronistes*, one of three chosen by his father and approved by the people. This ensured a continuance of the State ritual and the family tradition. He then began garrison duty at the gates of Munychia and the Acte. The following year, having received from the State his uniform and his arms, he went on guard duty at the frontier or at other strategic points. The State paid him four obols a day and the same amount to all military technicians and officials attached to the office of the *ephebia*.

Aristotle described the *ephebia* as first amongst the institutions of Athens, whereas in fact it was the last historically, in that it was the last attempt of the *polis* in its declining years to return to its origins by combining education and military training.

The circle was completed. Or, looked at another way, it was not completed if it is remembered that the *ephebia* had come to stay as a university-type cultural institution and therefore open to foreigners, who were always numerous in Athens. It remained as an institution to civilize the new Roman conquerors and made it possible for them to carry the torch of *humanitas*. Perhaps they too confirmed the truth of Plato's dictum in his *Laws*: ' *Paideia* [education] also brings victory... '.

A CITIZEN ARMY

Those who saved Greek civilization in the most dramatic hours of its history were not the trained soldiers of oligarchic Sparta who had grown up in the exclusive cultivation of force and the daily practice of arms. At Marathon, at Platea and at Salamis, on land and on the sea, the Persians were routed, driven back and disheartened by citizens of the Athenian democracy, soldiers by right and by duty, led by generals elected by the people. If Aristotle, in a late period of the city's history, considered the period of military training, the ephebia, *as first among Athenian institutions, though historically it was the last, it was because he virtually recognized the last attempt of the* polis *in its decline to return to its origins by combining education and military training. The Athenian recruit, in fact, was the man who, when his education was completed became also a soldier, having, during his compulsory two-year period of training, alternated gymnastic and warlike exercises with the study of music and letters. Thus the soldier was the man who realized to the full his own potentialities and, in this sense, could be said to be the symbol of a true civilian, or member of the* polis.
There were soldiers and sailors. The strength of Athens lay not only in the striking force of her companies of hoplites (heavy infantry) but also, and perhaps to a greater extent, in the strength and mobility of her navy, that ' wooden wall' against which, according to the sacred oracle, the waves of invaders would smash themselves to pieces and which also had the duty of protecting, in peace as well as in war, the vulnerable supply routes to the city.

When the historian Thucydides (*c.* 460 - *c.* 400 B.C.), our greatest source of information for the Peloponnesian War, came to relate the epic and exhausting conflict which swallowed up the greatest and the best part of the strength and wealth of the ancient Hellenic world, and led to its decadence, he said that the two rival cities came to wage war against each other when they were at the height of their power. He had Pericles say that he felt confident of victory because he judged that he had the necessary means to achieve it.

The might of Athens was impressive. Her empire embraced the Aegean islands north of Crete, except for Melos and Thera; most of the Chalcidice promontory in Macedonia (even after the defection of Potideas and Olynthus) and the Thracian coast from Strimon to the Bosphorus; almost all the Greek cities of Asia from Calcedon to Cnidos. In the west she was allied to Corcira and Xathintos, the Messenians of Naupaktos (Lepanto), the Acharnians, the Anphi-

locii, Reggio and Naples in Italy, Leontini and Segesta in Sicily. In naval strength and financial resources Athens far outdistanced her enemies: in addition to her considerable annual income she had a treasury of about 6,000 talents, stored on the Acropolis, inferior only to the treasuries of Imperial Persia and Carthage; there was a fleet of 300 triremes in the Piraeus, to which could be added the allied fleets of Lesbos, Chios and Corcira. Her land forces were not as numerous, considering the large population of her empire, which was twice that of the Peloponnesian League. Athens could count on an army of 13,000 hoplites and 1,000 cavalry, with in addition 1,800 mercenary archers and 10,000 cleruchs (Athenians holding allotments of land in foreign countries) scattered throughout the federal territory, and the territorial militia made up of very young conscripts and the older men.

Sparta went to war with an inferior fleet and financial resources, but with a decided superiority in military land forces. It is not surprising therefore that there were many Spartan voices raised, and some authoritative ones, for peace. The seas were open to her enemies, the military organization of the Peloponnesian states was incapable of supporting large-scale operations far from the home bases, was capable of besieging a fortified city, but not of taking it by assault. Sparta could only hope for victory by invading and sacking lands of the enemy and inducing their allies to desert. The war about to begin would therefore be a war-of attrition, with grave losses and dangers to the Peloponnesian League and her coastal cities.

Pericles, on the other hand, was confident that this kind of war would bring him victory. He knew

that he would never be able to invade his enemy's territory or attack their fortified posts, but he could rely on his navy to block their trade, interrupt communications with their overseas allies and lay waste their coastal areas. Eventually, not having the money to stand the cost of a long war, and probably abandoned by some of their allies, the enemy would begin to treat for peace. The one disadvantage was that the Athenians would have to watch, undaunted, the gradual loss of their resources and the destruction of their countryside.

FROM MARATHON TO CHAERONEA

We shall not trace the events of this bitter struggle, but rather follow the successive developments in the land and sea forces of Athens to see how they reached that peak of efficiency with which they confronted the strength of their enemy city.

In the free democratic republics of Greece, military service was considered not so much a duty as a right of every citizen. Perhaps more than that, it was a privilege. The several *poleis* were governed by a virtual oligarchy and the citizen's political rights were granted on the basis of a census, under which the heaviest obligations for military service fell on the wealthier, who thus paid for their political privileges whilst those who possessed nothing were exonerated from any kind of service whatsoever.

It could not have been otherwise, as the finances of the city were never able in the earlier period to stand the expense of maintaining a standing army, and citizens called upon to do military service had to provide at their own expense the costly armaments and their own upkeep. The tyrants, during the period of their rule over the city, were able to recruit large and well equipped companies of mercenaries (as did, for instance, Pisistratus and his sons in Athens) but this was generally done by levying a tax on the income of their subjects. The republican governments rigorously abstained from this, as far as was possible, considering that it was an affront to the liberty and the dignity of the citizen.

The earliest known military organization in Athens was that of the legislator Draco in the seventh century B.C. He linked the full enjoyment of political rights with the possession of the arms of a hoplite

The 'Miltiades' helmet (Olympia Museum).

The backbone of the Greek armies in general, and the Athenian army in particular, was the heavy infantry, or hoplites. The armament was designed to leave the soldier free to move, whilst also protecting the vital parts (see also p. 206). The helmet covered the whole face; the cuirass, of metal or of leather covered with metal plates, protected the thorax. The legs were protected by greaves, but only from the knee downwards. The shield was round and not cumbersome. Arms captured from the enemy, like the lance shown below, were put on view to the public with an inscription to show where they came from. (Olympia Museum).

Right: *a hoplite ready for battle. Note the 'episma' on the shield; this was a symbolic design which could have a ritual or a heraldic value (Kannellopoulos Collection, Athens).*

and the fulfilment of military service in the heavy infantry. The rank of officer, *strategus* or *hipparchus*, was restricted to those above thirty years of age, with a patrimony of at least 100 minae, and the fathers of sons of at least ten years of age.

Solon's constitution (594 B.C.) admitted to military service all those of the first three classes of the census (i.e. the *pentacosiomedimni*, the knights and the *zeugitai*), those of the last class, the *teti*, being exempt.

The democratic constitution of Cleisthenes (508-507) did not bring any notable changes in a citizen's mili-

tary obligations. There were, however, reforms in army organization. The citizenry was now conscripted on a tribal basis: each one of the ten tribes had to provide one of the ten regiments *(taxeis)* of hoplites of about 1,000 men each. The regiment was led by a *taxiarchos*, elected by the tribe. In the decade immediately following the reforms of Cleisthenes, the supreme commander of the army was the Polemarch (one of the three archons). In the period of the Persian Wars, when the archons came to be elected by lottery, the effective command of all the sea and land forces

The plain of Marathon as it is today. Here, at dawn on 10 August 490 B.C., within sight of the enemy fleet, the Athenian hoplites attacked and forced the Persian troops, commanded by Datis and Artaphernes, to run for their ships. Of the various Athenian battle plans, that

passed into the hands of the *strategi*. They too were elected by the tribes and had perviously served under the Polemarch. During the fifth century some detachments of archers totalling about 1,600 men were recruited from among the last class. They were paid and kept under arms even in peacetime.

Until the middle of the fifth century the cavalrymen apparently never exceeded 100 in number. They were recruited only for special service, and not for fighting, from the second class of the census, the knights. Later their number reached 1,000.

The Athenian civilian army of 10,000 hoplites, furnished by the ten tribes, first showed its paces, and brilliantly, at the battle of Marathon in 490 B.C. under Miltiades. Eight thousand hoplites from Athens fought at Plataea in 479 and many more embarked in the fleet or were left to garrison the city. When the Peloponnesian War broke out in 431 there were 13,000 hoplites under arms out of a possible total of just under 17,000.

The first great navy fitted out by Athens also dates from the Persian Wars, although there had been a fleet of some strength under Pisistratus of about fifty fifty-oared ships *(pentecontori)*. Two years before the second Persian War, Themistocles (d. 459) made the navy the principal arm of the city state. This allowed Athens to repulse the attacks of Xerxes and to contend with Sparta for hegemony in Greece. A hundred triremes were fitted out; the next year there were 200; at the beginning of the Peloponnesian War there were 300 and there was room in the dockyards for 400. During the fourth century bigger and faster ships were built. The Athenian navy will be discussed further below.

RECRUITING AND ARMING THE INFANTRY

All citizens liable for call-up as hoplites were enrolled on a list *(catalogos)* showing the first year of their service. Military service affected men from eighteen to sixty. For the first two years they were considered as recruits under instruction; from twenty to fifty they formed part of the army; after that they were used for territorial or garrison service, together with the young recruits. Except when the popular Assembly decreed general mobilization, the call-up was selective by year or by tribe.

of Miltiades was used. Instead of holding back the heavy infantry in the first phase of the advance, he allowed them to make a dash for the opposing enemy forces which they mowed down. 192 Athenians fell in the battle. Persian losses were very much greater.

Young Athenians were thus enrolled at eighteen, when their two-year period of military training began. Some of the wealthier families had their young sons trained by private tutors, even before they reached the call-up age. The military parade-ground in Athens was near to the Lyceum. Recruits between eighteen and twenty were known as *ephebi*. After the collapse of the Athenian empire and the disturbances under the oligarchic reaction, democracy was re-established in the early years of the fourth century B.C. The two years of the *ephebia*, the importance of which in the field of education has already been mentioned, became a stable influence on the life of a citizen and one of the most important institutions in the republic.

Before being admitted, the *ephebi* had to pass an examination called the *docimasia* to show that they had the necessary requirements of liberty, a legitimate birth, the required age and the appropriate physical state and development. If they could fulfil these requirements they then came under the supervision, distributed by tribes, of two special magistrates and in addition to their military training they received education in music and letters. In the second year of their service the young men received from the State their arms (a shield and a lance) and, after the ritual oath-taking, they served for two years in frontier defence detachments known as *peripoloi*.

Only in the last decades of the free republican institutions, that is during the course of the fourth century, were the *thetes* (small peasants and labourers) admitted to the service as hoplites or as infantry on ships of war. From the fifth century onwards foreigners domiciled in Athens were allowed to serve in the army as volunteers, first as *peripoloi* then as hoplites.

In the time of Pericles a start was made on paying citizens called up for war service. The hoplites got a drachma a day during the Peloponnesian War; later the pay was slightly less (two obols). The Republic provided for the funerals of those killed in action and looked after their families. The introduction of pay coincided with the setting up of a permanent armed force of some 2,600 hoplites and 200 cruising vessels for surveillance and policing duties within the maritime League.

The hoplites, or heavy infantry, wore a cuirass over a short woollen tunic *(clamides)*, greaves and a helmet and carried a shield. Even after the State started to provide the *ephebi* with lance and shield, the citizen still had to provide the rest of his armour himself and, for expeditions which took him outside Athens, provisions for three days. When the military situation demanded the recruitment of the poorer citizens, the Republic naturally took upon itself the cost of arming and victualling them.

The hoplite was armed with a lance about eight feet long and a straight pointed two-edged sword only about sixteen inches long, used more for stabbing than for cutting. Altogether his armament weighed between seventy and seventy-five pounds. He thus had to have one or more attendants, often slaves, to accompany him on marches and to carry his armament and sack of victuals.

The last stages of the Peloponnesian War saw the introduction of a lighter and more agile type of infantry known as *peltasts*, whose tactics came into general use during the fourth century. The famous Iphicrates was the leader of a force of *peltasts*. They operated with, and in support of, the heavy infantry and were armed with a sword, one or more javelins and a light shield of wood covered with leather (the *pelte* from which they got their name).

The light infantry also included detachments of archers, slingers, and stone and javelin throwers.

THE CAVALRY

From the age of Pericles to the time of Demosthenes the Athenian cavalry was maintained at a strength of about 1,000 men. Whereas the Spartans rather despised cavalry, the Athenians looked upon it with some pride. Occasionally this number was increased by the addition of a few hundred mounted archers. There were two cavalry commanders *(hipparchi)* and they were elected by the popular Assembly. They were responsible for seeing, amongst other things, that the force was always kept up to full complement. The young men assigned to the cavalry came from families on the census list which were obliged to maintain a horse. The maintenance for the cavalry corps in war, however, had to be assured by the wealthier families, who combined together in associations known as *liturgie*. This was also done for the fitting out and the maintenance of ships of war. On the other hand, there was no shortage of volunteers for the cavalry, where there was less hardship

This mound covers the remains of the *192 Athenian soldiers who fell at Marathon. Miltiades' victory was a triumph for the system of athletic training of the Athenian youth, who were used to competing against each other in armed races. The news of the victory was carried by an obscure hoplite who ran the forty-two kilometres from Marathon to Athens without stopping, then died from the effort. The Marathon event in the Olympic games was run over forty-two kilometres. Below left: a typical Persian helmet, conical in shape. Right: a Greek helmet.*

and danger than in the infantry. The tactical efficiency of the cavalry was far from good, and they were rarely used in Greece, except in Macedon and Thessaly.

MILITARY OPERATIONS

The art of warfare developed very slowly in Greece, as was shown at the time of the Persian invasion, when the only previously drawn up plan of campaign, duly modified as the action developed, was that of Xerxes and his generals. Tactics were limited to the infantry exclusively and based on the manoeuvre of a phalanx of hoplites drawn up in line eight deep. On either side of the phalanx and in front of it (sometimes behind as well) were detachments of light infantry, whose main duty was to engage the enemy in battle.

Before the fighting began the commander made sacrifices to the god to whom the outcome of the battle had been entrusted and the battle hymn *(peana)* was sung in his honour. After the approach phase by the light infantry and light armour, the phalanx advanced, then, at a signal from a trumpet, rushed towards the enemy phalanx, endeavouring all the time to keep in close formation and in a straight line and giving their war cry *(alala)*.

The phalanx was pivoted about its right wing, the position of its best troops and its commander. It often happened that its right wing would destroy the enemy's left wing and the success of the battle then depended on the combat between the two right wings.

A complete change in these traditional tactics was effected by Epaminondas, perhaps the greatest tac-

Reconstruction of a typical Greek fortress: the fortress of Eurielos built by Dionysius I of Syracuse on the natural terrace of Epipolae to protect communications between the city and the interior of Sicily. With its system

tician in ancient Greece before the Macedonian period. He heavily reinforced the left flank with a powerful phalanx fifty deep and limited the remainder of the army to harrassing tactics to keep the enemy engaged in the centre and on the left flank, whilst the enemy's right flank was attacked and crushed by the heavy column. In the history of warfare the new tactics of Epaminondas were called 'oblique order', as the various detachments of the line came into action one after the other and the enemy front gave way under the drive of the mass of hoplites.

of ditches, walls and towers, it was the most remarkable of Greek military works. Underground there were inter-connected galleries and arms depots. Below: a detail of the Eurielos fortress. In front of the forward spur there was a deep ditch and behind it were five towers, each manned by a contingent of archers. The inner fortress was linked to the outer wall by a drawbridge. (Museum of the History of Military Engineering, Rome.)

On the other hand, until the Greeks had a cavalry force which was efficient in battle and capable of consolidating the successes of the infantry by pursuing and cutting down the retreating enemy, such victories as their armies achieved were tactical ones only and could not serve any overall strategy.

For marching and pitching camp, the Greek army in the Classical age had none of the rules and regulations which were later to characterize the forces of Hellenism and Rome. They marched from twelve to twenty miles a day with a break for a meal at noon. One particular difficulty was the baggage train which, as there were practically no roads, was strung out in a line often longer than that of the army itself. There were of necessity very many non-combatants who followed the army. In addition to the porters of arms (and each hoplite could have two or three) there were the indispensable bakers, carpenters and smiths who had to build any military works which might be required and set up the camps. There were also the trumpeters who gave the signal for battle on a large trumpet *(salpinge)* or sounded the various camp calls on a curved horn.

The art of siege was virtually unknown before the Macedonian period. One notable exception was the siege of Syracuse in the middle of the Peloponnesian War at which the Athenian army under Nicias wore itself out. Generally speaking the besieging army built walls around its objective whilst those inside attempted to damage or destroy them by erecting their own outworks at right angles to them.

THE NAVY

Until the end of the sixth century B.C. the Greek navy consisted merely of long low boats with thirty or fifty rowers on one deck. They were called *tria-contori* or *pentecontori* (thirty or fifty oars). The navy could not, of course, use sail as the merchant ships did, since the manoeuvrability of a warship could not be left to the caprices of the winds.

Considerable attention was devoted to the technique of boat-building and this led to the invention of the trireme in about 500 B.C. According to Thucydides the first trireme was built by the Corinthian

Ameinocles in about 700 B.C. This date is very unlikely, and Thucydides contradicts himself by saying that triremes first appeared in the Greek navy at the time of Gelon of Syracuse and Themistocles (480 B.C.). From the time of the Persian Wars the trireme remained the classic warship in all the naval battles of the free republics from Salamis (480) to the Arginusae islands, Aegospotami (404) and Cnidos (394).

The Athenian trireme was a comparatively light ship about 130 to 160 feet long. It had a sail, but this was used only during voyages from one base to another and was furled when the ship was moving in battle formation. It had a crew of about 200, of whom 170 were oarsmen arranged in three tiers one above the other. There were some 20 sailors to attend to the sail and the rigging, and 12 soldiers, who could fight as either archers or light infantry when boarding enemy ships or landing.

The Athenians became experts in the use of the trireme as an instrument of war, manoeuvring it to ram the enemy vessels broadside on with its prow which was armed with a strong wooden beak covered with iron and placed just above water-level. There were two principal manoeuvres at which the Athenians were particularly skilled from the battles of the Strait of Artemesion and Salamis onwards. The first was

A swift vessel of war rebuilt from designs on pottery of the late sixth century from the Louvre and the Monaco Museum. The ladder in the stern was used for going on board. Slender, with flat sides, the vessel was built for military operations. Cargo vessels were of quite different construction, particularly in their length-breadth ratio which was four to one, whereas in warships it was seven to one. (The Naval Museum of the Piraeus.)

the *periplos* which consisted of taking action to avoid the enemy's prow by keeping alongside him. The second was the *diecplos* which was to rush the enemy, coming in parallel to his flank and withdrawing the oars whilst his oars were smashed to pieces.

When ships were brought in for repair they were hauled ashore and the work was done in sheds built for the purpose and arranged to radiate from some little port. Until the Persian Wars, the Athenians used the open roads of the Phalerum, later replaced by the great arsenal of the Piraeus, built by Themistocles, and the smaller ones at Zea and Munychia.

HOW MUCH DID WAR COST THE ATHENIANS?

As has been said, the Greek republics in the early years did not spend much on their military forces, since each citizen was supposed to arm and maintain himself at his own cost. The use of mercenaries, common during the reign of the tyrants, did not entirely cease on the return of the democracy. Thus in the fifth century Athens maintained a police force of Scythian archers bought as slaves on the Pontus market. The corps of 1,200 cavalry, which began to be kept permanently under arms at the same time, cost about forty talents a year.

Then when the Athenian government was obliged to arm a large number of *teti* to meet the demands of the navy and of the garrisons throughout the vast league, it had to provide itself the necessary moneys. It had to do the same for the wealthy citizens when wars came to last a long time and their theatres of operation were far from home. At the end of the fifth century an infantryman got about four obols a day and a cavalryman twice or even four times as much.

The State financed all the big fortification work such as the walls Themistocles built round the Piraeus, or the 'Long Walls' built by Pericles to link Athens with the port of the Piraeus at a cost, according to an ancient source, of 1,000 talents.

The expense of maintaining a strong navy was even greater. In the fifth century it could cost about one Attic talent to build a trireme. The crew received three obols a day, and they numbered about two hundred. The officers were paid very little more. Altogether to keep a trireme on a war footing cost about half a talent a month.

The siege of Poteidaia, which lasted two years (432-430) is said to have cost Athens 2,400 talents; the siege of Samos, which lasted little more than nine months, 1,200 talents; the operations around Syracuse from 415 to 413 cost well over 2,000 talents. The first ten years of the Peloponnesian War (431-421) cannot have cost Athens less than 12,000 talents (about £6 million, $15 million).

POLITICAL INSTITUTIONS

Goethe said that the Greeks dreamed the dream of life in the most wonderful way. Applying the same sentiments to political life in Athens, it could be said that the Athenians dreamed as no one else has ever done the dream of democracy. From Solon to Cleisthenes, from Cleisthenes to Pericles, Athenian political institutions gradually but irresistibly progressed towards an ideal of equality which they reached, often through contrasts of tolerance and cruelty, time and time again, only to find it successively betrayed, perhaps because no ideal can co-exist with reality. It would be difficult to imagine a setting more worthy to represent the slow and painful development of a democracy in action than the Greek polis, a little state of scarcely more than a hundred thousand citizens, each one fully conscious of his own rights and duties to the community and of the part he must play in maintaining public life in the city. The polis of Athens was a state in miniature in which, in the course of one century, many minds and talents were at work to give meaning, both for itself and for mankind, to an ideal of controlled strength and liberty.

In that city-state, where it would have been the wish that the voice of the town-crier could reach all the citizens from the public square, a group of men learned and taught others to live democratically, in harmony and moderation, though they did not always follow their own rules.

The most ancient records of the social organization of the Hellenes speak of the sub-division of the population almost everywhere into families *(gene)*, brotherhoods *(phratriai)* and tribes *(phylai)*. According to tradition these were artificial divisions brought about by the necessities of internal organization at a certain moment of development, and were the work of one legislator. Tradition, however, was wrong and these sub-divisions, which were more like associations, date back to the most ancient times and were spontaneously formed. They preceded any higher forms of organization such as the state.

The *phratries* were certainly the oldest forms of family association. The lack or insufficiency of any central controlling power explains the necessity for certain families to group themselves together in an association to provide for the common defence and the common needs for a collective life. Within the *phratries*, personal relationships between the members were regulated by ceremonies presided over by the phratriach: marriage, the presentation by the father of his legitimate children or the recognition that a youth had attained manhood and his admission to the exercise of civil rights. In the nomadic period when Greek families moved from one part of the country to another, members of the same *phratries* travelled together. When the community settled down they would live near each other and fight together in war.

From the beginning *phratries* had their own cults in honour of the gods who were deemed to protect them. Zeus was regarded as their particular protector; he was worshipped as Zeus Phratrius and was often associated with other deities such as Athena Phratria, Poseidon or Apollo Phratrius and so on.

As time went on it became opportune for several *phratries* to unite and form larger groups more capable of acting as a central organization and of dealing with

The Parthenon by night.

gradually evolved, the tribe must have been given military functions, and it no doubt furnished cadres for the recruitment of the army and the commanders, members of the *gerusia* (a kind of senate) and the popular assembly as well as persons who could serve on certain commissions and magistracies.

There is no doubt that the *phylai* as well as the *phratries* preceded, at least in their original form, the settlement of the Greeks in their definitive areas of the peninsula and the colonies across the Aegean, and the fragmentation of the Greek people into the innumerable little Mycenaean states. We know from Herodotus that all the Ionians were distributed, like the Athenians before Cleisthenes, in four tribes: the Argadei, the Haegicorei, the Geleonti and the Hopleti. These tribes existed not only before the Ionians emigrated from Attica but also before their original settlement in Attica, where they originally formed many separate political entities.

The names of the four Ionian tribes were derived from the names of deities, except the Hopleti, which probably meant 'Armed Men' or 'Bearers of Arms'.

THE ARISTOCRACY OF THE *GENE*

After the Greeks had come to organize permanent settlements and the Mycenaeans had established a monarchy, *phratries* and tribes were finally recognized by the state, which found in them an excellent basis for a rudimentary organization for recruitment and taxation purposes. The *phylobasileis* eventually became state magistrates, collaborating with the king, or acting for him, in public religious practices, in the administration of justice and in the command of the army. They then became the focus of all the jealousy and hostility felt by the aristocracy against the king's powers and the authority.

The main element in this aristocracy was the nobility, the *gene*, or great and powerful families which had gradually arisen, by differentiation and development, out of the mass of small families of the ordinary people. It should not be thought that the *gene* dated back to the earliest times, as the word's association with the Latin *gentes* might lead one to believe, or that they were the first elements of the *phratries*. On the contrary, the families which joined together to form the ancient *phratries* could not have done so on the

problems affecting the whole community such as, for example, putting into effect the vendettas, or acts of justice, in accordance with the judgements of the *basireus*. This person became a chief, or a king, and would be recognized as such by a family, an entire people, or a section of the people. These larger associations were called *phylai*; we call them tribes, after the Roman name for apparently similar organizations.

The oldest of the tribes had their own chief, the *phylobasileus*. In addition to settling blood feuds over the heads of the *phratries*, these tribes would intervene also in questions concerning family rights and would organize the celebration of common cults. The four *phylobasileis* in Athens had sole jurisdiction in cases of premeditated murder. As the institutions of the state

basis of distinction, as they were only rudimentary social groupings, and in a few generations, with the inevitable ramification of the family stock, the units soon lost track of their common origin. Later, when they were no longer nomadic, they gradually consolidated their ownership of property, not only of their flocks, slaves and other possessions, but also of land, which single families succeeded in holding and dividing up amongst themselves as their own property *(kleroi)* after surrendering the due portions *(temene)* allotted to the gods and the king. These families who were evidently able to impose themselves on the others because of their superior strength, courage and intelligence, consolidated their position with the land and property they owned, and were able, in fact, to increase these in times of war, as only the rich could maintain costly stables and buy arms and equipment *(panoplie)*.

It was therefore in the interest of these privileged families to stick together even when their descendants multiplied and spread in successive generations. They therefore devoted some of their efforts to the preservation of their family tree, enriching it with legendary ancestors and generally taking it back to some divine source. Thus there arose the *genos*, with its own family religion, its own patrimony, its own standards of justice administered by the head (also a *basileus*) on behalf of all its members. The head of the *genos* was also its military leader and he commanded its members in war operations in the ranks of their own *phratrai* or *phylai*, under the overall command of the king. The authority of the head of the *genos* was transmitted in order of seniority to his descendants in the male line. The landed property of the *genos* was originally collectively held and as such indivisible, inalienable and hereditary.

Once the *gene* had been formed and their position consolidated, it was not long before an aristocracy was constituted. This was an association of the *gene* into a closed society. Its purpose was to ensure for itself every kind of privilege over the rest of the people and to hold fast to its prerogatives, even when in conflict with the king. In some cases the tendency of the *gene* to exclude those who were not noble, from membership even of the *phratries*, led to a reaction and the formation within the *phratries* of associations of a religious character called *thiasai* and more restricted ones known as *orgeonai*.

THE *DEMOS*

The king now felt that he was being watched over and that his power was being restricted by the continued presence and the increasing strength of the nobility. He turned for help and support to the *demos*, that is, as the word came to mean, those who were left outside the *gene*, the great families, just as the Roman *plebs* formed a class apart from the patricians. But the aristocracy knew how to make itself indispensable and soon got the better of the king and the

demos: as the state institutions became more complex, a powerful central organization was necessary and only the aristocracy was able to find the men needed to run it from among the *phylobasileis* and other heads of the *gene*. Thus the king faded out: the Mycenaean monarchy, which in Greece had been so different from the showy, theocratic, absolute monarchy of Crete (though at one time it had wanted to copy its external trappings), also came to an end. In its place there arose the aristocratic republics.

Naturally the monarchy did not disappear all over Greece at the same time. Its decline was most rapid in the more culturally and economically developed regions, where the great families had increased more quickly in power, wealth and activity. This was the case in Ionia, where the rise of the nobility was favoured by the continual state of warfare between the Greek cities and their neighbours, and by the economic development which required continual intervention by the central authority in disputes between private individuals and between opposing group interests. In Ionia the powers the state had to take upon itself were more important and more varied than elsewhere. They were entrusted partly to the ancient *gerusia* (a kind of senate) presided over by the king as in Athens at the Court of Areopagus, a Council of State held on the hill of that name, and partly to magistracies created for the purpose, like the office of archon in Athens.

The republics which arose out of the remains of monarchical regimes taken over by local aristocrats were governed by a particular class and safeguarded the privileges of this restricted society. It was this society which had provoked in its own interests the decline and fall of monarchical government.

The ordinary people, who in the last years of the monarchy had often found in the king a natural ally against the capricious domination of the nobility, were now oppressed as never before. They were excluded from all forms of government, either because this was restricted to the nobility, or because they lacked the independent means to undertake any political activity. They could, it is true, take part in popular assemblies to elect magistrates and to approve laws (though a rigidly conservative state would neither need nor desire new laws), but even here they were inhibited by their fear of the nobility whom it would have been imprudent to displease.

The condition of the *demos* deteriorated politically under the new aristocratic regimes. It also deteriorated economically. There was, however, a substantial change in the economy in Greece with the development of the cities.

THE *POLIS*

The various nomadic groups in Greece settled in definitive areas throughout the peninsula for various reasons, amongst which the more important were the complicated geography of the country and the great difficulty in communications between the various settlements. The political and economic links which had existed between the members of one group grew weaker and other links were formed, which were closer, but limited to smaller groups. New community units grew up, each one of which was like a miniature state in itself, presided over by a king who lived in his fortress on a prominent feature (a rock or an acropolis) whilst his subjects inhabited the surrounding plain, scattered about in numerous villages. In the case of enemy invasion the people were always ready to abandon their villages and take refuge, with their families and their possessions, in the impregnable acropolis, such as the ones at Tiryns (in southern Argos), Mycaenae, Athens and Thebes, and there prepare for defence under the command of the king.

These Mycaenaean kingdoms were numerous and small, and they will best be illustrated by the case of Attica which, it will be remembered, was for a long time divided into twelve autonomous regions.

As long as the Mycaenaean monarchy flourished, there were strictly speaking no true cities in Greece, although there were rudimentary forms of a more stable kind of life when the population of the surrounding villages collected together in the king's acropolis.

As the monarchy declined, the Greeks began to adapt themselves progressively to a civic life in the colonial territories. Here the inhabitants had found, particularly in the Eastern Aegean, in Crete and along the coast of Asia Minor, a more progressive civilization, a higher standard of living and a level of commercial and industrial activity unknown in their countries of origin. They had gone there as simple farmers and shepherds, and had become sailors, mer-

Stele inscribed with a law against tyranny (Agora Museum, Athens).

fied areas became towns with their own walls and defence works. They also began to attract the wealthier landowners who lived out in the country. It became even more urgently necessary for the nobility to transfer their dwellings to the town when political power passed into their hands, and the new republics had to have an official residence for their magistrates and for the meetings of the councils and the people.

The true city, or *polis*, thus arose on the model of the cities which the Greek colonists had found in other areas of the eastern Mediterranean, particularly in those parts where Greeks themselves had settled. It was a political, economic and military centre, usually surrounded by a protective wall, with, at its centre, an altar dedicated to its god, with an acropolis for its defence, an *agora* for its market and a place of assembly for the people. Often it had also a port on the seashore or at the mouth of a river. Soon, following the example of the nobility and their hangers-on, people of more modest means also came to settle within its walls. Notable amongst these were the rootless ones, those who owned nothing: they easily found work and gradually became tradesmen and craftsmen. This does not mean that there was a general exodus from the countryside; agriculture lost none of its importance in the state economy and for many years the census of individual citizens was drawn up on the basis of their revenue from farming.

The radical political changes which characterized the end of the Mycenaean period were accompanied by equally radical changes in the economic conditions and the various forms of life of the Greek people. From the eleventh century B.C. there was a decline in Greek maritime activity, and expansion in the eastern Mediterranean came to a halt. Naval supremacy in the Aegean was lost to Phoenician navigators and merchants.

With the settlement of the aristocracy within the *polis*, agriculture also underwent a change. The family and patriarchal systems gradually declined and the collective property of the *genos* gave way to individual ownership, increasing the economic gulf between the landowner and the dispossessed. The wealthy man could always bring pressures to bear on the weaker and force him to give up his possessions. The small holder declined and large-scale landowners thrived. A large class of free men arose who owned nothing. Some of them took up a trade and became smiths,

chants and artisans, adapting themselves to living in the towns which had grown up in considerable numbers in the colonies. They also took to living in captured towns, and themselves founded others, some of which became very wealthy.

All this was naturally to have an influence on the mother country, and especially on those areas along the east coast from which the colonists had originally set sail. As trade and industry developed, those inhabited zones which had sprung up around the forti-

carpenters, potters, soothsayers, doctors, and came to be called *demiourgoi*, 'those who work for the people'. Others worked for pay in the fields and were called *thetes*; they formed the lowest class of society. Between these different social classes, between the nobles with their selfish attachment to their lands, the *thetes* and the *demiourgoi*, who with a miserable pittance were just able to satisfy their daily needs, there soon arose a bitter hatred. The aristocrat's disdain of any form of manual work, in contrast to the Homeric age when the *paterfamilias* was not ashamed to take a hand in the farming with members of the family and paid workers, created an ever-widening gulf between the landowners and the humble, despised labourers, weak and poor and exposed to the whims and cruelties of the noble members of the *gene*, particularly after the disappearance of the monarchy and the advent of the rigid government of the aristocrats.

Meanwhile, whilst the nobility grew weak and inefficient in their proud but sterile idleness, the vast numbers of humble, persecuted commoners toiled on in silence. Work sharpened their wits and developed their muscles. They became industrious and enterprising. Living frugally, they were able to accumulate their earnings. Driven off the land, they turned to trade and navigation. There thus arose, alongside a class of landed proprietors, a class of property owners. The *demos* took on a new meaning as an assembly of people excluded from the power of governing, but having nevertheless the economic and intellectual means to exercise it; it was a meaning close to that of *bourgeoisie* or *tiers état*. It gave help and protection to the *kakoi*, or the poor and oppressed, and received from them sufficient support to combat the dominant aristocrats. The first conquests, in both the social and the political fields, were not long in coming.

FROM MONARCHY TO DEMOCRACY IN ATHENS

When the nomad Greeks who, from their later colonization of the coast of Anatolia opposite, came to be known as Ionians, had settled down in parts of Attica, they set up in the Mycaenaean age numerous little states governed by kings. One of the most important of these, both from its strong position and the advantages of its surrounding countryside, must have been Athens. Huge walls and the remains of an ancient palace would seem to bear this out.

In addition to Athens, so-called after the goddess worshipped on the rock, there were several other notable centres in Attica such as Decelea, Aphydna, Brauron and Cephisia. Tradition has it that there were twelve cities based on the twelve cities of Ionia and, which is more likely, that there was an independent state of Eleusis and a Tetrapolis in Marathon with three adjacent villages.

There was also a decisive move towards bringing the separate Attic towns and villages under one city based on the *polis* in Athens. This must have entailed some struggles and even warfare between the larger and the smaller towns, and the last resistance seems to have been by the *polis* in Eleusis.

In Attica also we find the population linked together from the earliest times into *phratries* and in the four Ionian tribes of the Geleonti, the Hopleti, the Argadei and the Haegicorei, each led by a *phylobasileus*, showing that these associations go back to the period of the monarchy. Attica too reached the constitution of the *gene*, each with its head of a family who gave his own name to it and a collection of more or less mythical ancestors. Members of the *gene* were called *eupatridai*. Those excluded from the *gene* organized themselves into *orgeonai* and *thiasai* for mutual defence and communal worship.

There were traditionally four kings before Theseus: Cecrops, Erichthonius (or Erechtheus), Pandion and Aegeus. All were worshipped as local deities in Attica and the surrounding areas. The control of the towns and villages by one city is said to have happened under Theseus. Tradition has made Theseus the most popular king of Athens. He too was a god and his

Harmodius and Aristogiton, revered by Athenians as liberators since they killed the tyrant Hipparchus. They figured in a bronze group by Antenor; placed in the Agora in Athens, it was carried off by Xerxes and subsequently restored. (Copy in the National Museum, Naples.)

225

cult flourished in and around Marathon. Patriotic legends sprang up around him, one of which tells how he fought the Minotaur to deliver Athens from a hateful tribute imposed on her.

Other kings followed Theseus: the seventh was Codrus, who was said to have sacrificed himself to save his country from invasion by the Dorians. The line of hereditary kings is thought to have come to an end with one of the successors of Codrus, Medontis or Acastus. They were followed by a series of seven archons, elected for life in the same dynasty, who ruled from 1038 to 753 B.C., a series of archons who held office for ten years, ruling from 752 to 682, after which the archon's term of office became annual. There is little of historical value in this artificial and illogical account of pre-classical Athens which has been handed down by tradition. Yet it does help us to see how gradually, as the state progressed and became more complex, the king was assisted then superseded by magistrates such as the polemarch, who commanded the military forces, and the eponymous archon, who gave his name to the year and was the supreme judge. The *basileus* was left with only the religious duties.

When these magistracies had come to be elected annually, the king also being considered an archon, six additional officials were appointed, called *thesmothetai*. Their duties were to act as codifiers and guardians of the law. The eponymous archon, the polemarch, the *basileus* and the six *thesmothetai* came to form a single college known as 'the nine archons'. All those who had held one of these offices had right of entry to the Council of the Areopagus, which was probably a continuation of the ancient royal *gerusia*, a kind of Senate. The Council, presided over by the king archon, dealt out punishment for crimes of blood and watched over and conducted the *dokimasia*, an examining of the nine archons.

Although Athenians could and did write, there were still no written laws by the seventh century. This was true of most Greek cities, and it made it very difficult for the ordinary people to protect themselves against abuses of power by the magistrates, who came from the nobility. They accordingly asked for the laws to be written down, and this was done. In 621 a citizen by the name of Draco was charged with codifying the laws for the uniform administration of justice. In later times these laws were judged to have been severe, but they corresponded to the needs of society and the customs of the times.

If Draco's code of laws brought a better administration of justice, this did not materially affect the living conditions of the poor. The government was in the hands of the nobility, and many families were reduced to selling their lands in an attempt, often vain, to keep out of debt. Debtors who did not pay up on time were treated cruelly: their creditors could seize them and make them work as slaves, or even sell them into slavery outside Attica.

Those who settled in the town and were able to adapt themselves successfully grew in numbers and wealth by engaging in business and in seagoing trade. They too demanded a constitution more in keeping with the real conditions under which they were living. Finally the different interests concerned agreed on the choice of a just man to bring about the necessary reforms.

The man in question was Solon. He was of noble family, an expert in politics and trade, and a man of culture and considerable poetic gifts. Elected archon in 594, after issuing certain decrees designed to better the lot of the debtor and to provide cheaper food for the poor, he reformed the Athenian constitution democratically. The population was divided into four classes, graded from the rich, through the less wealthy, to those who possessed nothing (the *thetes*). The first two classes could be elected to the highest magistracies, the third to less important offices, whilst the *thetes* had the right only to attend meetings of the popular assembly and vote.

Solon's constitution may have satisfied the demands of the middle classes and improved the living conditions of the poor, but it did very little to meet aspirations towards political equality, and once again dissent and disorder broke out. The continued unrest amongst the lower classes fed the political ambitions of an energetic leader named Pisistratus, who rose to power on the support of the masses and by overcoming the resistance of the aristocrats. He was proclaimed *tyrannus*, or lord, of Athens.

The rule of Pisistratus began in 561 and lasted, with minor interruptions, for many years. He governed wisely and promoted the development of trade and shipping, both the merchant marine and the navy. Under him the Athenians acquired their first colonial possessions on the coasts of Thrace and Asia Minor.

Bowl used in the citizens' council (the Boule) in Athens discovered during excavations by the American School. It is stamped with a symbol indicating 'public property', as was everything for use by representatives of the people. (Agora Museum, Athens.)

The city grew in size and beauty: it was enriched with fountains and elegant public buildings. Artists and men of letters received state protection. The constitution was left virtually unchanged. He exercised his power by having himself legally appointed as army commander, and carried out this function through ten generals, nominated and appointed by him, called *strategi*.

During the rule of Pisistratus, Athens prospered at home and was respected abroad. His popularity ensured that his son Hippias should succeed him on his death. But Hippias had few of his father's good qualities and soon incurred the hatred of the people, particularly when he was implicated in the assassination of his brother Hipparchus by a band of conspirators. The Athenians sought the help of Sparta and forced Hippias to abdicate, together with his family.

When Hippias had been driven out, the republic returned to normal, but the people were then able to achieve certain democratic reforms. A new democratic constitution was drawn up by Cleisthenes, one of the members of the noble Alcmeonid family.

Cleisthenes began by determining the condition and the political and administrative competence of the single Attic *demos* (equivalent to a parish). He then fixed the number of these and their boundaries. The whole territory was then divided amongst ten tribes *(phylai)*, forming the basis on which the population took part in popular assemblies and elected magistrates.

The magistrates, elected by the people, were required simply to be the executors of the people's will, and to this end a central organ of government was set up. This was a council, called the Boule, and it was decidedly popular in character. It had 500 mem-

227

bers, each tribe electing 50, and it prepared the laws for submission to the popular assembly, known in Athens as the Ecclesia.

To thwart the ambitions of any future leader such as Pisistratus who might seize power, the Ecclesia was empowered at its meetings, which might attract no less than 6,000 citizens, to name any citizen whom it had reason to suspect and send him into exile for ten years. The name of the man to be denounced was written on a potsherd called an *ostracon*: hence the word ' ostracism ', which originated in this procedure.

The basic elements of Cleisthenes' constitution remained permanently in force. Subsequent modifications were made, and these were always in the direction of a more democratic application.

The characteristic circular building called the Tholos in which at least a third of the prytaneis (officers) were always in residence, day and night. In cases of enforced absence they could delegate their duties to substitutes who had executive powers. The building was equipped with a kitchen, crockery and other accommodation requirements. (Model in the Agora Museum, Athens.)

ATHENIAN DEMOCRACY IN THE AGE OF PERICLES

The word 'democracy' has more than one meaning. It is 'power in the hands of the *demos*', 'government by the *demos*'; as the word *demos* ('people') took on different meanings in different period of history, democracy itself has had various interpretations. According to Aristotle, there are two basic factors in democracy: the liberty and the sovereignty of the majority. When these are established everyone can express his own opinions, all have equal rights and all can aspire to public office. There are other essential characteristics: the institution of people's tribunals, each formed by a college of citizens, or in certain cases (especially for political trials) by all the citizens gathered in a popular assembly with judicial functions; the responsibility of the magistrates who, on leaving office, are called upon to render an account of their conduct and activities during their term.

In Greece the concept of democracy was always linked to that of the *polis*, or city-state. It if appeared obvious to the Greeks that all the citizens of a *polis* should be able to exercise the same rights and be subject to the same duties, whatever their social status or their economic position, it was not admitted that foreigners from another city who had settled in their midst should enjoy the same rights of citizenship. Foreigners remained foreigners, though they were treated with the highest regard, enjoyed the protection of certain laws and were often especially rewarded for their services to the city of their adoption by the granting of some rights of citizenship, but these were only ever conferred as a privilege.

This was the form of Athenian democracy after the introduction of Cleisthenes' constitution, and it was similar in many other Greek *poleis*. The bases of the new political structure were the tribes, established in their allotted lands, and the appointment to offices by the drawing of lots.

The aim of Cleisthenes' reforms was to break the power of the nobles, who until then had controlled most of the political life of the *polis*. To this end he divided the State into ten tribal areas which cut across the boundaries of the ancient family groups.

The country was then further divided into about 150 smaller districts, or *demoi*. These were grouped together to form 30 larger divisions, 10 in the Diacria (the region of Mount Parnes and Mount Pentelicus) 10 in the Paralia and 10 in the central plain. These districts were known as *trittyes* because the tribes were formed from them in groups of three, one from each division. Athens itself, it should be noted, was divided between the ten tribes and sub-divided into *demes* which, like all the others, had autonomous administration. Thus was the aim of the reforms secured, better than was ever thought possible, and the citizenry were shuffled about as at the beginning of a card game.

Each *deme* was under the leadership of a *demarchus*; all the citizen were enrolled on the register of one or other of the *demes* and this was the basis of the civil list of the *polis*. The *phratries* continued and Athenians continued to present to them their wives and sons.

The *trittyes* were led by *trittyarchoi*, magistrates whose duties were predominantly military. The tribes were governed by 'curators' with mainly financial responsibilities, but they were also the source of recruitment for the army, each tribe having to supply one of the ten regiments of hoplites, each commanded by a *strategos*, elected first by popular vote within the tribe, then freely by all the citizens of Athens.

The tribal organization was also the basis of the new organ of government created by Cleisthenes, the Boule, or the Council of Five Hundred. The members were drawn by lot, fifty from each tribe. Each *deme* put up a number of candidates according to its population. This is the first example in history of an assembly elected on the basis of proportional representation. Each of the ten groups of fifty members was called a *prytaneia* and it collectively held the presidency of the Council for one tenth of the year (this period also being called a *prytaneia*). It drew up the agenda for the meetings of the *bouleutai*, as the tribal representatives were called, and for the popular assemblies. Its chairman, who held office for only one day, was called 'President of the *prytaneia*' and he lived in the building where the meetings were held.

All the other magistracies were also appointed on a tribal basis. Each of the nine archons and their secretary, all elected annually, had to come from one of the ten tribes.

Sovereign power now resided in the popular assembly (Ecclesia) of which all citizens over the age of twenty were members. At the beginning of each year, the assembly deliberated about the upholding of the laws; at the beginning of every *prytaneia* they discussed whether or not to keep certain magistrates in office. The assembly could approve on reject the draft laws presented to it by the Boule, and to make the sovereignty of the people even more effective, there was the system of ostracism. It is not clear whether this was introduced in the time of Cleisthenes or some twenty years later. Every year, at the beginning of the sixth *prytaneia*, the people were asked if certain citizens should be ostracized; if this was

their wish, they were invited to write the name of the person concerned on potsherds at the meeting held in the eighth *prytaneia* (in April).

Ostracism became a dangerous weapon in the struggle between political factions and had the opposite effect to that intended. It enabled anyone with influence to get rid of his adversary and deprive his rivals of a leader.

When demagogy became rampant in Athens, Cleisthenes' constitution, which still left the highest magistracies in the hands of the rich and prevented the poor from ever actually exercising justice, was looked on with nostalgia by some of the Athens oligarchy. It is, however, understandable how Herodotus, writing at a time when such processes of levelling down had never been thought of, could think of Cleisthenes as the true founder of democracy. One section of the community, the least well-to-do, may in fact have been denied executive and judiciary powers, nevertheless every Athenian citizen could take part directly in the government of the state through the drawing of lots within the Boule. The lottery was so arranged that every citizen with the requisite qualifications could occupy an office at least once in his life (more than twice was not allowed). As the presidency of the *prytaneia* lasted only for one day, something like two thirds of the population who enjoyed the necessary rights could in fact have the honour at least once in their lives of governing the state as President of the Republic.

The constitution of Cleisthenes nevertheless did not satisfy all the requirements of a perfect democracy. Not all the magistracies were accessible to citizens not owning property. In fact, as public offices were unpaid, they were virtually barred to anyone who had to earn his own living.

The work of Cleisthenes was devotedly taken up in the middle decades of the fifth century by Pericles, son of Xanthippus who had commanded the Athenian fleet in their victory over the Persians at Mycale. He was little more than thirty when he entered political life and he soon showed tendencies towards democracy, helped by family tradition and the education he had received. Insinuations were made later that he had decided to take the democratic line because the conservative faction was headed by Cimon, a man of great reputation whom Pericles could never have hoped to equal.

Potsherd (ostraka) used by citizens for the ostracism of Themistocles and Aristides discovered during excavations of the Agora. Every year the general assembly of the sixth prytaneia was asked if it was opportune to apply to any citizen the system of ostracism. If the vote was affirmative (a quorum being six thousand), procedure was set up for the operation to take place the following April. Below: a list of taxpayers and their contributions (Agora Museum, Athens). Below left: Themistocles (a statue in the National Museum, Naples).

It is a fact, however, that when he took over the government of the republic in about 460 B.C. (and he held it almost without interruption for thirty years) he completely won over the Athenian populace with his daring democratic reforms, to the extent that they felt as never before that they were the complete arbiters of their own destinies.

The first measure which Pericles presented to the people for their approbation was the introduction of payment for magistrates. The assembly voted them two obols a day, not a very generous payment and less than the average daily wage of an ordinary workman, but it did at least allow any ordinary person to give up a few days to the exercise of an office to which he now had the constitutional right. Pericles' reform did, therefore, put the administration of justice in the hands of the people, but it should be remembered that they could be people who might not be able to curb their party passions and who were almost totally lacking in culture and experience.

Once the principle of payment for public office *(mystophoria)* was accepted and extended to the archons, who were paid four obols a day, to the *bouleutai*, who got five and the *prytaneis* who got a drachma, there was no longer any reason why even the office of archon should not be open to the lower-class citizens. Thus, in 457-456 members of the *zeugitai* class (owning property yielding two hundred measures) were admitted to the office of archon. This was a foretaste of the eventual admission of the *thetes* (peasants and labourers) to all magistracies appointed by lottery. The political powers of the Areopagus were suppressed and its jurisdiction remained so limited that it was considered essential as a safeguard for the republic that citizens should retain their power of private accusation. This turned out to be a disaster, as it soon came to be abused by gangs of blackmailers and extortioners *(sycophanti)* ever on the lookout for objects of personal attack whom they could turn to personal profit or political advantage.

The kleroterion, as explained in the chapter on the Agora, was the mechanism for the appointment by lottery of various officials and public servants within the Boule from among the twelve tribes. Bronze identification plates bearing the names of the bouletai (members of the Council) were arranged in any order in columns according to their tribe. The prytanei, or tribe providing the officers for the period, were excluded. A number of small white balls were taken corresponding to the number of bouletai to be elected. These were then mixed with a number of black balls and put

These constitutional reforms clearly undermined the authority of those magistracies chosen by lottery. This was much to the advantage of the Boule, which gave the necessary instructions for the exercise of such functions, and for the few elective offices which remained, all of them demanding a high degree of competence from their holders. First of these were the *strategi*, whose board came to exercise control over all other magistrates and had the greatest authority in the assembly and in the Boule, where it was the centre of executive power. Pericles was elected *strategos* in 460 and, for the greater part of his thirty years' reign, was president of the board of *strategi* and ruled, in a perfectly constitutional manner, as head of the Athenian republic.

The government of Pericles soon exhibited all the tendencies of radical regimes: the unbridled pursuit of imperialist ambitions and an unrestrained, almost inhuman, selfishness in its relations with allies, subject peoples and weaker states. Only later did Pericles realize the effects of an omnipotent populace on the government of the state, when there was no one to control it and to 'face up to its anger'. The greatest success of his policy was that it created a regime based on a diarchy (the populace and its demagogue). When this failed, with the defeat of the demagogue, the state inevitably faced a crisis.

THE ORGANIZATION OF TAXES

What did their democratic regime and the imperialistic policy of their republic cost the Athenians? As in all Greek cities, the main burden on the finances in Athens from the fifth century onwards was the upkeep of the military forces, especially after the use of mercenaries, introduced by the tyrants and extended under the democracy.

Another considerable item of expenditure, introduced by Pericles and extended after his time, was

into a kind of long funnel on the left of the kleroterion. The balls came out of the bottom through an opening in the left-hand side. If the first one was white this meant that the first horizontal row of names was chosen: if black, the first row was eliminated. The second ball to emerge determined the election or otherwise of the second row, and so on. A similar procedure was adopted for the election of judges. Opposite: *bronze name-plates and a ball.* Above: *the kleroterion. (Agora Museum, Athens.)*

the payment of public officials. One drachma a day to the 500 *bouleutai* and the maintenance of the *prytaneis* in the *prytaneum* cost altogether 30 talents a year. Magistrates earned at first 2 obols a sitting, then half a drachma from the time of Cleon (d. 422 B.C.), and this entailed an expenditure of 90 talents a year. Expenses connected with the religious cults were also considerable, but these were borne by the temple treasuries.

What income did the state have to cope with this varied expenditure? The most regular source of income for the tyrants, a direct tax on revenue, had been suppressed by the democracy as a hateful affront to the citizen's personal liberty. Nowhere in Greece, and not even in Athens, which was by any standards a progressive state, was there any state budgeting or accounting until the fourth century B.C. Each magistrate met the costs of his office from a particular fund supplied from particular revenue. The only controlling body in this anarchical arrangement was the Boule, which watched over the distribution of the funds available, met the demands of single magistrates and collaborated with the thirty accountants *(logisti)* who, at the end of each *prytaneia*, audited the special funds of individual magistrates.

Like every other democratic Greek state, Athens could rely on three sources of revenue: from state-owned land and property, from indirect taxation and from the personal contribution of private citizens. From 500 B.C. the most lucrative state-owned property was the Laurian silver mines. Indirect taxation consisted mainly of duties of various kinds: the duty levied on the use of ports at from 2 to 5 per cent of the value of the goods imported or exported (though there were no customs offices at the borders); the 10 per cent tax, imposed during the Peloponnesian War, on all goods passing through the Bosphorus to or from the Black Sea; the duties on market sales, collected at the gates of the city immediately as the goods were brought in. In addition there were special taxes levied for the exercise of certain trades or callings which required police supervision (such as prostitution) and the payment of legal costs by those who had recourse to the tribunals. The possessions of bankrupt debtors and of those condemned for political reasons also went to the state.

Personal contributions from individual citizens were called *liturgie* in Athens. The richest were the *penta-cosiomedimni*, or those with a personal wealth of at least twenty talents. The *liturgie* were of two kinds: the ordinary and the extraordinary. Among the first were the *choregia*, or the provision of a chorus for one of the lyric, tragic or comic contests on the occasion of the various annual festivities in the city, and the *gymnasiarchia*, or the provision of one of the athletic contests. Of the second, the most costly was the *trierarchia*, or the fitting out, the maintenance of both equipment and crew, and the personal commanding of a trireme during the whole period of any operations. Because of the heavy burden this imposed it became necessary to share it between three wealthy citizens.

THE ATHENIANS JUDGE THEIR OWN INSTITUTIONS

The citizens of Athens were always proud of the free institutions of their country and never failed, when the opportunity presented itself, to praise and glorify the deeds and the virtues of those who had deserved well of the republic by defending its liberty and independence.

The occasion for these celebrations was the feast of the Epitaphie, held annually with official ceremony around the tombs of those who had fallen for their country or who had in some other way deserved public esteem. An essential part of the ceremony was the speech by some illustrious citizen in praise of those for whom the ceremonies were being held.

The most noteworthy regular Epitaphie feast in Athens was held on the seventh of Pyanepsion (that is, at the end of October) at the public graves of soldiers who had died in the wars and were buried in adjacent tombs in the Ceramicus cemetery. Five *epitaphi*, or speeches in honour of the dead, have come down to us: Pericles' funeral oration for those Athenians who died on the battlefield in the first year of the Peloponnesian War, as reported by Thucydides; that which Plato puts into the mouth of Socrates in the *Menexenus*; the speech attributed to Lysias for the dead of the Corinthian War (394-387 B.C.); that of Demosthenes for the Athenians who fell at Chaeronea (338 B.C.), where he himself fought with the hoplites; and finally the *epitaphios* spoken by Hyperides in praise of Leosthenes and those who fell with him in the war at Lamia in Thessaly (322 B.C.).

The oration reproduced by Thucydides in the second book of his *History of the Peloponnesian War* as that of Pericles may be considered as the classic model of the Greek *epitaphios*. Pericles, the orator deputed by law to praise the fallen, feels above all the moral obligation to pay a tribute of honour and gratitude to those of their predecessors who, first, defended the liberty and independence of Athens, then, setting the standards of life and of government, led the city to its present greatness and splendour: 'Our constitution is not an imitation of any other. Rather do we set the example to others. Its name is Democracy, because we entrust the city not to an oligarchy but to a vaster circle of citizens; but in reality its laws give all without distinction the same rights in their private life; and as far as honours are concerned, men are chosen for the fame they have won and not because they belong to one or the other party. Nor can poverty stand in the way of a man's reputation or prevent him from following a career which may bring good to the city. The political life of our city develops freely, and as for prying into the daily habits of the citizens, we do not become irritated with our neighbour if he indulges in some pleasure, nor do we frown upon him, which may not harm him directly, but is unpleasant. We do not place restrictions on our private lives, but in our public lives we do not transgress the law because we revere it; we obey the magistrates in office and the various laws, especially those which protect the oppressed, and those unwritten laws whose universal sanction is dishonour.

'Not only this, but we have procured many diversions for the refreshment of the spirit, with games and religious festivals throughout the year, and elegant private houses, the daily enjoyment of which puts melancholy to flight. Moreover the greatness of our city is such that products flow to it from all parts of the world, and with the enjoyment we take from them we claim as ours the good things which other lands produce, as well as what our land gives us'. And again: 'Our city is worthy of admiration from other points of view. Love of beauty does not lead us to ostentation, nor does culture make us weak. Wealth is for us a stimulus to action, not a motive for garrulous pride. As for the restrictions of poverty, it is humiliating to us not to confess them, but not

Terracotta name-plates for the appointment by lottery to public office (Agora Museum, Athens).

to know how to overcome them by work. In our same persons we combine both family and political preoccupations, and though each of us is concerned with a different private life, yet we can all show a not inconsiderable capacity for public office, and we count the citizen who cannot undertake public duties not as an inoffensive man but as a useless one.

'Even when we show nobility of soul towards others, we do it differently. We seek friendships that we might give, not receive benefits. He who has done a man a good turn is a better friend, as he has the gratitude of the receiver. He who only gives in return, however, is more slothful as he knows that he does not give freely, but only to wipe off a debt. And we alone are fearless in our giving because we do it, not from calculation but from the trust we have in ourselves as free men.

'I will say, in a word, that our city is, in its whole complex, the school of Greece, and that each one of us, it seems to me, develops in it an autonomous personality, an elegance and a versatility which can adapt to the most varied ways of life'.

THE ADMINISTRATION OF JUSTICE

Athenian poets and philosophers discussed among themselves Justice, the Law, Equity, Harmony and Concord, yet the city did not fully develop a sound legal system. Perhaps this was because of the nature of the Athenian genius and in particular its human qualities. A science of law could have developed gradually in the set framework of a life of unhurried labour. Their constant and conscious exaltation of the spirit, their ever restless imagination and their passion for beauty hardly disposed the Athenians to weigh up coolly and calmly the pros and cons of an argument. This lack of detachment was inimical to any sound legal system.

Although the spirit of the times acted against the creation of a true science of law or a body of legal practitioners, through lack of a concrete system of positive law, the fact nevertheless remains that Athenian law greatly influenced the Greek world and Hellenic civilization in general, and inspired both Roman law and modern jurisprudence.

It is surprising that such a high order of culture as that of Classical Athens should not have a word to describe its juridical system. This was true for the whole of Greece, and it is all the more surprising in that Greek thought, exemplified at its highest in Athens, was preoccupied more than any other with the problems of justice and the law. When the Greeks came under the beneficial influence of Roman Law, they were at a loss to express in their own language the Latin word *ius* and fell back on *dicaion* (normally used with some qualifying adjective), which in classical Greek meant 'justice' or 'just'.

The fact is that the Athenians could not conceive of positive law outside statute law. In Athens justice was rigorously bound to the law; it was in the highest sense 'legal' justice. The great Greek lyric poet Pindar, born near Thebes, who often wrote in praise of Athens, could rightly claim that the law, though he meant it in a different sense, was sovereign over both mortals and gods.

It could have happened, certainly, that some judicial terms did not come from the law but arose from everyday life and current vocabulary. Similarly the customs and the notions of equity and natural law, or, more accurately, natural 'right', created by the philosophers and the men of letters, might have had some bearing on the creation of the body of laws through the observation of the customs and habits of the ancients in the sphere of sacred and public law (which often went together in the *polis*). The course of private law and of punitive justice was also influenced indirectly by the judgements given by the heliasts, the members of the Heliaea, a judicial tribunal in which each one voted according to his conscience and within the terms of an oath he had sworn. Custom seems to have played an equally important part in the development of commercial law in

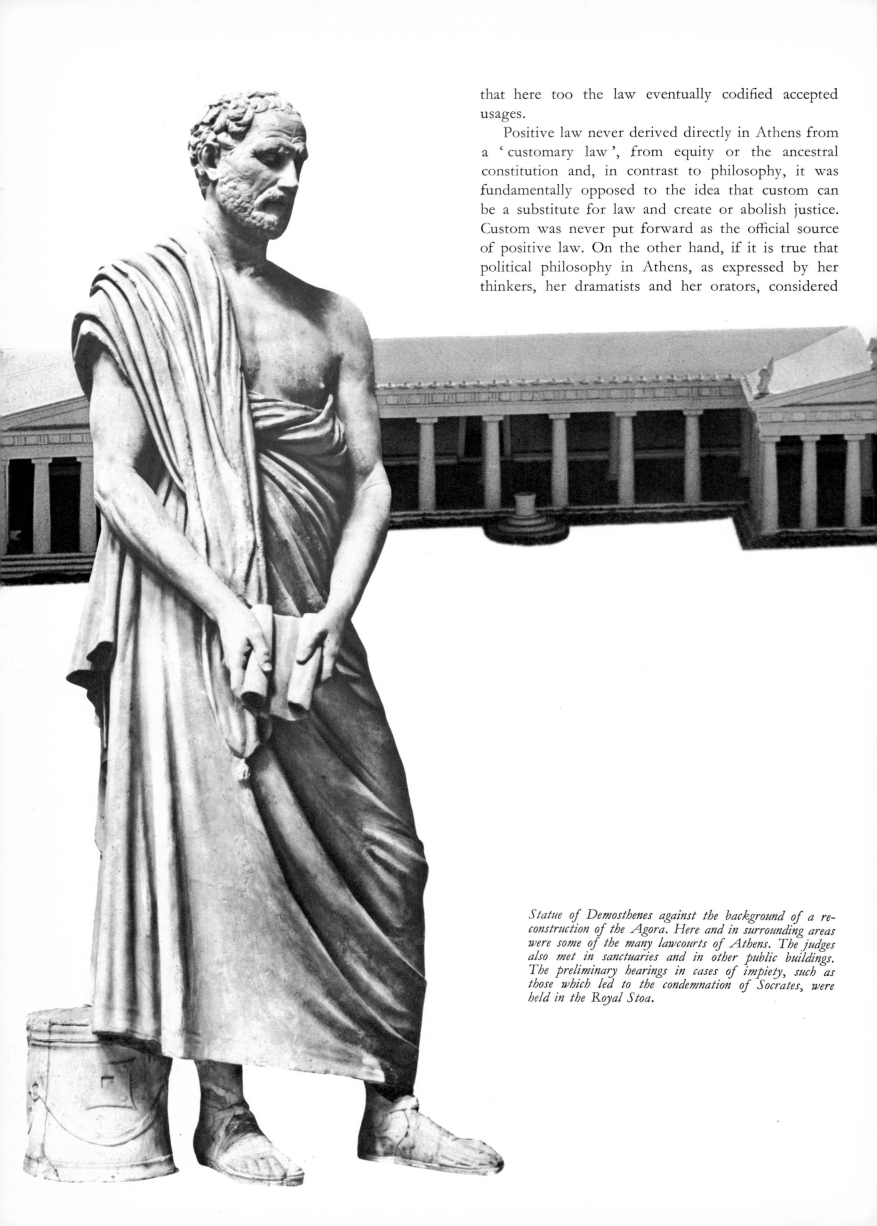

that here too the law eventually codified accepted usages.

Positive law never derived directly in Athens from a 'customary law', from equity or the ancestral constitution and, in contrast to philosophy, it was fundamentally opposed to the idea that custom can be a substitute for law and create or abolish justice. Custom was never put forward as the official source of positive law. On the other hand, if it is true that political philosophy in Athens, as expressed by her thinkers, her dramatists and her orators, considered

Statue of Demosthenes against the background of a reconstruction of the Agora. Here and in surrounding areas were some of the many lawcourts of Athens. The judges also met in sanctuaries and in other public buildings. The preliminary hearings in cases of impiety, such as those which led to the condemnation of Socrates, were held in the Royal Stoa.

law as an instrument of character-building and a model of ideal conduct rather than a set of rules for building up the state, it is also true that positive law never came into this order of ideas. The divine, sacred origin of the law, which evoked fear and respect, and its mission as an educator, remained always on the speculative level.

Athenian law, or Attic law, as it is usually called, is the most developed and the best known amongst all systems of law in Greece because it had to adapt itself, and it did so admirably, to the demands of a highly mercantile city. This flexibility, moreover, has also caused it to be regarded with some doubt and reserve. It served as a model for many cities of Classical Greece, especially those on the islands, and formed the basis of a common Hellenistic law. Finally, although few purely legal texts have survived, it is the best known because of the copious references to it in literary texts: in the speeches of orators, in Plato, Aristotle and his school, in the dramatists, the lexicographers, the scholiasts, the historiographers, and especially the chroniclers of Athens. It is also referred to by Latin playwrights and rhetoricians.

There are many inscriptions which throw light on the legal system of Classical Athens, but the literary texts are still the most important source and make Attic law the best documented of all in Greece.

LEGISLATION

Athens was one of the first Greek cities to move towards the making and enactment of laws. As in the rest of the Greek world, this arose out of political and social struggles and the appearance of a monetary economy, trade and a craftsman class. The gradual emancipation of the citizen brought a desire for equality. On the other hand, the social and economic changes taking place made the surrounding countryside, which was quite incapable of keeping step with these advances, increasingly dependent on the city. The nobility, in spite of their imminent decline, were still the owners of most of the land. In spite of many democratic reforms, the powerful families still governed effectively until the Peloponnesian War. This was the general situation which gave rise to the legislator.

The oldest set of laws in Athens was that of Draco and it dated back to about 624 B.C. He was particularly concerned with criminal law and his most lasting reform dealt with homicide. The cruelty of his measures has made his name legendary, but his code of laws clearly assisted the establishment of state authority and did away with private vengeance.

The greatest Athenian law-giver, however, was Solon, one of the seven wise men, whose constitution dates from 594/3. He is one of the most famous figures in the history of Athens and is the embodiment of the Greek spirit of harmony and control. It was he

who gave the city her political impetus, her regime and her system of laws. His constitution survived to classical times and was regarded as the greatest of all the ancient constitutions. All political parties recognized it, respected it and put their trust in it.

THE LAW

Solon's constitution must not, however, be taken as a constitution in the modern sense of the term, as this never existed in Athens. It was not a closed system of rules and laws. Although these were not codified they did, however, provide a set of standards for reforming the structure of the state and of society. It was a constitution based on wealth (Athens became a democracy only in 508/7 after the reforms of Cleisthenes and others who followed him) and it embodied the noble principle of equality before the law, of which the Athenians were justly proud, and the prohibition of individual and retroactive laws. It was pervaded by a spirit of equilibrium between the state and society on the one hand and the individual on the other. Solon's laws became an example in the Classical and the Hellenistic periods, and continued to be an inspiration to the Romans and to succeeding ages up to our own, whose right of association looks back to the time of the Greeks. The laws were written on portable wooden tablets which disappeared with time. Later they were copied on to stone and displayed under the royal portico.

Solon's legislation paved the way for positive law in Athens but did not set the pattern, and there was a considerable revision of the constitution in 402/3 after the Peloponnesian War. Athens was one of the Greek cities which had a comparatively flexible legal system. It was a common Greek concept that the law could not be changed or repealed, and this was particularly the case in Sparta. In Athens, however, it was possible to promulgate new laws and abolish old ones and one session of the popular assembly was devoted to this every year. Every citizen had the right to propose a law, provided that it did not contradict an existing one, unless it was also proposed at the same time that the existing law should be repealed. Failure to do this could lead to the charge of illegal proceedings (a reform probably due to Ephialtes in 462 B.C., or even earlier) which could lead to a fine

and the annullment of the proposed new law. Athens therefore held to the principle of *lex prior derogat legi posteriori*. The accusation of illegality was typical of Athenian public law and was found scarcely anywhere else; in this respect it resembled the system of ostracism during the first half the fifth century.

The new laws proposed were not decided upon by the assembly of the people, but in the form of a trial by a body of legislators chosen from the members of the Heliaea. The value of this procedure was to some extent lost by the fact that the popular assembly could publish decrees as well. Decrees and laws were the exclusive sources of positive law, and there was, to all appearances, no difference between them, though this point has been argued fiercely over the years. Decrees also had to conform to existing laws and follow a special legislative procedure, otherwise they ran the risk of annullment and the corresponding charge of illegality. Radical democracy in Athens did not, however, care very much for legality and placed the popular assembly above the law.

THE MASTERPIECE OF GREEK ORATORY

One accusation of illegality gave rise to the masterpiece of Greek oratorical art in the shape of Demosthenes' speech 'On the Crown', a defence against the accusation of illegality brought by Aeschines against Ctesiphon in 330.

After the Athenians' defeat at Chaeronea in 338 by Philip II of Macedon, Demosthenes, the champion of liberty and democracy, proposed the hurried rebuilding of the city walls against a probable invasion by Philip. The proposal was accepted, and a decree charged each of the ten tribes to supply ten citizens to supervise the labour and the finance necessary for the work. Demosthenes was chosen by the members of his tribe, the Pandionids. Not only did he perform his duties well, but he made a personal contribution of a hundred minae.

Ctesiphon, a friend of Demosthenes, proposed to the popular assembly that Demosthenes should be given a crown of gold and crowned with it in the theatre during the Greater Dionysiac festival when the new tragedies were to be performed in March 336. The reason for the decree was 'Demosthenes works and advises in the interests of the people'.

Aeschines, a ruthless adversary of Demosthenes and one of the pro-Macedon faction, seized the opportunity to accuse Ctesiphon of illegality. The trial, however, was not held until six years later, in 330. The accusation was made formally against Ctesiphon, but it was Demosthenes whom Aeschines was attacking.

This provoked Demosthenes' intervention and Ctesiphon chose him to defend him. Because of the great interest aroused by the trial, and because the two greatest orators of the time were to face each other, two whole days were devoted to the proceedings, each one having a day to present his case.

Excavations have brought to light many of the implements in common use in the lawcourts such as the kleroterion, the little bronze voting-discs and the klepsydra, or water-clock, which fixed the time for speeches by both prosecution and defence counsel. The discs, which date from the period of Demosthenes, are mentioned by Aristotle in his 'On the Constitution of the Athenians'. Those used for acquittal had a stub in the centre, those for condemnation a hole. They were made so that they could be easily hidden in the fingers before being placed in the urn. Above: klepsydra and discs (Agora Museum, Athens).

241

The accusation was made under three headings: Demosthenes was to have been crowned whilst still in office, and public coronations were forbidden before the holder had accounted for his term; it was to be held in the theatre, which was against the law; finally, and this was the most important, the reason behind the decree was untrue: Demosthenes did not work or advise in the interests of the people, and the law did not allow decrees based on false assumptions.

The result of the trial was catastrophic for Aeschines. His charge, together with his authority, crumbled completely and he had to go into exile in Rhodes, where he founded a school of rhetoric. One day when he had delivered in front of his audience in Rhodes his oration against Ctesiphon, he was asked how it was that such a remarkable speech had not won him the cause and he replied ' You should have heard the wild animal!... ' clearly meaning Demosthenes.

The acquittal of Demosthenes was at the same time the finest prize which Athens could award the great orator, her most brilliant son, particularly at a time when his policy had completely failed and Macedon was at the height of her power.

TRIALS, PUNISHMENT AND THE RIGHT
OF THE CITIZEN

In public law (the concepts of public and private law were created by the philosophers) the most notable of Solon's reforms was the institution of the *ephesi*, incorrectly translated as ' appeal ', against decisions of the archon which brought prejudice to the citizens. This meant that suddenly the status of rights and the rule of the law were fixed, because in the last resort the judges resolved controversies by executive power based on the laws themselves, the violation of which would naturally provoke recourse to *ephesi*.

Criminal law arose from the generous fount of legislation provided by Solon. It was not, however, criminal law as conceived today on the principle of *nullum crimen nulla poena sine lege*. Neither crime nor punishment was strictly defined, and the nature of an offence could be uncertain. Moreover, where there was a loophole in the laws the judge had to act according to an oath he had taken and according to his own conscience, thus becoming himself the lawmaker.

When the punishment, or, in private law the indemnity, was not defined, accuser and accused each proposed a penalty and the judge had to choose, without being able to modify either. This is why the same crime could carry the death sentence or an insignificant fine. Penalties were either capital or pecuniary. The Athenians' feeling for liberty did not allow punishments which restricted a man's freedom, except indirectly.

The office of Attorney General, or State Prosecutor, was unknown in Athens. Solon had introduced a popular system, which bore the marks of the disreputable action of the sycophants, whereby anyone could bring an action against a fellow-citizen, whether he was directly concerned or not in the affair. If, however, the prosecutor failed to obtain one fifth of the votes he was liable to a fine of a thousand drachmae. The parties had to conduct their own cases and bring forward evidence and witnesses. They also had to prove that the law applied in their case because *iura non novit curia*. There was also the possibility of the charge of bearing false witness.

Although contractual law in Athens fully met the demands made upon it and was wide-ranging in its application, private law in general was elementary by comparison with modern legal systems and even with the Roman law which followed it. Cicero's contempt for Greek laws is well known. Land in Athens seems to have been in general inalienable between living persons at least until the end of the fifth century B.C. There seem to have been no beginnings of a theory of obligation, credit or contract. These were apparently met by a series of legal fictions; procedures for selling, buying on credit and establishing trust were largely empirical.

The rights of a family and of succession have to be examined within the context of the family as part of the city-state. This has been fully dealt with in the chapter on family life.

Judiciary protection was rigorously legitimate. There was a whole series of litigations *(dicai)* which were similar to the Roman system of legal actions. Outside the *dicai* recognized by law, there was no protection within the sphere of private law. In civil procedures the value of proof was open to free assessment. The law was an object of proof. After Solon it was no longer legal to seize the person of an insolvent debtor.

JUDGES

Although political philosophy in Greece dealt with the concept of the separation of powers, these were, in fact, not distinct in Athens. The judges sat both in the courts and in the popular assemblies and the executive functioned within the organs of justice more than in the framework of a general administration.

The archons could not be judges, not because of any distinction between the legislative and the executive, but because of the supervision which they exercised over the courts of justice.

The organization of justice goes back to Solon and Cleisthenes. It had a popular quality and used the jury system, with a few exceptions, the most important of which was for cases of homicide which continued to be dealt with mainly in the private sector and, after Draco's reforms, by the Areopagus. There were about a dozen courts with a body of judges varying at about a hundred. The main court was the Heliaea, whose members were known as heliasts or judges. This was under the control of the *thesmothetai*, archons charged with the guardianship of the law. Heliasts were recruited from citizens over the age of thirty who had full civic rights, and it would appear that most of them were volunteers. There were about six thousand of them all together, divided into ten sections of fifty, with the remainder as a kind of reserve. Each section was designated by a letter of the alphabet, and for this reason the section came to be known as ' the letter '. When there were important cases to be heard, further sections were added which could bring the numbers up to a thousand or 1,500. If the case was unimportant a mere fraction of a section would suffice. Every year the heliasts swore an oath, the most important clause of which confirmed their attachment to the law and a promise that, where there were loopholes, they would give their verdict according to the most just opinion, that is, according to their conscience. The heliasts from every section who were to sit in court were drawn by lots every morning. In this way it was hoped to avoid corruption, the real scourge of Athenian public life. As a result of a democratic measure passed under Pericles, heliasts were paid according to the number of sittings they had done and on production of their token of attendance. Their pay was temporarily suspended in 411 by the conservative regime.

Solon (National Museum, Naples).

Sittings were public and could not last for longer than a day, the time being measured by a *klepsydra* (water-clock). Courts did not meet on feast days, or on days of mourning and probably not on days when the assembly was held. The voting was secret and had to be done without consultation or deliberation, which would have presupposed a legal training which no judge in Athens could have had, as there were no professional lawyers. The judge was not expected to know the law; it was up to the parties to prove that the right law existed for their case. Any attempt to interpret it might have revealed the judge's incapacity. This clearly reflects the attitude of the Athenians towards the law which was required to regulate

everything and foresee everything, otherwise they would have made the judge's verdict dependent on the most just opinion, a principle which precluded the possibility of the judge's interpreting the law himself and directed him towards justice rather than to the law. Plato and Aristotle proceeded in roughly the same way and to restrict the application of a law which was too general they created a fictitious law such as a historical legislator would have created where he faced the same problem. The all-embracing character of the law prevented any restrictive interpretation which might have been taken as a partial abrogation of the law. It was exceptional for jurisprudence in Classical Athens to be really creative.

LAWYERS AND JURISTS

Although there was in Athens no body of lawyers such as there was later in Rome, there did exist, nevertheless, a number of citizens whose knowledge of legal matters was above the average: those who expounded the law and those who wrote speeches for the litigants *(logographi)*.

The former were concerned with the interpretation of ritual and sacred law, and they were required to have a considerable knowledge of legal matters in general, especially those which affected religion, such as homicide cases. They could, however, hardly be considered as expert jurists: they would be consulted on legal matters rather as one would turn to any cultured man. They were *prudentes* rather than *jurisprudentes*. On the other hand, any Athenian who aspired to public office had to have some knowledge of the city's laws. Menander in his ' Sicionius ' speaks of ' those who know the law ', meaning presumably this kind of person, unless he is reflecting some idea in Platonic philosophy.

The *logographi*, on the other hand, could well wear the mantle of the jurist, if this term is not too pretentious. They made their appearance in Athens towards the end of the fifth century and functioned as advocates, or rather as defending counsel, as there was no order of advocates or prosecuting counsel in the true sense of the word. They were orators more or less versed in legal matters. Because judicial proceedings did not allow of proxies, except in certain exceptional cases or where women were concerned,

the litigating parties had to appear and plead their cause in person. When the litigant felt incapable of writing his speech he got the *logographos* to do it for him, either for a fee or for nothing. The most famous *logographi* were great orators such as Antiphon (*c.* 480-411 B.C.), Lysias, Isaeus (*c.* 420 - *c.* 350), Dinarchus (born *c.* 360), Hyperides (born 389), Demosthenes (383-322), and Isocrates (436-338). Andocides (born *c.* 440) and Aeschines (born *c.* 390) both pleaded *pro domo sua*.

The *logographi* were not responsible for the outcome of the cases and did not show themselves officially. Theirs was a questionable profession, as they freely traded their liberal art. They endeavoured to carry out their mandate using every kind of sophism and subtle or specious argument. Taking advantage of the general lack of legal training among the judges, they would not hesitate to draw on jokes and absurdities or even to ridicule their clients. There was much appealing to sentiments, especially in criminal cases where politics were involved, and this has left us some speeches of great beauty. Although some of these orators might have been talented interpreters of the law, they were few and far between. There was no sign anywhere of that creative spirit which would have caused them to ponder over the concrete case, deduce all its consequences in law and arrive at a synthesis and a system, in a word to bring law out of the realm of practice into that of the intelligence. So long as law was not studied in itself, such a spirit could never arise; orators were trained through practice, experience and example.

Yet the intellectual climate of Athens, with its concentration on philosophy, dialectic and rhetoric, was ideal for the cultivation of jurisprudence. The Romans took advantage of their Greek heritage and achieved incomparable supremacy as lawgivers. The material was there in Athens for the training of lawyers. In both the Academy and the Lyceum it would have been possible to teach comparative law and a theory of law and justice. Theophrastus (*c.* 371-287 B.C.), practically the only jurist in ancient Greece, is an isolated example. Unfortunately his writings on legal subjects have been lost, apart from a few fragments salvaged by Stobaeus (*fl.* A.D. 500), which afford glimpses of his method, apparently based on a comparative study and on some ideas of his own, rather than on deduction.

Theophrastus (Villa Albani Museum).

CHARACTER OF ATHENIAN LAW

There are many reasons for the deficiencies of Athens in the sphere of justice. First of all was the belief in the omnipotence of the law, which was to govern everything; this arrested development of legal thinking. One proof of this is the way the philosophers legislated and theorized to cover up loopholes in the law; there was a never-ending recourse to legislation by decrees where, to our modern way of thinking, a simple act of private law, of administration or of interpretation would have met the case and would have strengthened the juridical processes. Another example is the accusation of illegality which makes no sense if people know the laws in force. It is a well-known phenomenon that all diffuse and sporadic legislation acts as a brake and an obstacle to legal thinking.

In the second place the hundreds of jury members in the courts, none of whom knew anything about the law, turned the courts into popular assemblies. In these conditions there was no possibility of a reasoned, dignified debate. The judge had to decide between two opposing and mutually exclusive propositions and could not modify the sentence or influence it in any way; this again was scarcely conducive to good jurisprudence.

The political and social structure of radical democracy in Athens gave rise to a spirit which, if not exactly hostile, was at least indifferent, to strict judicial training. This, by its very essence, could grow only in a conservative, virtually aristocratic atmosphere. The absence of legal studies reflects this mentality. Jurisprudence presupposes a long tradition and great patience. But Athens, whose advent in history was meteoric, had neither the time nor the will to create a legal system. When the truth is told, it will be seen that the history of Athens is concentrated in merely two centuries.

Finally every nation exhibits certain natural tendencies of its own, and again amongst peoples of the same cultural and intellectual levels there is a difference in the way they develop their legal systems.

In spite of her deficiencies in positive law and in legal discipline, Athens was the leading city in Greek law and had an indirect influence on law elsewhere and on jurisprudence. The Athenians were masters in philosophy and in the philosophy of law, and Plato and Aristotle were their two greatest representatives. Athens's gifts to jurisprudence were the idea of law, the interpretation of law, equity, the theories of the will, of guilt and of error, and, in general the theory of law.

These great achievements of the mind, which go beyond the formal concept of the law, but which were incapable of influencing positive law in Athens, passed into Roman law and have left their mark on modern jurisprudence.

ECONOMIC LIFE

A country which, according to Herodotus, 'always had a sister called poverty': this was Greece. It was a country which did not know the beginnings of either capitalism and industrialization or a so-called slave economy, although it did exploit a slave labour-force. Its society, and this is true even of its greatest city Athens, was organized on a predominantly agricultural basis.

But the difficulties of communication in a dry, mountainous country, whose roads were little more than rough tracks, and the nearness and hence the temptation of the sea could not fail to encourage a systematic development of imports, exports and re-exports overseas which laid the foundations of the economic and social progress of Athens. The city, in fact, kept itself going principally on its trading and maritime activites, and constantly encouraged the producers and traders among the foreigners who came to live within its walls. No restrictions were placed on foreign residence within the community, and foreigners played a principal role in the banking and financial activities of the republic. The development of the various social classes within a regime of considerable general poverty, but equally of considerable egalitarianism, allowed the institutions to function freely for two centuries and avoided, or mitigated, many crises and disadvantages.

'Poverty is, and always has been the sister of Greece'. These words were attributed by Herodotus to Demaratus, the exiled Spartan ruler. The phrase can be truly applied to Greek economic history in the two centuries of Athenian domination, from the days of Marathon to those of Chaeronea, from the victory of Miltiades to the defeat of Demosthenes.

To the Greeks poverty is a thing of nature, the result of a given fact, the consequence of a circumambient reality to which man adapts his own activity. *Natura non vincitur nisi parendo.* What is true of nature is also true of that which, amongst all the sciences invented by man, is closest to the nature which conditions him: economics.

A country's economic history is therefore a history of its rate of progress, be it ancient Greece or modern Switzerland. There is much in common between these two: both are poor in raw materials, difficult to reach: their population is mixed and often politically divided,

yet, out of sheer talent and hard work, careful economy and courageous energy, both have exploited to the full the possibilites nature has offered and the inventive capacity of man.

Here, however, the parallel ends, as Switzerland, which at least until the end of the eighteenth century produced and exported virtually nothing but mercenary soldiers, was able, with the onset of the industrial revolution, to profit from the generally improved standards of living of the continent and developed firstly her transport, especially her railways, then her tourist industry and finally achieved a prosperous market in foodstuffs. During the First World War Switzerland's tourist trade suffered, and she wisely undertook a wide programme of industrialization, especially in the fields of precision engineering and chemicals. Mechanization and industrialization are, of course, factors of our modern age and were unknown in classical Greece, or indeed in the economy of the entire ancient world.

There was virtually no developing technology in ancient times in the sense of the creation of machinery of production, even in agriculture where there was a marked evolution. It would be doing an injustice to the intelligence and the inventiveness of the ancient Greeks and Romans to say that they deliberately turned their backs on discovering, if not machines, at least, implements for better and more productive work. It would seem, however, that at times they showed some reluctance at sailing the seas to increase their trade and their foreign earnings, or to dig metals out of the earth, or to open up roads for trading, not only in goods, but in men.

This point of view could be dated back to certain Greek philosophers of the fourth century B.C. who declared that a free man should not work, that trade and labour were incompatible with personal liberty, and to Roman moralists of the ages of Augustus, Nero and Tacitus, who deprecated any keenness for work and any activity which led to technical discoveries or to civic development.

NATURAL RESOURCES

Any treatment of the economic history of Classical Greece must take account of the limitations of the

on Mount Pentelicus in Attica and on the island of Paros which gave marble. Greece had to look to the sea, both on it and beyond it, therefore, for her development, and in her darkest days the sea brought a remedy to her poverty and overpopulation.

The sea was known to all Greeks as a means of communication, even to those who lived in the mountains of Epirus, to the shepherds of Arcadia and Acharnia, of Aetolia and Phocis, but only the most enterprising and progressive of the inhabitants yielded to the temptation to explore it. These were the Greeks who, in an earlier phase of their history had set out on voyages of colonization which eventually spread to all parts of the peninsula, including agrarian, sedentary, militaristic, oligarchical Sparta. In the classical period these colonists started an embryonic industrialization as they developed into craftsmen and traders and they became an important formative element in Athenian democracy.

It is to be supposed that from the beginning of the organization of towns and cities the Greeks, especially those of the Peloponnesian league and Sparta, were well aware of the consequences of developing sea trading. The landowners must have known about it too, solidly entrenched in the colonized territories, be they the ' barons ' of Thessaly, to whose strongholds the peasants brought the fruits of the earth, or the ' peers ' of Laconia who enjoyed the fruits of the labour of the Messenian helots and benefited from the vast network of the *perioeci*, or ' dwellers around ',

Greece was a country with particularly difficult internal communications. Roads, built with an eye to the strictest economy, were virtually tracks of beaten earth, often with very difficult gradient, and were too narrow to allow vehicles to pass except in the small open squares in towns. In the middle of the road ran two parallel ruts about three feet apart, and this became the standard width between wheels as vehicles were made to fit them. Opposite left: a typical Greek landscape at Delphi. Above: a Greek chariot-wheel from the Museum of Science and Technology, Milan. Below right: small model of a votive cart (Corinth Museum).

subject imposed by natural restrictions and human insufficiency. The errors of modern ideological and conceptual interpretations lie in the refusal to recognize these limitations.

It was a mountainous, roadless country, without plains, except in Thessaly, in which nature favoured, on the one hand the breeding of horses, and on the other the creation of serfs. The land was difficult to cultivate except in Boeotia, where the eels of Lake Copaides, whose waters have now been drained, prospered more than the wits of men. There were no mines, except those of the Attic district of Laurium which produced silver, and no quarries except those

citizens, that is, of the towns of Laconia, all of which paid tribute to Sparta.

Sparta, tenacious of its hegemony and anxious to secure a way of life commensurate with its leading position in Laconia, had no qualms in the early years over importing whatever it thought fit to develop its agrarian economy, to embellish its city and to educate its citizens. Thus, although Sparta never even achieved a craftsman-type industrial production and there were no means of exchange, it being forbidden to own or to import money (all trade being done by barter), there was nevertheless at the end of the sixth century B.C. some evidence of luxury and art such as might be associated with a successful economy. This was copied to some extent by Sparta's rivals, first by Corinth then by Aegina and by Athens whilst these belonged to the Peloponnesian league. Sparta first accepted this as inevitable but then retreated into her shell, protected by her military discipline and the efficiency of her victorious phalanxes of hoplites, and certain of immunity from dangers which in fact only began to touch her in the later years of the Peloponnesian War.

The problem which then overtook Sparta, and brought with it the danger of a revolution, was the complete lack of any *homo oeconomicus* within the confederation. The eventual rise of this class of administrator, especially if he had political gifts also, could not fail to undermine the stability of Lycurgus' regime and fan the flames of opposition, rebellion and conspiracy, as happened in the cases of Pausanias and Lysander, two Spartan commanders punished for intrigue and insubordination.

The same problem was generally avoided in the other cities, especially where there was a democratic regime and a long experience of sea-trading. Their difficulties were of another kind and arose from differences between economists and politicians with the frequent predominance of the former.

These differences arose out of the gradual development of economic institutions away from their mainly agricultural origins. Whereas closed societies, such as Sparta and its league, never even allowed the rise of a *homo oeconomicus*, the open societies of the maritime republics were forced to open up sea routes to survive and virtually had to create an economic organization.

A POOR ECONOMY

The constant paradox of Greek history and economy lies in its agricultural character, in the fact that wherever and whenever Greek society was democratic, it was always a land-owning democracy.

In the age of Pericles there were about 30,000 male adult citizens in Athens, and most of them were poor. They formed a homogeneous stratum of modest land-owning peasants who possessed, dreamt of possessing or still remembered that they once did possess, a house and a few acres which they cultivated alone or with the assistance or their wives and children. They may have had, in some cases, the help of slaves or free men. There were, however, no slaves in Socrates' house: he was the son of a craftsman and a craftsman himself, making statues and figurines in his father's workshop. It would seem that Sophroniscus, the father of Sophocles, did not make enough in his workshop to provide for his family and that his wife, Phaenarete had to take in washing, the only honest toil allowed to a free woman in Periclean Athens. Socrates also said that he derived much of his *maieutica* from his mother (the word, which means 'obstetrics', was used figuratively by Socrates in the sense of helping people to bring out ideas and concepts which were latent in their minds).

The house which the citizen-proprietor owned has been described elsewhere in this book. It was small, uncomfortable, built by an individual craftsman, generally of one storey and was virtually indistinguishable architecturally from that of any other citizen or peasant. The big town houses which began to be built in the first half of the fourth century always remained exceptions: even in 349 they were a subject of argument in Demosthenes' *Olynthiacs*. At cock-crow there was no time to turn over in bed or hang about the house: you had to be out in the streets, off to work in the countryside or to the *agora* to take part in politics, administration or judicial affairs.

And what did the countryside yield? Barley, in limited quantities, the food of slaves and women, and fruit, especially grapes and figs. It was traditionally believed that the latter were so essential to the diet of the Athenians that, although they were produced in copious quantities, it was forbidden to export them. Hence the origin of our word 'sycophant' which in

The sea was not only Athens's great communication route, but also an essential element of her economy. Fish was a main feature of her food and it was eaten fresh or preserved. Preserving fish allowed it to be sent to inland districts far from the sea. Above: *Roman copy of a Greek statue (Capitoline Museums, Rome).*

Greek meant ' one who informed against an exporter of figs '. Olives were produced for eating or for the extraction of their oil in a rudimentary press; there was an abundance of this celebrated oil which, incidentally, was the only oil or fat, edible or otherwise, known to the Greeks. Wine too was plentiful and for the sake of economy was never drunk undiluted. It was imported and exported throughout Greece. The mountain district of Hymettus east of Athens produced a famous bitter honey; this was the only sweet substance the Greeks are known to have used, although it is likely that they knew about sugar. There was

fresh fish in abundance, but the Athenians seem to have preferred it pickled; most pickled fish was imported and may possibly have been cheaper. In the more wooded areas of the countryside, such as the district of Acharnia at the foot of Mount Parnes north west of Athens, the peasants cut and burned wood to make charcoal. Where the land allowed of grazing there were sheep which provided milk and cheese and on special occasions the lambs were eaten. There was one essential thing missing which the soil of Attica did not produce and which therefore had to be imported: grain for bread.

Great expanses of olive trees everywhere: the olive was one of Attica's few riches. It was used as a food, or put through a rudimentary press to make oil. Greece was renowned for olive oil, the only oil or fat material known and used for every occasion, not only for cooking, but also for lighting the flickering lamps which burned in every Athenian house. Above: the olive groves of Arachora, between Delphi and the sea.

IMPORTS

'More than any other people, we use imported grain', said Demosthenes in many of his orations, but particularly in his 'On the Crown', in which he claimed for himself the merit of having frustrated the plots of Philip of Macedon against Byzantium, thus keeping open for Athens the grain route from the Black Sea. Grain imports were a necessity economically, politically and commercially. It was therefore essential that the supply routes should be kept open between Athens and the grain-producing countries. Over half the annual requirement of 800,000 *medimni* (well over a million bushels) came from the Black Sea. A merchant fleet and an active navy were therefore essential to her survival.

Official dry measures (for cereals, vegetables and so on). The smallest measure was the cotule. After the reforms of Solon four cotulai made a choenix, which was the common measure for a day's ration of cereal. The largest measure was a medimnos, or 48 choenix (1.4 bushels). Intermediate measures were the hemiecton and the hecteus. Athens imported every year 800,000 medimni of grain. (Agora Museum, Athens.)

The question of grain imports thus had important political, social, economic and strategic consequences and was a determining factor in the structure of the *polis*.

How did Athens pay for these 800,000 *medimni* of grain? How could she ensure their constant supply? There had to be friendly relations and commercial treaties with the producing countries, especially with those in Thrace, on the Bosphorus and the Hellespont. The fleet had to be kept up to the mark, both technically and in its men, and there had to be an efficient administration to ensure the proper unloading, storing, sale and contracting of imported grain, the payment of dues, both for passing through the Bosphorus and landing at the Piraeus, and the availability of sufficient moneys. Officials and magistrates had to be on the spot to settle immediately any arguments about the quality or the quantity of the loads and their prices and to secure the observance of any contracts or regulations in force.

Thus there derived from the necessity to import grain a whole politico-social structure, an entire programme of government and a succession of legal structures, of administrative procedures and of organizational processes covering military, financial and social affairs. This, in a nutshell, covers the whole history of Athens and explains the reasons, not to mention the moral urge, behind her resistance to Macedon whenever her trade routes were in danger,

real, suggested or imaginary. These routes could be used to bring wood from inland Vardar through the port of Amphipolis, or the many products of Thrace, which like Amphipolis was half peopled by Athenian colonialists, or imports from the Black Sea which Philip could have controlled, not only for his own profit but to suit his own politics once he had gained control of the Straits.

Eight hundred thousand *medimni* of grain to be imported every year and equitability distributed at a free price fair to all and requiring, at least in the lean years, to be controlled by an appropriate commission: this was the centre of the economy of classical Athens. From the figures of grain consumed it is possible to deduce the number of inhabitants and their economic conditions: the yearly average was seven and a half *medimni* (ten and a half bushels) for an adult male and about five (seven bushels) for women and children. Taking into account the need to feed the slaves (and this was usually with the remains of imported grain, local barley and inferior corn) this would give a population of 30,000 adult males, as many or slightly more females and about 60,000 children, 20,000 slaves and 10,000 resident foreigners, or metics. These figures agree roughly with the census statistics of the Macedonian viceroy Demeter of Phalerum, who governed Athens from 317 to 307, and of Antipater, Alexander's regent of Macedonia.

STATE REVENUE

If the State had to be in a position to acquire and to import 800,000 *medimni* of grain each year, the inhabitants of Attica on their part had to be in a position to earn their living. The State managed it by collecting revenue of various kinds from various sources. As all transactions were in cash there had to be sufficient ready money available and income and expenditure had to be kept in constant balance. As was explained in the chapter on political institutions, apart from revenue dependent on the political situation, such as levies paid by allied navies, the main sources of the State's income were excise and customs duties, taxes on the Laurian silver mines and on building, harbour dues from the Piraeus, obligatory taxes on foreign residents, contributions from wealthier citizens (virtually voluntary as there was no efficient system of proportional taxation), the confiscation and sale by auction of the property of convicted persons or insolvent debtors, and the collection of fines. Certain modern historians have claimed, with some exaggeration, that Greece's only nationalized industry was war, as this brought in booty, plunder, indemnities from the conquered enemy and an abundance of slaves to be sold on the home or the foreign market. It should be pointed out, however, that traffic in slaves in classical Athens was less than that resulting from the Roman conquest of the Hellenistic rulers and other Roman expeditions overseas.

The State of Athens was thus manifestly compelled to promote trade and to open its port to foreigners whom at the same time it could not allow to possess property. In the classical age only as a special concession or by special treaty was it ever possible to own property in a foreign country. The more foreigners there were living in the Piraeus, the more taxes were collected and the greater was the economic and commercial development of the city, as metics engaged almost exclusively in trade. The war effort of the State required a war industry with naval and land armaments to which the metics could not fail to contribute and from which in their turn they could not fail to profit. It was not by chance that the wealthiest foreigner resident in Athens, both during and after the age of Pericles until the terror of the Thirty Tyrants in 403 B.C., was the Syracusan Cephalus. He had an arms factory, which he handed over to his sons Lysias and Polemarcus, employing 120 workers, both free men and slaves. Similarly most of the wealth of Demosthenes (the father of the orator) came from a workshop built on to his house in which he employed more than thirty swordsmiths and cutlers.

MARITIME TRADE

It will not be surprising to learn that amongst the commoner and more profitable forms of investment was the financing of imports and exports. Risks were considerable, but the rate of interest was high: between 20 and 30 per cent. This gave rise to the most progressive innovations in the economic history of Athens and Greece in the fifth and fourth centuries

Official liquid measure. The smallest measure was a cuathos (about an eighth of a pint) and the largest a metretes (about eight and a half gallons). Intermediate measures were the cous and the hemicous with their subdivisions (Agora Museum, Athens).

B.C.: credit, the banking system, insurance, credit and cash transfers. The system developed without the intervention of the State, either restrictively or protectively, in the search for new markets and new products or for monopoly control.

The Athenian navy was something of a private concern in that the wealthier citizens had a duty to provide for the upkeep and the increase of the ships, the moneys they paid being considered in lieu of taxes. The ships remained under State control and were the effective property of the Republic, registered in its shipyards and subject to inspection by its politicians and legislators.

It was therefore an attractive position to individual citizens, to metics and noticeably even to slaves, to invest capital in maritime activities, both public and private, to give credit to shipbuilders and merchants and underwrite their various projects and plans. This was a business involving people from the most varied social classes.

The man who had the capital and was responsible for supplying the ship, taking upon himself all the risks and expenses and doing it all in the form of a gift in lieu of taxes, was completely dependent for the success or otherwise of his enterprise, and ultimately for his own solvency or insolvency, on the existence and the activities of the metic tradesman and the ordinary worker, who generally belonged to the lowest social class of the *thetes* and were exempt from both taxation and military service. The worker also would have found it difficult to make a living had he not been taken on as a member of the crew, or given work in the shipyard either to built the ship or to maintain it during the months when the sea was not navigable.

INVESTMENTS

An ex-slave named Pasion who became first a metic then an Athenian citizen in recompense for his generous services to the State as a banker, industrialist and landowner, rose to the highest position and wealth in the Athens of his day and left estate valued at seventy to eighty talents. He had given financial assistance to Timotheus, the victor of Samos in 365 B.C. and the son of Conon, and other contemporary Athenians who, because of the onerous nature of their office, were frequently short of ready cash, though they were men of considerable wealth. In cases such as this a credit was opened and the rate of interest was at least twelve per cent. In the rudimentary capitalist system of fourth century Athens there was virtually no arrangement for bank deposits or for a quick withdrawal of funds. This meant that substantial capital had to be kept tied up in the form of silverware, objects of luxury or artistic value, gold, jewellery, and so on, and this in spite of the lack of security in the house, of threats from extortioners and of thieves or agents sent, or at least tolerated, by the State to denounce tax evaders or lawbreakers in general. A man's patrimony, in a word, had to be such that it could easily be turned into cash, an operation in which brokers and money-changers took their profit and, from the middle of the fourth century, began to invest money themselves in loans to farmers, buying and selling land and property and negotiating mortgages, and so on.

The last, and most typical form of capital investment was that suggested to the moderate post-civil-war government of 355 B.C. by the Spartan sympathizer Xenophon in his little treatise on the *Poroi*: the

Series of official weights found during excavations in the Agora. Weights and measures were supervised by five magistrates in Athens and five in the Piraeus. In Athens the basic unit was a stater (a little over a pound and three quarters) which was marked with an astragal as an emblem. The subdivisions of the stater were stamped with shields, tortoises and so on (Agora Museum, Athens).

purchase or hiring-out of slaves (as mentioned in the chapter on the life of slaves and their employment) for the exploitation of the Laurian silver mines, traditionally worked on contract for a fixed annual amount by an entrepreneur or a financier. Now Xenophon proposed that the State should turn industrialist and itself exploit the mineral resources of the country, or eventually cede to others for a compensation not only the mineral wealth but also the labour force. There had already been an example in the previous century under that tragic idol of the moderates and of Thucydides, Nicias, the wealthy commander of the Athenian expedition to Sicily whose timidity and lack of resolution had been mainly responsible for the disaster of the Great Harbour (Syracuse) and the Assinarus (413 B.C.). Nicias, with his great wealth and his many slaves, was a precursor of the metic-demo-

cratic capitalism of the fourth century and an example which shows how citizens of any class were prepared to enter into economic and speculative activities. To maintain her existence Athens had to have an adequate and a stable economy, and at the same time develop a certain internal and external policy to give shape to her institutions and her society.

Once more, then, Athenian democracy was shown to be a necessity in that maritime trade in Athens required to be conducted by democratic means. The agrarian oligarchy could choose to ignore these until the end of the Persian wars, or at the most until immediately after the Peloponnesian War, but, as the example of Nicias showed, they well knew the advantage of turning to industrial enterprises, as it is unlikely that their capital would have survived the fatal consequences of the Spartan invasion of Attica and the blockade of Athens. When it became evident that any 'conditioning' of the city into an economic programme based on landed property would be impossible, because any such programme would not guarantee the material existence of the majority of the population, the moderate leaders of the restored democracy, such as Archinos and Trasibulos, saw that the future of the republic lay in renewed industrialization and economic expansion and not in a restoration of landed property.

In fact, either because they did not survive the Peloponnesian war or because the new men bent on a new expansionism and a new militarism were progressives and cultural and political technocrats (sophists, *logographoi*, teachers, leaders of mercenaries, and so on), the rich now found themselves reduced to a very small minority amongst the many citizens who took turns to control the State and to exercise political power; they were no longer able to organize themselves to defend their position or to develop economically their own interests. Yet they did not become the target for the hatreds, the appetites or the fears of a 'proletariat'. The small property owners and modest craftsmen in Athens were ignorant of the principles of trade union organization, and thought of the State either as an enemy to be overthrown or as a machine which should be made to work for their own advantage.

It is therefore untrue that the rich were narrow-minded conservatives. To this category of the wealthier citizens there belonged the successors of Pericles, mocked and detested by Aristophanes because, lacking blue blood, they engaged in profitable trade (Cleon the tanner, Lysicles the cattle-breeder, Hyperbolos the proprietor of a lamp factory), the men of the moderate faction such as Timotheus and Isocrates and those of the anti-Macedon faction such as Demosthenes, Hyperides, the aristocratic Lycurgus and their supporters and financial backers.

There was thus little solidarity of interests or of class between the so-called Three Hundred. These were the representatives of the 300 wealthiest families most frequently liable to be called upon to carry the financial burdens of peace and war, the patriotic and the religious liturgies, including the *trierarchia*, the special contributions, the ransoming of prisoners, and so on. Nor should it be thought that the rich, or only the rich, had a direct interest in non-resistance, in the appeasement of Philip and the eventual victory of Macedon. This was a policy which had the support of half of the popular classes, continually threatened by compulsory military service at their own expense (to be a captain of the hoplites now needed a capital outlay of no more than twenty minae). War brought the spectre of famine to those left at home, the fear of failure if the smallholding was left untended. The soldier's wretched pay and an eventual share of the booty were little compensation for virtually certain bankruptcy. This is why Demosthenes met with such extraordinary difficulties when he put forward a programme under which citizens were to contribute money and soldiers their own arms towards resistance against the Macedonians. These measures caused De-

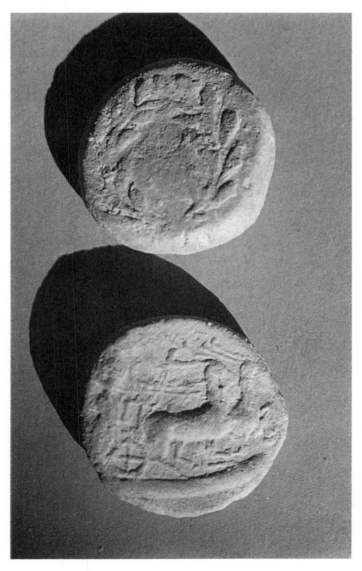

The monetary unit of the Greek world was the drachma. In Athens there were two- three- and ten-drachmae coins (didrachmon, tetradrachmon and dekadrachmon, respectively) and the commonest subdivision was the obol, or one sixth of a drachma. A hundred drachmae made a mina

mosthenes great trouble and could never be satisfactorily imposed.

PAUPERISM AND POVERTY

Pauperism was certainly widespread in Greece in the fourth century B.C. Very little of this was due to incipient industrialism and it occurred mainly in economically backward areas or predominantly agricultural parts of Greece rather than in Attica. It may have fed the armies with mercenaries and provided the backbone of the imperialist propaganda of Philip and Alexander of Macedon, who opened up the whole Persian Empire to the numerous Greek colonists and

eliminated the fear of unemployment, yet it never had more than the slightest effect on the social and political fortunes of Athens. The more socially developed and efficient Athenian democracy was, the more capable she showed herself of resisting the strength which Macedonia mobilized against her, often taming it and using it to her own advantage.

In Athens, 150 years after Demaratos and Herodotus, the problem was not pauperism but continuous poverty, a poverty which the State tried to mitigate with assistance to the war disabled, by giving away its budget surpluses, by ensuring that an adequate price was paid for labour, whether of free men or of slaves, and above all by payments to those who performed their civic duties and undertook public office.

and six thousand a talent. Towards the middle of the fifth century there were half-drachma and two-obol coins in circulation, amongst others. Most coins were stamped with the head of Athena and the owl. The owl on the deka-drachmon differed from the others in having its wings open. The Corinthian didrachmon had the head of Athena on the obverse, but on the reverse Pegasus, the winged horse. Opposite: coins of Darius found at Marathon. Above top: Athenian didrachmon; below: Corinthian didrachmon. (Museum of Numismatics, Athens.)

259

In spite of claims to the contrary by both ancient and modern authorities, it is not true (and statistics bear this out) that this modest relief was sufficient of itself to provide a livelihood and bred an indifference to work in the middle and lower classes, thus increasing the need for and the risk of slave labour.

Athens had a substantially stable economy and a substantially equal society.

Poverty, work, a progressive levelling-out of society, deprecated during the war against Archidamus of Sparta by the anti-democratic author of the pseudo-Xenophon treatise on the Athenian constitution, brought together free men, slaves and metics. All of them worked together for their own profit, against the background of the Periclean temples on the Acropolis, on an arid soil and amidst chronic poverty.

Lead weights hung by wires (Agora Museum, Athens).

The words of Herodotus on poverty in Greece, on the antithesis, or the correlation, between poverty and virtue, may rise like a symbol half way through the history of the Peninsula, between the stern warning of the archaic Boeotian poet who said 'the only idleness is shame' and the magnanimous proposal of the orator Hyperides, the day after the Macedonian victory at Chaeronea, to grant Athenian slaves their liberty. The freeing of the slaves had held off the verdict of the fates with the victory of the Arginusae islands (406 B.C.), and it might be held that Athenian society and its government were now historically justified and that the last battle which Athens lost was in a sense a democratic, libertarian vindication of its policies.

EARNINGS

To give a clearer idea of the economic and financial situation of fourth-century Athens and of how greatly it differed from the economic realities of today we have availed ourselves of certain statistical data collected by H. M. Jones.

After the revolt against Macedonia which ended in defeat for Athens at Lamia in Thessaly in 322, the

Left: *goldsmith's anvil and small hammer (Olympia Museum)*. Above: *hammer and mallet (Benaki Museum)*.

Macedonian regent Antipater imposed on Athens a constitution based on a franchise of twenty minae (or 2,000 drachmae). According to the Sicilian historian Diodorus Siculus (*fl.* 40 B.C.) who quoted Hieronymus of Cardia (third century B.C.), this restricted the rights of citizenship to 9,000 adult males and deprived of these rights some 12,000 who had been recognized as full citizens during the liberal democratic regime.

How much was twenty minae, and what would it buy? What did it cost to keep house? How much did a salaried worker earn? Land cost 360 drachmae (or over three and a half minae) an acre. The *ephebi* were paid four obols (two thirds of a drachma) a day merely for their keep, whilst in the same years of Macedonian domination, from Chaeronea (338 B.C.) to Lamia (322) a skilled worker earned between two and two and a half drachmae a day and an unskilled worker one and a half drachmae. At the end of the fifth century, before prices went up and wages followed suit, a woollen cape cost twenty drachmae and a pair of shoes eight. It is not surprising therefore that Socrates went about barefoot, though some of his wealthier and more refined pupils such as Alcibiades took this as a confirmation of his eccentricity. To keep a family of three children, two girls and a boy, a manservant and a maidservant cost one client of

Lysias 1,000 drachmae a year. In 363 Demosthenes calculated that it cost him about 700 drachmae a year to keep himself, his mother, and his sister whilst they were under his care.

In both these cases there were more females than males in the household, and women consumed five *medimni* of grain a year as opposed to a man's seven and a half. On the other hand, Lysias' famous disabled soldier who fought hard for his State pension of one obol a day (raised to two during the fourth century) could not possibly live on it, but used it to eke out his modest earnings from a small business or from casual labour.

Jones shows that the moneys paid for civic duties could not and were not intended to be considered as a salary or the equivalent of a salary, but merely as a reimbursement of expenses. The members (drawn by lot) of the Council of Five Hundred, which no one could belong to for longer than two years in his lifetime, received five obols a day (about half the average earnings of a workman), which would explain why there was in the Council a preponderance of influential and relatively wealthy men with a real passion for politics, whose interest lay in party issues rather than in any monetary gain. The 350 magistrates were paid in the same way as the members of the

As far as technology was concerned, Greek metallurgy was no further advanced than that of other Mediterranean countries. Some metalwork, particularly in bronze, reached a high artistic level, though by traditional methods: chill casting by the cire perdue *method (in which a wax model was made, coated with clay and baked; the wax ran away leaving a hollow mould), pressing in a fireproof mould and the making of reliefs. Opposite: some particularly beautiful bronzes: a satyr, a lamp, a lamp-holder and a votive statue. On this page, bottom: a bronze relief; top: a mould for projectiles used in slings (Kannellopoulos Collection, Athens).*

Council; although many of them were of modest means only, they made no complaint about serving on the Boule, or perhaps did not dare to. Jury members collected three obols (half a drachma) a day, as much as the State allowed for a day's food for the slaves hired in Eleusis, but these were also clothed and housed free. In the comedies of Aristophanes and in anti-democratic propaganda in general, members of a jury were always made out to be greedy for power, gluttonous and ever eager to condemn the accused so that his patrimony could be confiscated and divided out amongst them: it should be pointed out, however, that the fruits of the confiscation were shared not only amongst the members of the jury but amongst all the citizens of the republic. Finally, anyone taking part in the ordinary debates of the Assembly was paid a drachma and a half. Here again, the very modest sums paid out compared with what a worker or an agricultural labourer received shows that this was intended not as a salary but as a kind of payment of expenses.

Jones comes to the reasoned and convincing conclusion that 12,000 out of the 21,000 Athenian citizens (about sixty per cent of the entire population) 'earned their living on smallholdings of not more than five acres, as qualified craftsmen or shopkeepers, assisted by not more than five servants, or as day-labourers '.

In confirmation of a thesis both aptly maintained and convincingly demonstrated, Jones adds that ' even the richest of the Athenians were persons of comparatively modest means '. This is borne out by the following statement of Demosthenes senior's liabilities and assets at the time of his death, compiled from figures given in speeches by his son against the dishonest trustees.

PERSONAL PROPERTY AND POSSESSIONS OF DEMOSTHENES SENIOR

I) *Items bringing in a profit*

1) Two workshops
   a) with 20 carpenter-joiners engaged under guarantee of a loan of 3,000 drachmae — 4,000 dr.
   b) with 32 or 33 cutlers and swordsmiths valued at 500 to 600 drachmae each — 19,000 dr.
2) about 6,000 drachmae invested at 12 per cent giving a net yield of over 700 drachmae a year — 6,000 dr.

Total income-yielding patrimony of Demosthenes senior — 29,000 dr.

II) *Items which do not bring in a profit*

1) a house (dwelling for family and workers) — 3,000 dr.
2) iron, ivory and furniture bought for — 8,000 dr.
   gall-nut and bronze bought for — 7,000 dr.
3) cellar — 8,000 dr.
4) furnishings, silverware, jewels, clothing — 10,000 dr.

Total patrimony which does not bring in an income, that is, the house and its annexes — 36,000 dr.

III) *Investments*

1) with the banker Pilas — 600 dr.
2) credit with Xutos for maritime transactions — 7,000 dr.
3) with the banker Pasion — 2,400 dr.
4) loan to Demomeles — 1,600 dr.
5) miscellaneous (credits with various persons, each of 200-300 drachmae) — 6,000 dr.

Total investments — 17,600 dr.

Total patrimony of Demosthenes senior — 82,600 dr.
   or 13 talents, 46 minae (one talent equals 60 minae or 6,000 drachmae).

SHIPS, PORTS AND SEA ROUTES

Athens was at one and the same time a city, a stretch of countryside and a port. The city and the Piraeus, in fact, joined by the famous three ' long walls' which cut them off from the rest of Attica, formed an organic whole and were virtually an island open on to the sea. Attica was arid, harsh, impenetrable: its internal communications were extremely difficult, consisting of rare, irregular tracks with impossibly steep slopes over which carts could be dragged only at the cost of great labour, taking an enormous length of time to cover short distances. Athens was able to communicate easily with the rest of the world only by her fleet.

The squat ships with their many-coloured square sails voyaged incessantly over the sea routes to the Black Sea, Egypt and Sicily to supply Athens with the grain she needed, and to carry almost everywhere on the shores of the Mediterranean the oil, wine and craftwork of Attica. The Piraeus was not only the busy centre of this traffic, but the driving and the organizing force behind it all. Here Athenians and foreigners lived in substantial agreement, united in purpose, and here Athenian democracy, especially in the time of Pericles, showed its maturity in its enlightened policy towards foreign residents.

It was significant that during the years of the reactionary tyranny of the Thirty the Piraeus, traditionally a free refuge for many different peoples, should become the stronghold of rebellion.

The little land of Attica was soon unable to feed its population, lacking as it did fertile plains for growing cereals, the basis of food in ancient times. On the other hand it produced considerable quantities of goods for which there was some demand: oil, wine and honey. Athens thus came to build up her international trade on the importing of cereals and the exporting of oil and wine, to which was added, especially when the city grew prosperous in the fifth century B.C., the importing of luxury goods and the exporting of useful and artistic products such as pottery (for which Athens had become the prime producer in the sixth century, soon overtaking Corinth). In the ancient world the sea was the natural trade route, especially for Greece where the difficult nature of the terrain was compensated for by the presence everywhere of the sea. Attica soon became a seafaring country and by the fifth century the Piraeus was the greatest commercial port in the Aegean.

The principal merchant vessel in Athens, and in Greece in general, was the ' round' or ' hollow' ship, the trireme, or polyreme, of the navy. The method of construction, however, was similar for all ships; they were usually made of red pine, though some were made of spruce, cypress, elm, ash or sycamore and sealed with oakum, wax, pitch or red lead (the greatest producer of the latter being the island of Chios, and Athens soon acquired the monopoly). The shape and the technical characteristics varied considerably. Warships were required to be fast moving, easy to handle, strong enough to withstand frontal attack and independent of the vagaries of the winds. The ' long' ships therefore had a length to breadth ratio of about seven to one; they were armed with a spur for ramming and were driven by oars, the sail being used only as an auxiliary to lighten the work of the rowers, and never in battle.

34.

Detail of a model of the Piraeus shipyards. The keels were laid with trunks of cypress, larch or red pine, connected horizontally with deep joints. On to this were built the ribs of the hull, then the deck planking (The Piraeus Naval Museum).

These 'long' ships must have had a very shallow draught as they could be drawn up on any beach for the night. The merchant ships, on the other hand, served quite a different purpose: they had to be very stable and capable of carrying loads, and speed and manoeuvrability were of secondary importance. Sea routes for merchant ships were fixed, in contrast to those of warships, and the question of mobility was different. The merchant vessel was 'round', with a length to breadth ratio of only four to one, much heavier and with a deeper draught. The stern and the bows were simple and roughly shaped and did not have the characteristic design of warships.

Oars were used only in cases of emergency and for manoeuvring in port. Normally merchant ships were driven by sail.

For a long time the 'round' ship had one mast and a square sail. Towards the end of the classical period a second smaller yard was added. On merchant ships the mast was fixed, whereas on warships it could be dismantled in combat, a cumbersome and often highly dangerous arrangement as it was liable to be knocked down by collision.

Greek merchant ships had a large square sail, which was generally coloured and scarcely ever white, and the sailors decorated it in various ways with festoons or pennants made of animal skins.

In the classical age the displacement of a merchant ship varied from thirty to a hundred tons, the average being around sixty. The small or relatively shallow draught was obviously aimed at a greater loading potential. It is admittedly difficult for us to know the technical characteristics of Greek merchant ships. There is little information available, and what there is is not easy to interpret. We therefore have to try to reconstruct data from indirect sources on which scholars are not always agreed. We also know very little about the period before the fifth or the fourth centuries. For example Hieron II of Syracuse (269-216 B.C.) had a great ship called the *Syracusia* built in 240 to carry grain. It could take 1,000 tons of cargo and was also used for pleasure cruises. This must have been an exception even in that age, and ships of this size were unheard of in the earlier classical period, when most vessels were of 70-80 tons, and later, in the Hellenistic period, little more than 130 tons. There were occasionally ships of as much as 250 tons, but these were not common.

The speed of these vessels was about three or four knots and they would cover some ninety miles in

Model of a monoreme cargo vessel. Merchant ships had a fixed mast and were propelled by one or two banks of oars. The rudder usually consisted of two long-bladed oars fixed to the stern. Cruising speed was three to four knots (The Piraeus Naval Museum).

twenty-four hours. In favourable weather conditions a merchant ship would take seven or eight days by the most direct route from the Piraeus to Naucratis on the Nile delta.

THE PROTECTION OF TRAFFIC: CONVOYS

The Athenian mercantile marine was not very different from all those which have sailed the waters of the Mediterranean up to the present day. It was always sufficient to carry the cargoes required at the time; under the protection of the great navies, convoys from Athens came home from distant shores with their precious cargoes of grain or luxury goods and left again loaded with pottery, oil and wine. We have some idea of the size of these convoys from the destruction of the Athenian fleet by the Spartan general Lysander (d. 395 B.C.) in the battle of Aegospotami in 404, when he intercepted and captured a convoy of merchant vessels carrying grain from the Black Sea to Athens: there were 170 ships.

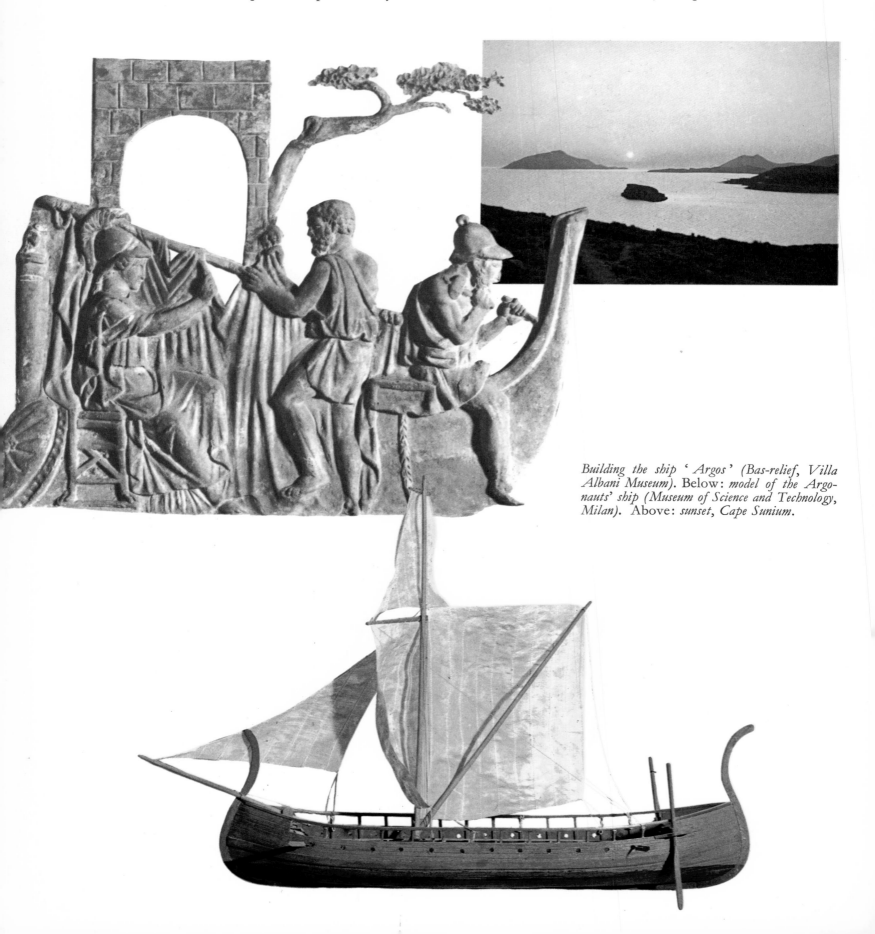

Building the ship ' Argos ' (Bas-relief, Villa Albani Museum). Below: *model of the Argonauts' ship (Museum of Science and Technology, Milan).* Above: *sunset, Cape Sunium.*

This was no exception, even though Athens was reduced to extremes at this historic moment and had to resort to massive protection of her grain fleets from the Black Sea area. There was a similar example in 340 when Philip II of Macedonia was operating in the straits of the Bosphorus, in spite of his naval inferiority. Just before the outbreak of war, or during the very first days of the conflict, profiting from the temporary absence of the supreme commander of the *Hieron Teichos*, he took by surprise at the entrance to the Bosphorus some 230 merchant ships all loaded with grain, timber, victuals and other war material.

Philip sorted out and confiscated the cargo he wanted and set free fifty of the 230 ships he had captured, still with their cargo aboard. These must clearly have belonged to cities with which he was not at war. Many cities would take advantage of the superiority of Athens to protect their merchant fleets even though they did not always support her policies. There was thus a kind of implicit distinction, which was generally well observed, between political and economic matters and the activities of the merchant fleets and the navies were often quite distinct. Apart from certain specific cases of intimidation or retaliation, naval blockades with their consequential harm to the civilian population were not practised in ancient Greece. Nor was there any limitation or prohibition of imports between one *polis* and another, except for certain monopoly goods and in the grain trade, although even here such prohibitions as there were affected the exportation and the re-exportation of foreign grain rather than 'Attic' grain itself.

Naval protection, especially Athenian, of merchant fleets, and in particular those sailing from the Pontus Euxinus (Black Sea) through the Bosphorus, where a heavy toll was imposed by the Byzantians (the ancestors of the present inhabitants of Constantinople or Istanbul), was clearly a very necessary precaution as it was very difficult to police the seas. Athens did her task well in this respect during the two centuries of her hegemony in the Aegean, but the convoys were subject to frequent raids by pirates both from the European coasts of Thracia and the Anatolian coasts of Cilicia.

The pirates boarded the captured ship, confiscated it and sold, or attempted to sell, the passengers into slavery.

The risk of piracy, either tolerated or openly encouraged by the enemies of Athens, explains the difficulties of navigation, the large profit margins required and the high insurance rates charged by the shipbuilders and the entrepreneurs.

THE PORT AND ITS ECONOMIC LIFE

Athens, unlike any other Greek city, was able to deal with the problems of its ports as a whole. It was soon able to establish the Piraeus and Phalerum as two naval roads with easy communications with Euboia, Thessaly, Macedonia, Thracian Chersonese and the straits of the Hellespont. The Piraeus became the more important of the two at the beginning of the fourth century and was from then on the principal port of Athens.

The town of Piraeus, built towards the middle of the fifth century, stood on the peninsula (*Akte*) surrounded by fortifications and linked to Athens by the famous three 'long walls' built first by Themistocles and then by Pericles. It was built on a chequerboard plan and opened on to three ports: that of the Piraeus itself, which had a naval and a mercantile sector, and the two naval ports of Zea and Munychia. The shipyards were built by Pericles at a cost of 1,000 talents and were rebuilt, enlarged and modernized, after Lysander, by the restored democratic government. The work went on for the whole quarter century of this government and gave the yards a capacity of 400 ships. The Piraeus was made the location for the arsenals, the warehouses, the customs offices, the money-changers and the merchandise market. Ships from all over the Mediterranean came to unload their cargoes, and it was here that all kinds of goods were handled and distributed.

The organizer or director of maritime trade was called an *emporos*, and the market or the building on the Piraeus where the trade was carried on was known as the *emporion* (hence our 'emporium'). Here the merchandise was exhibited for sale and it would include both imports into Attica and exports from Attica (agricultural and, mostly, industrial) to places throughout the Greek world as far as the Black Sea and Scythia (the coasts of the Sea of Azov and Southern Russia) as well as to the Nile delta and Cyrenaica. The goods were displayed and sold in warehouses known as *deigmata* and were provisionally exempt from duties. As soon as they were taken out of the *deigmata*, however, they were subject to a two per cent tax (the so-called *pentekoste* or one-fiftieth) whether they were for import into Attica or for export, directly or indirectly, from the Piraeus.

Much use was made of the free port as a weapon of policy especially by the Romans who abolished all duties on the islands of Delos, where there was a Roman settlement (166 B.C.), to counter competition from Athens at a time when that city was following a policy displeasing to the Senate. The importance of the *pentekoste* and the threat from a free port can be judged from the simple fact that the two per cent duty brought in an average annual income of 30-36 talents to Athens, which means that the annual turnover in the port of the Piraeus was in the region of 1,500-1,800 talents. In classical times a family with a capital of one talent was considered rich.

Amphorae and jars were used to hold a wide variety of things: oil, wine, vegetables and cereals.

THE PEOPLE OF THE PIRAEUS

The Piraeus was thus a great seaport and a meeting place for foreigners of all nations, speaking all languages. It swarmed with inns, gaming dens and brothels. Its inhabitants lived almost entirely on the activities of the navy, the merchants and the shipyards.

The shortcomings of other ports favoured the development of the Piraeus and the growth of Athenian production and trade, attracting more foreigners to the port. These, with their different habits and customs, together with the native Greek merchants, soon began to form a distinctive community in Periclean society and a symbol of the liberty and the liberality of the metropolis. There arose, in fact, a separate class of self-sufficient foreigners domiciled, some of them for generation after generation, in the Piraeus. The very strict laws governing citizenship did not allow, except in the most exceptional circumstances and for outstanding merit (as in the case of Lysias), the descendants of foreigners to be admitted from the class of metics to that of citizens.

Although they existed on the fringe of political life and could not officially work for the State or hold any public office, the metics, or at any rate the wealthier among them, achieved high positions in society thanks to their intensive mercantile activities in the Piraeus.

The case of the family of the Syracusan arms manufacturer Cephalus in certainly not an isolated one. He himself enjoyed the friendship of Pericles, and Plato, although not caring much for the eloquence or the style of Cephalus' son Lysias the orator (see Plato's *Phaedrus*), nevertheless put him and his brothers, with Socrates, into his *Republic*, which is set in the house of Cephalus in the Piraeus. At the beginning of the *Republic* Socrates says that he came down to the Piraeus the previous evening with his young friends not especially to converse with Cephalus but to take part in the festivals of the Thracian goddess Bendis. These were spectacular and consisted of rituals, races and torchlight processions.

There were cults and temples of foreign deities in the Piraeus (Thracian, Phoenician and so on), brought into the area by the various foreign communities which had settled in the port, or perhaps officially introduced by the Athenian republic to encourage the

immigration of metics. This liberality was the only example of its kind throughout Greece and may be taken as symbolical of Athens.

Finally, as a proof of the close link between democracy and the sea-faring life in Athens, the Piraeus became the focus of resistance to oppression, and it was from here that Thrasybulus set out in 403 with his exiled companions to liberate Athens from the Thirty Tyrants.

If the Piraeus was, as has been aptly remarked, the lung of the city, then the warehouses in the port were its capacious stomach. Athenian merchant ships sailed from early spring to late autumn, supplying Attica with cereals and carrying away the products of its craftsmen. Above: model of a warehouse showing the outside and (below) a section (The Piraeus Naval Museum).

SHIPOWNERS AND CONTRACTORS

The difficulties of navigation and the relative insecurity of sea voyages owing to storms, piracy, inadequate navigational instruments and lack of any weather forecasts, hindered the development of sea trading and enormously raised its cost. The burden fell on those who fitted out the vessels, either as owners or as contractors with a share in the profits of the undertaking, though a contractor could be granted exemption from sharing also in the risks.

The technical term *naukleros*, originally meaning only 'ship's master', soon came also to indicate the so-called *fortegos*, or the man responsible for transporting the cargo, and the captain and charterer who could be, but was not necessarily, the *fortegos* to whom the owner entrusted the merchandise for shipment and handing over at its port of arrival. The *fortegos* could have a share in the profits if he had also shared the cost of chartering the ship.

The largest Greek merchant ships usually had two anchors, the subsidiary one being fixed in the stern (The Piraeus Naval Museum).

In general, however, the trasporting of the cargo, which was strictly the duty of the *fortegos*, gradually became the responsibility of the owner-captain or the owner and the captain jointly, each taking an equal share of the profits and the risks of loss or damage to the cargo, half of any eventual loss always being the sole liability of the owner.

Charting costs affected the price of goods and therefore the profits. Athens, for example, soon acquired a monopoly in red lead which could only be shipped to the Piraeus in Athenian vessels or in vessels expressly authorized by the Athenian government. Charting costs ran out at one obol per talent (58 lbs) and then there would be the two per cent duty. It cost Timotheus 1,750 drachmae to have a load of timber, given to him by Aminta III of Macedonia, sent by ship to the Piraeus and he had to borrow the money from the greatest banker and business man in Athens at the time, Pasion. For the same high level of taxes, the profits were proportionate to the risks. Lucian mentions the owners of a large merchant vessel of the second century A.D. who made an annual profit of not less than twelve talents.

Transporting passengers, on the other hand, was fairly cheap, as there was no system of life or accident insurance. A passage from Egypt or from the Black Sea to the Piraeus, or vice-versa, does not seem to have cost more than two drachmae for a family and its luggage. This would not, or course, include meals and there was little cabin accommodation on board, what there was being reserved exclusively for the crew. Ships did not normally sail at night and passengers would sleep in ports or on the open beach.

The risks of sea trading and the uncertainty of making a profit on cargoes led at the end of the fifth century to a system of export credit called the *nautikon* which gave cover of up to thirty per cent of the combined value of the ship and its cargo. Credit was granted against a kind of insurance policy under which the creditor covered himself up to half for any loss of the money lent or, if this were part of the agreement, for any loss of profit if the goods were damaged in transit or failed to reach their destination. He was not, of course, able to claim against the ship's sinking or the total loss of the cargo.

As well as being at the heart of Athenian trade, the Piraeus was also the city's shipyard. Timber arrived here from Thrace (it was scarce in Attica) and from

PRINCIPAL GREEK TRADING AREAS
AND SUPPLY ROUTES FOR GRAIN TO ATHENS

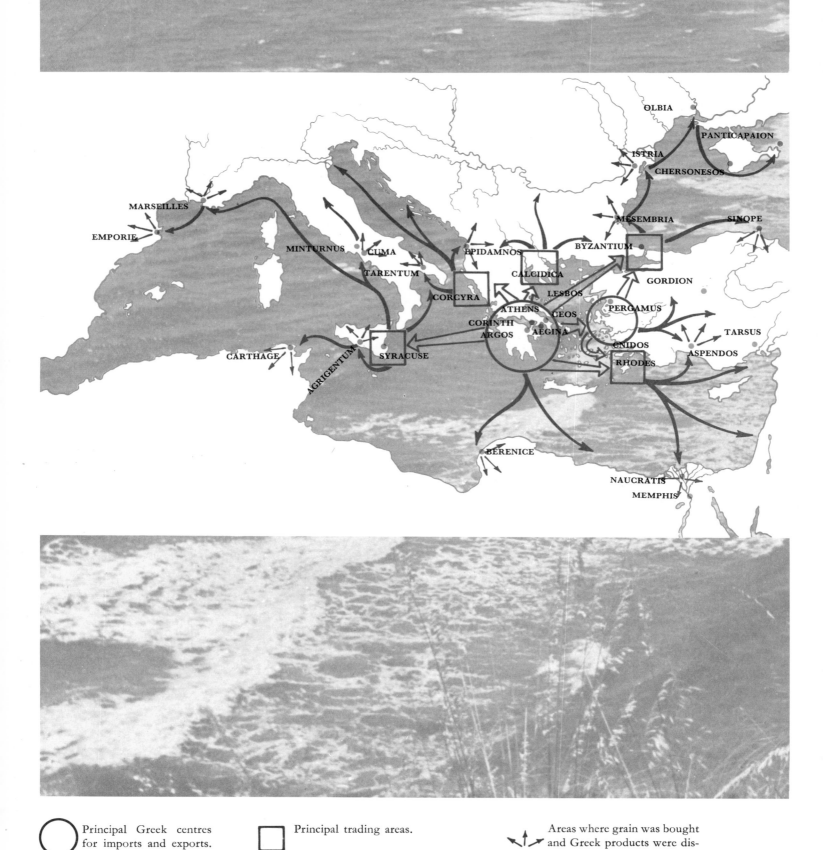

OLBIA

PANTICAPAION

ISTRIA

CHERSONESOS

MESEMBRIA

SINOPE

MARSEILLES

BYZANTIUM

EMPORIE

MINTURNUS

CUMA

EPIDAMNOS

GORDION

TARENTUM

CALCIDICA

CORCYRA

LESBOS

ATHENS

CEOS

PERGAMUS

TARSUS

CORINTH

ARGOS

AEGINA

CARTHAGE

AGRIGENTUM

SYRACUSE

CNIDOS

ASPENDOS

RHODES

BERENICE

NAUCRATIS

MEMPHIS

⭕ Principal Greek centres for imports and exports. ⬜ Principal trading areas. ↖↙↗ Areas where grain was bought and Greek products were distributed.

other areas, to be used by the hordes of carpenters for building new vessels and repairing old ones. The Piraeus and Athens together, isolated from the rest of Attica by the Long Walls, were a kind of island open on to the sea.

When Lysander blockaded the port of the Piraeus in 404 the clumsy merchant ships of Athens were either stranded in harbour, or at sea and could not get in. Although she had put up with a land siege for many years, the blockade forced her to capitulate out of hunger.

SEA ROUTES

Where did Athenian merchant vessels sail to and where did they return from? There were three principal sea routes for trading in the Mediterranean and all of them followed the coasts. One went to the north east; Thrace, the Bosphorus, the Black Sea, the Crimea and the Propontis (the sea of Marmara); another to the south and the south east, Egypt and Cyrene especially; the third to the west: Sicily and Italy and ports of call in Spain, Gaul (Marseilles) and Africa. These were all grain routes from the Scythian shores of the Black Sea, Egypt and Sicily. The two great naval expeditions which Athens undertook in the fifth century, one to Egypt and the other to Sicily, were both intended, amongst other things, to strengthen relationships with the grain-supplying countries, which also took craft products from Athens. Athens was always sensitive to the Northern Aegean, the Straits of the Bosphorus and the coast of Thrace with its offshore islands, as these lay on the route from the Black Sea, a trading area for Athens since pre-classical times before Egypt and Sicily.

A critic of Athenian democracy, who could not be unaware of the great advantages of sea power, wrote towards the end of the fifth century: 'The principal cities of the continent can manage to survive only after the greatest sacrifices of the crops sent to them by Jove, whereas those cities which have dominion over the sea have a better life. Not all the region is a victim of misfortune and those parts which have had an abundant harvest send their products to those which can trade by sea. And if we wish to speak of less important things, we can also say that sea power and trading with many nations has brought products of great refinement and the greatest delights to be found in Sicily, Italy, Cyprus, Egypt, the Pontus, the Peloponnese and elsewhere. Moreover, listening to all the varied tongues, these trading cities have taken habits and customs from everywhere, so that only the true Spartans speak, live and dress in their own characteristic way, the Athenians now speaking a tongue contaminated by the languages of other Greeks and barbarian peoples '.

There was thus a clear realization, even though in this case it was a critical one, of the importance to Athens of sea power and the great merchant fleet. These brought her not only the possibility of survival and a higher standard of living than that of other Greek cities, but also close contacts with other peoples which enriched her religion and her civilization. The critic of the democracy and of the great sea trade of Athens did not take into account the reverse of the process, which was that the heavy merchant vessels which set out from the Piraeus took out all over the Mediterranean world the flower of civilization as expressed in that golden age of the city of Pericles.

THE GOLDEN AGE OF ATHENIAN ART

Just as the age of Pericles was the period of the greatest splendour in Athens, so the Parthenon was at one and the same time a point of arrival and a point of departure not only for Attic art but for the art of all Greece. The experience of the previous centuries in the moulding of forms and the balancing of masses culminated in the supreme harmony of this building, which pointed the way for all the successors of Phidias, the greatest Athenian artist of the time.

For over twenty centuries the Parthenon was admired ' as intact and as little injured by the passing of time as if it had only just been built ', as the ambassador of Louis XIII of France, Louis des Hayes wrote in 1630, until that fatal day when the Turks' gunpowder exploded inside it during the siege of 1687. The patient labour of Greek and foreign archaeologists has restored the scattered marble of the Acropolis and strengthened that which was left standing, so that once more it is the centre from which radiates the Hellenic spirit, the symbol of the supremacy of the logos: « There is one place where perfection exists, not two, and that one place is here... It was the Ideal materialized in the marble from Mount Pentelicus that I was being shown » (Renan, ' Prayer on the Acropolis ').

The ' Hellenic miracle ' achieved the height of its artistic expression, the goal to which it had been led by the tentative experiments and touching uncertainties of the archaic period, in Athens in the age which has taken the name of its most inspired political leader, Pericles.

This is certainly the great period of Classical Greek art when, fully aware of human anatomy, it found a perfect balance between form and content, between rationality and inner feeling, and its artists strove to capture all the elements of the surrounding world in their purest essence, looking at them with a clearer eye and expressing their movement in a style free from the restrictions of convention. It was an art which has been called the most realistic of antiquity, but it has equally justifiably been called the most idealistic by someone who is considered to have been the father of archaeology, and could more rightly be considered to have formulated the first of

the ephemeral theories of ancient art, Johann Joachim Winckelmann (1717-68). The artist in the Periclean age struck a balance between intuition and reason, though he was fully aware of nature's many manifestations, and reproduced the ' ideal ' image, excluding the accidental, the transitory, the casual and the decaying. It was the age of Plato's youth, and, as the philosopher was to say later, the artist saw in his earthbound imagery the reflection of the divine world of ideas. Plato too knew about moderating the expression of one's sentiments by what he called *metron*, an essential of the *kalokagathon*, or the ethic ideal, which is also the aesthetic ideal, so that the harmony of forms achieved by nature shall not be upset by the disorder of doubt, pain or anguish. Only inferior beings express their feelings violently, and when Phidias designed the Parthenon metopes he gave violent expression to such animal-like figures as the centaurs.

Yet is it true to say that with the explosion of full Classical art, which covered not the whole fifth century but only the age of Pericles, there was a sudden and complete break with the past and the traditions of Archaic art which the Greeks of our age consider to have been the mere fumblings of adolescents and despicably primitive? Shall we have to return — contrary to all modern aesthetic theory — to the neo-classic critics who saw in classicism the final perfection of ancient art, the peak of its expression, before which there were only anxious searchings and after which there could be nothing but decadence? Must we really believe that artists in the pre-classical era never ceased to be painfully aware of the shortcomings of their work and of the great gap which separated them from the goal for which they strove so fruitlessly? And at what precise moment must we place this peak of expression, this achievement of the keenest realism in the representation of nature? We shall see that in sculpture this does not coincide with the summit of classicism. In painting we find artists striving for three-dimensional representation from the late sixth century with ceramists such as Euthymides. In the mid fifth century these attempts were carried a stage further by Polygnotus of Thasos who, to give an illusion of space, arranged the figures in a circle, introduced curved lines to give an idea of landscape, and broke with the ancient tradition of using flat colours. Other Athenian artists who also worked along these lines were Mikon, who collaborated with Polygnotus in a 'Battle with the Amazons' and a 'Battle with the Centaurs' in the Theseum in Athens, and Panainus, the brother of Phidias. In the second half of the fifth century the representation of space was also encouraged by attempts at scene-painting in the theatre. Yet the achievement of real spatial depth, with figures in different planes in accordance with an accurate mathematical perspective, had to wait until after the Classical age and even after the Hellenistic period until the art of Imperial Rome. It is therefore impossible to select any one moment at which the artists might have felt that he had reached the height of perfection and that his art had come to a stop. Every artistic creation has value in itself according to the way it expresses the artist's intuition and re-creates his vision in the mind of the beholder, regardless of the state of evolution of the artist's technique and the state of his knowledge of the object he is representing. One may thus legitimately feel the greatest admiration and the strongest affinity for the ingenuousness, the immediacy and the freshness of a work of art from the Archaic period, or for the inner pathos of those of the second Classical age from the beginning of the fourth century to the age of Alexander. For the origins of the high Classical style we must consider certain works produced before the mid fifth century.

SOME PRECURSORS OF CLASSICISM

Shortly after the First World War there came to light from the sea bed near Cape Artemisium on the northern tip of Euboia one of the few original large bronzes which have survived from ancient Greece. It was amongst the booty being transhipped to Rome and was a statue, probably of the god Poseidon (Neptune) hurling his trident to placate the fury of the storm. The might of the god is shown merely in the stance of the perfect human body, balanced, vigorous and full of vitality, expressing in this alone his dominion over the elements. There is nothing in this representation of the human body, which reveals a complete mastery of anatomic detail, of the rhythm of movement and of the way the skin reveals the bone structure underneath, which could not be said to obey the strictest canons of Classical art. Yet there are some almost imperceptible details which show that this statue was made in an early period. One of these was the *krobylos*, or the way of dressing the hair with a short plait at the back of the neck. Although this and other similar details were to appear in later art it is only shown on old men on the Parthenon frieze, which dates this statue to the period when Phidias was only just beginning and it has, in fact, sometimes been attributed to Calamides, considered to have been a precursor of the manner of Phidias.

If we go back to the end of the Archaic period we find that during the reign of the tyrant Pisistratus and his sons early Attic art was subjected to a wave of foreign influences. The tyrants, as part of a far-seeing political programme, had proposed the embellishment of their city and had encouraged the erection of sumptuous buildings. For the refinement of their court life they had attracted artists from the Aegean islands and from Ionia, and they had introduced a

The colossal statue of the god Poseidon hurling his trident to placate the storm is thought by some scholars to be the work of Calamis, the supposed teacher of Phidias. It was found in the sea, amongst the wreckage of a ship near Cape Artemesius (National Archaeological Museum, Athens).

new style of dress. It was thus the mid sixth century, the period of the Pisistratids, which saw the importation of Ionic art and left the many graceful *korai* on the Acropolis. These were statues of maidens pictured as making offerings to the deity, Athena. Their pose was affected, they wore a thin Ionic *chiton* of linen and over their shoulders a *himation*, one edge of which was almost invariably held up to give a striking interplay of crossed folds and complexity of surfaces, concealing the structure of the body and the proportion of the limbs. The portrayal of the face shows none of the ancient Attic austerity, the features being modelled with a tenderness typical of the Asiatic Greek school, the glowing skin seems to be shaded here and there, the cranium is excessively long under the thick mass of hair in stylized waves, the eyes look askance and the extremities of the mouth are turned down in what has come to be known as the 'archaic smile'. Towards the end of the sixth century these characteristics, so contrary to the Attic spirit, began to disappear, but the last two of the *korai*, which must date from shortly before the Persian destruction, show quite a revolutionary style. On the 'kore of the polis' the affected smile has give way to the earlier severity of expression, the face is now square, not long, with wide, well-balanced features and the lips are merely two broad arcs which meet in the centre. The sim-

plicity of the modelling is not a repudiation of the subtleties of mature Archaic art, but a mastering and refinement of them. In the *kore* of Euthydikos we can see this evolution also in the wonderful portrayal of the body, which is not based, as previously, on a radiation from the central area but on horizontal and vertical axes. It is a body which discreetly reveals its plasticity through the whole harmonious articulation of the limbs, which is a solid whole, with its wide rounded trunk, its firmly modelled breasts and a series of minute details such as the slight swelling of the flesh around the tight edges of the clothes, the hint of concavity between the ribs under the cloth and the way the shoulder-blades stick out under the *himation* which follows the hollow of the back and is caught in round the waist. The eyes are deeply shaded by the eyebrows and give the face an expression almost of withdrawal and displeasure. The same square structure and the same severe expression which seems to shun any ostentation or frivolous gaiety are found again on the male head known, from the remains of colour still to be seen recently on the hair, as the 'fair-haired *ephebus*'. In the *kore* of Euthydikos, in other words, there can still be seen, especially in the design and the accentuated width of the shoulders, the traces of a declining style, but in its spirit the statue belongs not to the Archaic, but to the Classical world. The change of style seems too sudden and too radical to be explained as a natural evolution of Archaic art. This did not, in fact, slowly decay. It would appear that there was a clear break, as if there had been a clear decision to turn away from the past.

With the *kouros* called 'of Kritios' we reach the last example, dating like the two *korai* from about 480, of the long series of Attic *kouroi*, stylized figures of men bearing offerings, which show how Greek sculptors mastered the secrets of the human anatomy and the representation of volume, from the 'cubic' approach with a frontal view and two side views placed at angles to it, to the all-round presentation which permits an infinite number of viewpoints. The artist's knowledge of the human body was achieved gradually, and the proportions were at first sacrificed to an unnatural relation of masses, the line and the muscular features subordinated to the rhythm of the decorative elements. Yet it is not true that every concrete detail of archaic art was transformed into an abstract one, or that the subject was not considered

The severity of expression of the Kore of Euthydicos, one of the last of a series of statues of maidens offering gifts to the gods, brings us from the Archaic era to the spirit of the Classical world. (By courtesy of the German Archaeological Institute, Rome.)

The same facial structure and expression of restraint are seen in the fine head of the 'Fair-haired Ephebus', so-called from the traces of colour still to be seen in the hair. (The Acropolis Museum, Athens.)

as the juxtaposition of details all of equal importance. From the beginning of this development of sculpture as representing the whole, however bound by conventions, there clearly began to emerge an irrepressible inner energy, expressing the joy of a living being placed simply at the centre of nature. At the end of this development the mastery of human anatomy was complete, to the last muscle, the last tendon, the last vein. The artist would seem to have revelled in his knowledge to such an extent that he sometimes showed all the muscles in movement at once. A good example of this 'écorché' style is found in the depiction of two teams playing a ball-game on the base of a statue set into a section of the wall built by Themistocles immediately after the battle of Platea (479 B.C.). Some of its vivid colouring remains and it was carved at about the beginning of the fifth century. In the *kouros* 'of Kritios', however, the knowledge of the structure of the human body is taken for granted and we have reached the stage, the beginning of classicism, in which the artist can play down the secondary de-

tails, the lack of which helps to accentuate the essence of the organic whole of the subject. The hieratic immobility of the archaic *kouros*, standing firmly with his legs together, here gives way to the new position, which opens the way to a whole series of statues showing figues in motion, with the weight of the body on one leg thrust forward, giving a subtle play of curves and asymmetry in the limbs. The *kouros* takes its name from the similarity of the head with one of the group of the Tyrannicides which Kritios and Nesiotes remade after the victory over the Persians to replace an original by the sculptor Antenor which had been carried off by the barbarians. The original dated from the late sixth century. It is possible that some of the artistic innovations noted on the later statue could also have been found on the original.

THE SUPREMACY OF ATHENS

With the expulsion of the tyrants and the institution of democracy under Cleisthenes (510 B.C.) the whole political and intellectual life of Athens underwent a profound change which very soon made the city supreme in the artistic world of ancient Greece. Cleisthenes is credited with the plans to transform the Acropolis and with the beginning of work on the large new temple to the goddess of the city in the central area near the southern edge. This was to replace the old Hecatompedon of the Pisistratids and to herald the new era of democracy. It was to be more magnificent than the temple of Apollo at Delphi which had been renovated by his own family, the Alcmeonids. The supremacy of Athens was confirmed in 490 when she alone, aided only by the little town of Platea, withstood the onslaught of the Persian invasion on the plain of Marathon and threw the enemy back into the sea. The eyes of all Greece were on her when, ten years later, the farsighted Themistocles created his grand fleet and transformed her into the greatest naval power of Hellas. This brought further disaster to the Persians at Salamis and Platea.

Without wishing to imply that there was any complete break in the eternal evolutionary processes of art we could justifiably maintain that in Periclean Athens Hellenism became fully conscious of its role and its destiny, signed and sealed its achievements and sang a hymn of glory to the triumphs of its own genius which it opposed to that of all other peoples, all of them 'barbarian', over which destiny had decreed that Athens should prevail for ever in the domain of the intellect as well as on the field of battle. It was quite appropriate therefore that immediately after Salamis and Platea, when the new outer wall of the Acropolis was begun, there should be built into it pieces of the buildings destroyed by the enemy, pieces of the columns of the Hecatompedon and of the partly-built Parthenon. A piece of the frieze of an ancient temple in *poros* stone was set into the wall near the projecting upper part so that it could be seen from a distance by everyone on both the approach road and on the Agora, to act as a warning to the foreigner that the spirit of victorious Athens was ever on the alert, and that any further threat from the east would inevitably be destroyed by the indomitable will and spirit of the west. A similar warning and a similar expression of the city's indomitable will was also to be implied by the new complex of buildings being erected within the walls.

A kind act of fate decreed that this complex, such as the visitor sees in the ruins today, should have been conceived by one man and, in broad outline, executed by one artist. In the eighth year after Salamis, when work was beginning on the new walls, young Pericles put on at his own expense a performance of Aeschylus' *The Persians*, a foretaste, perhaps, of the lead he was soon to take in artistic affairs. Themistocles, who had hastily built the previous rampart, had also begun building the Acropolis wall and during his rule and that of Cimon this was finished. The Acropolis terrace had then taken on its definitive shape. Cimon was also responsible for the first versions of other important buildings on the Acropolis such as the Brauronium and the Chalcoteca. Further reconstruction was prevented by wars against the Medes

and their allies and against some of the allies of Athens herself. The year following Platea saw the creation of the grand maritime league against the Persian threat. This associated Athens with all the Hellenic centres in the Aegean and the Delio-Attic league which at first had its centre on Delos, the sacred island as the centre of the Cyclades. The league soon became an Athenian empire, as the largest of the Allies, with her great fleet, increased by the common fund of the league, took over the protection of the smaller states, imposing her will on them, suppressing their defections or rebellions with the help of the democratic parties in individual cities and installing her own garrisons on their territory.

About twenty years after Salamis, Cimon and his aristocratic party suffered a sudden eclipse. An Athe-nian expedition led by Cimon to assist the Spartans, who were being threatened by a revolt of their slave class, the helots, was summarily dismissed. As a result of this outrage Cimon was sent into exile, the democratic party came into power and a new constitution was promulgated. On the horizon of Athens there arose the star which was to guide the city's fortunes for thirty years: Pericles.

PERICLES AND PHIDIAS

In this citizen of Athens, who from his youth had espoused the democratic cause, the city's entire population was able the recognize the incarnation of their own spirit, a spirit of balance, finesse and control, of

A ball-game shown in a relief on the base of a statue. A similar interest in the detailed representation of the human anatomy is found in the vase-paintings of the same period. (By courtesy of the German Archaeological Institute, Rome.)

natural elegance shorn of ostentation, of justice and incorruptibility, of universality and idealism. With the farseeing foreign policy with which he proposed to bring the ancient world under Athenian domination, with the many courageous reforms which he planned for the city's internal administration, he combined a radical programme for making Athens a beautiful place to live in. To pay the enormous costs of this programme he seized the entire funds of the Delio-Attic league which had been brought to Athens from Delos in 454 B.C. In his life of Pericles, Plutarch has him say, in defence of accusations by his opponents of treachery and squandering public funds, that this colossal artistic and architectural undertaking was urgently necessary as an economic measure to provide employment for the increasing number of workers in the city, artificers, craftsmen and labourers, just as the expansion of the fleet, the maintenance of the freedom of the seas and the urge to trade, the importing of all the raw materials necessary for this programme of public works, the establishment of garrisons and the founding of colonies, had all found employment for those classes particularly concerned with military and naval affairs. In fact to Pericles the splendour of his grandiose works of art was another contributing factor to his city's strength and defence. It was one more, and perhaps the most efficient, way of ensuring for Athens peace and prosperity, proclaiming her watchfulness and her supremacy and seeking to spread her spirit throughout Greece and hence throughout the world, both for the present and for the ages to come.

Where there is an inspired creative will, fate always sends the right man at the right time to put its ideals into effect. In the case of Pericles it was Phidias, son of Charmides. He was above all a sculptor, but also a painter, and for antiquity was one of those universal geniuses which we usually associate with the Italian Renaissance. He succeeded in gathering about him and inspiring for the great undertaking a team of the finest artists in Attica. He drew up, from the plan given to him by Pericles, a complete new scheme for the buildings on the Acropolis, both those already in existence and needing to be renovated, and those newly built. Within this overall plan he was able to give directions to his architects for single buildings, suggesting the general theme to the sculptors and painters called in to embellish them, and leaving each

artist with the satisfaction of developing and perfecting his part according to his own tastes and personality. Some of these artists were collaborators and former pupils of the master and, though their own reputation was established, they felt no loss of dignity at accepting his firm yet tactful guidance. Phidias directed everything, Plutarch tells us, but he left to other artists the execution of independent and personal works of art such as the statue of the great Pericles himself, to be placed at the entrance to the Acropolis from the Propylaea. This was to be made by Cresilas, a sculptor born in Crete but brought up in Athens.

The great buildings on the Acropolis were begun only towards the mid fifth century when Pericles had been in power for ten years, as were also the Long Walls linking the city with the Piraeus. Shortly after 432 B.C. Phidias left the worldly scene soon after he had been prosecuted for embezzlement as a consequence of a gold and ivory statue to Athene which he had made. This prosecution was clearly an attack, through him, on the whole of Pericles' schemes of finance and city planning. The overall plan was beginning to emerge, and its principal architect after Phidias was undoubtedly Ictinos; even so, some of the buildings were greatly delayed and others were put off until the end of the century. Although a great many men worked on them, they show a dominant sense of balance and practicality. Behind the solution of their many individual problems, one senses the presence of a single controlling mind, overflowing with energy, despising traditional methods and conventional canons of art, rejoicing in the anomalies it must resort to to solve the difficulties of nature. In obedience to some higher impulse it introduces Ionic elements in a Doric temple, and virtually everywhere on the Acropolis takes a delight in marrying the austerity of the one style with the slender delicacy of the other.

THE ACROPOLIS

Thus, stamped by the genius of Pericles and Phidias, the Acropolis, formerly the city itself, became the sacred precinct, the abode of the city's gods, the receptacle and symbol of its spiritual power. It is this which the modern visitor sees when he gazes upon the spur of rock jutting out into the narrow plain of

Aerial view of the Acropolis from the west, showing the Propylaea, the Parthenon and the Erechtheum.

The Acropolis seen from the colonnade of the Hephaestium in the Agora.

Attica and giving the illusion that it rises higher than the surrounding mountain peaks. The hill, crowned with the brilliance of its ancient marbles, seemed destined by nature to influence the future of the world, with its delicate but indissoluble mingling of the honey-coloured stone from Mount Pentelicus, the yellow *poros* and the pinkish-blue limestone from the Acropolis itself.

The perfectly thought-out adaptation of the architecture to the ground on which the buildings were to be laid, whatever the irregularities of the latter and the difficulties of the former, the rhythm of the masses and the things which the eye sees as it moves from one to the other, linking them together in an indissoluble unity, all these factors are present in the first building we see as we climb the Acropolis. This is the Propylaea, the triumphal entrance-gate, designed by Mnesicles when the Parthenon was nearing completion and built between 437 and 432. In its essential plan it was a type of structure which dated back to the pre-Hellenic period. It had two porticos with colonnades standing back to back, with a dividing wall, one opening on to the exterior and the other on to an ensemble of enclosed structures. There was a similar building at the entrance to the Mycenaean palace at Tiryns, a very ancient city in Argos. The style reaches its most elaborate example with Mnesicles. Apart from

an occasionally almost impassable path up the side of the rock, the only way of getting on to the top of the Acropolis was up a rather steep slope through the two strong points on the west side. To emphasize the rugged nature of the terrain the architect built two wings on to the central portion of the Propylaea. These also had columns and started from the western portico, giving an open view down the slope. Anyone approaching from below or looking from the hills opposite, the Areopagus, the Philopappus or the Pnyx, saw a gently sloping path winding between terraces, corresponding to practical necessities and at the same time to the requirements of the solemn Panathenaic procession which took this route, and found his gaze led upwards to the crown of the rock, the superb mass of marble where the path ended. All the visible part of the Propylaea, in common with that of other religious buildings erected on the Acropolis in the same period, was in Pentelicus marble, whereas the wall foundations were in *poros*. The rows of marble blocks in the foundation wall above the limestone clearly show the outline of the steps and the terraces on both sides. A touch of colour on the white of the marble was provided by the bases of some of the walls and by the occasional Eleusis stone with its light streaks of bluish-black half way up the walls.

The largest of the bastions, that on the south side of the Acropolis, the pivot of its defence since the Mycenaean age, had been refaced with *poros* and adapted to fit into the new axis of the general plan. In 448 Callicrates presented his plan for the little temple of Athena Nike (' Victory ') to be built on top of it. The southern wing of Mnesicles' building, called the Pinacoteca, was intended to be an art gallery for the showing of famous paintings. Behind the Doric portico of the Propylaea, with columns slightly smaller than those of the central portion, a door and two slender windows open on to the ' gallery '. The two windows are not symmetrical with the door, and these three openings do not correspond with the columns in front of the portico, which have irregular spaces in between them. The object of this was to afford a view, through the space between the columns, to anyone coming up the central axis of the slope or standing on the terrace of the Athena Nike, of the Panathenaic procession. Here is a prime example of the way in which Greek architects did not, in fact,

The Propylaea as seen from the slope leading up to the Acropolis. On the base under the columns the line of the original flight of steps and the terrace, covering what is now bare rock, can clearly be seen where the marble meets the limestone of the foundations.

The Propylaea showing the side which looks in towards the Acropolis. This east loggia, in the Doric order, brings the entrance portico up to the level of the interior. Behind the columns can be seen the five doors, all of different sizes. The largest one in the centre was probably opened only for processions.

slavishly follow the demand for symmetry and the correspondence of the various parts of their buildings. It is an attestation of the true principle which guides the artist, and of which we shall find so many examples: to offer to the viewer the most favourable prospect of his work.

There is a somewhat more striking asymmetry in the two wings of the Propylaea, the southern one having only the atrium, or passageway behind the colonnade facing towards the terrace of the temple on the bastion. This may account for a well-held theory that Mnesicles' original plan was not completed through strong opposition from the priestly class or the conservative party, or because of the difficulties experienced by the State at the growing threat of the Peloponnesian War. This original design was completely symmetrical and would have given the building a southern wing identical to that of the Pinacoteca, completely covering the view of the open space in front of the Athena Nike which could then only have been seen obliquely; its altar would have been hidden, and there would have been no shrine to the Charites (Graces) built up against the south side of the central portion of the Propylaea; alongside the east front of the Propylaea there would have been two more immense porticoes which would not only have spoiled the enclosed area of the Brauronia and entailed the destruction of part of the sacred ruin of the Mycenaean wall, but the long line of their low columns would have made the inner face of the Propylaea itself seem less imposing. Such a plan could never have originated in the mind of Mnesicles: it is more like that of some modern architect, inured to the cold, leaden, useless symmetry of certain neo-classical buildings or the formalist Doric of some Chamber of Trade or House of Parliament.

We should therefore resist any suggestion that the artist is to be blamed for any asymmetry in his designs. This would be to judge the work of Mnesicles by a pedantic application of the criteria of traditional construction methods. Nor should we think of Mnesicles as a revolutionary brushing aside accepted solutions in search of surprise, displacing elements and deliberately breaking up the balance of traditionally repeated features. There are no sudden leaps forward in Hellenic

The Acropolis as seen from the Propylaea. Against the wall in the background, which hid the Erechtheum, stood the colossal statue of Athena Promachos. (Reconstruction by Stevens.)

architecture; it is an uninterrupted process, of inexhaustible energy and infinite variation, moving steadily towards the solution of themes of the utmost grandeur. The Greek architect found a satisfactory expression of his genius in the designing of his buildings to harmonize with their surroundings and to suit the demands of religious cult and ritual, then in shaping his material with patient loving care, so that one block fitted perfectly on top of the other, each one being immaculately polished.

To anyone climbing up to the Acropolis, the Propylaea offers a facade with perfectly balanced north and south wings. Behind the front is a simple antechamber, a pause to prepare the eye for a different artistic vision and a different religious emotion. Between the two wings a majestic series of four steps leads to the central Doric colonnade. Behind, two

transverse colonnades of slender elegant Ionic columns offer the first perfect combination of the two orders. The section dividing the two facades has five doors, a huge one in the centre with the side ones decreasing in size: the well-worn threshold in Eleusian stone of the northermost door shows that this was the one which was open every day, whereas the central door must have been opened only for the most solemn religious functions. Owing to the steep slope of the ground the eastern gallery, which opened on to the interior of the Acropolis, rested on the rock itself, whereas the western gallery required a steep flight of stairs.

As they look out from the eastern gallery towards the interior of the Acropolis the crowds of visitors who today stand before the magnificence of the view of Greece's greatest sanctuaries would be astonished to know that this view was not in fact intended by Pericles' architect-planners. They did not have that 'chthonic sense', that respect for the warm, coloured bareness of the surface of the Acropolis rock which was almost covered with terraces, each containing individual sanctuaries, enclosed by walls which were high enough to conceal all but the tops of the two tallest. Right opposite the entrance, at the end of a long courtyard, the top of the Erechtheum rose up above a high wall, which probably marked the boundary not only of the terrace of the Hecatompedon built by the Pisistratids, the charred ruins of which, set on fire by the Persians, were still visible in the time of Herodotus, but, from even further back in time, also of the area of the Mycenaean royal palace. With its back to this wall and on an imposing carved pedestal, traces of which can still be seen today, there stood the colossal statue of Athena Promachos ('the Champion'). This was the work of Phidias, and the last before he began work on the Parthenon. Athena was the silent ally of the Athenians on the battlefield and stood there, an ever-watchful sentinel on her fortress of rock. The golden point of her spear could be seen from the sea by mariners returning home. It was their first landmark and was visible, not, as legend would have us believe, from Cape Sunium, from which it would be hidden by Mount Hymettus, but after rounding Cape Zoster, where the last spur of the Hymettus comes down to the enchanting bay near the sanctuary of Apollo Zoster by the isthmus of Vouliagmeni. Carried off to Constantinople by

Justinian, the statue, according to a Byzantine chronicler, was pulled down by the angry populace during the Fourth Crusade as it was thought that the pagan goddess's uplifted arm (the lance and shield having long since disappeared) acted as a signal to the approaching invaders.

This celebrated hieratic statue can only be dimly imagined today. On the other hand, thanks to several Roman copies (the most faithful of which is in Dresden) we have a good idea of another of the works of Phidias' maturity. This is the Athena Lemnia, a statue which he finished shortly after the Promachos. It was placed immediately on completion on the left of the entrance to the Propylaea, not far from Cresila's bust of Pericles. It was a bronze statue dedicated to the Athenian cleruchs (citizens holding lands abroad) in Lemnos and was the most admired work of the sculptor's in ancient times. According to Pausanias (second century A.D.) it was the most worthy to be seen. This would be the first to be noticed in a whole forest of statues, representations of gods, votive offerings and mythological groups, scattered all over the top of the sacred hill, enclosed within walls but also exposed to view between the columns of the Propylaea, at the end of open spaces and flanking the principal street leading direct to the Parthenon, the route of the Panathenaic procession. This street would be the only bit of bare rock showing, a narrow strip marked with hollow lines to make an easier climb for the animals sent up for sacrifice. At the beginning of this street, standing against the first column on the right of the Propylaea gallery, inside its little sanctuary, stood a statue of Athena Hygeia. This was the work of the sculptor Pyrrhus and, according to legend, was dedicated by Pericles himself to the goddess of health after a workman had fallen from the roof of the Parthenon and miraculously escaped injury. This little sanctuary at the southern end of the Acropolis was built up against the tall boundary wall of the precinct of the very ancient sanctuary to Artemis Brauronia which, as we have said, was rebuilt after the Persian wars by Cimon and re-aligned to the general overall plan of Ictinus. The wall, however, was not so high as to prevent the view from the sea of the tip of the lance of Athena Promachos. The rocky path between the two side terraces did not go right up to the facade of the Parthenon, but turned to the right, through a small portico into another courtyard bounded on the west side by the wall of one of the colonnades of the Brauronia and at the far end by a civic building, the Chalcoteca, built up against the southern outer wall.

The Parthenon as seen when approached from the Propylaea. The flight of steps, covered with steles and monuments, accentuated the grandeur of the building. (Reconstruction by Stevens.)

THE PARTHENON

Those taking part in the Panathenaic procession would only see the Parthenon after passing through this small portico and coming out into the courtyard (that part of the procession with the animals for sacrifice having gone straight on along the north side towards the front of the temple) and the building would then reveal itself suddenly, standing high and firm on its terrace. Each of the other temples and sanctuaries, isolated within its precinct wall, took on a separate religious significance of its own. The procession climbed the Parthenon terrace through a narrow gap in the centre of a monumental flight of steps, cut out of the rock at the bottom and at the top made of blocks of limestone. The steps would be difficult to see in their entirety as they would be

The eastern end of the Parthenon, which was also the entrance. The carvings on the pediment showed the birth of Athena. These, together with sculptures from the other pediment, are in the Acropolis Museum and the British Museum. Under the cornice is the Doric frieze whose triglyphs and metopes show the struggles against the giants.

thickly covered with votive offerings, steles and statues. This terrace had been made by levelling off a stretch of the hill which sloped steeply towards the south, causing long delays to the first plan of Cleisthenes. This very wide platform was abandoned after Salamis when it was proposed to build a temple entirely in precious Pentelic marble. This plan in turn was abandoned after the Persians set fire to the original building. It was then decided to shorten the length of the temple but to extend the foundations on the north side with rubble from the older building; this patchwork, very clearly visible today, was then hidden by the level terrace which went up as far as the three steps of the marble base.

The exceptional width of the temple, which has seventeen columns on the long sides and eight on the short ones, was clearly designed to leave ample space

within its cella on the east side — the 100 foot cella, or Hecatompedon, which by itself covered the whole of the former temple of the Pisistratids — for Phidias' colossal god and ivory statue. The first complete view of the temple which those taking part in the Panathenaic procession would see, however, was that of the western side. Anyone coming out of the entrance portico into the courtyard in front of this side would see, under the sloping roof with its series of painted acroteria, the sculptural decoration of the pediment. This was the first verse of a hymn glorifying, through the various symbols and images of the goddess, the great patroness of the temple. The carvings on the pediment told a purely local story, the struggle between Athena and Poseidon for the sovereignty of Attica. In the centre the god called up the lake of salt water and the goddess of the sacred olive tree

Row of columns on the south side of the Parthenon. On the left: *the wall of the cella.*

(both these attributes being preserved in or near the Erechtheum) whilst at the sides sat the ancient tutelar deities and the local heroes of the Acropolis, witnesses and arbiters of the great event, Cecrops and his daughters, Erechtheus and, at the ends, the rivers of the city, the Cephisus, the Ilissus, the Eridanus and the Callirhoe fountain.

The idea, born of the fascination of the pale marble of the ruins, that there was no colour in the original building, has long since been discredited. Under the brilliant Mediterranean sun the whole top part of the temple, from the entablature upwards, shone with bright colours, with red and blue predominating and alternating with bands and fillets of gold. The clothing, arms, implements and accessories of the sculptured figures would also be coloured and would set off the clear, waxen, honey-coloured flesh. The figures on the pediment were carved completely in the round

Detail of frieze and columns on the front of the Athena Nike temple.

and were enhanced by the constant play of light and shade. On the pediment the triumph of Athena was celebrated, a triumph which bound her to her people from the beginnings of the temples. Underneath the pediment there could be seen from the entrance to courtyard of the Parthenon the decoration beneath the Doric frieze, or, to be more precise, the fourteen metopes on the west side and the first few of the thirty-two on the north side. Here too, as on the

pediment, Phidias kept to a long tradition and exalted the temple's titulary goddess with episodes from her myth, or through subjects in some way related to the city or under whose mythological mantle he could by allusion glorify the national pride. This ample Doric frieze with its ninety-two metopes recounted the isolated episodes of the myth and arranged them rhythmically in single figures or groups. Unfortunately the frieze and all the metopes, including those least visible on the south side, were savagely mutilated and broken, probably during the Turkish occupation. The metopes on the southern side relate the myth of the Centaurs and the Lapithae who also recur on the western frieze of the so-called Theseum (in fact the temple dedicated to Hephaestus, the patron god of smiths). This temple is still standing and was the only remaining temple converted into a Christian church, the Church of St George. It is on the top of the Hill of the Nymphs, overlooking the western side of the Agora. The long series of metopes recounting the battles of the Centaurs was broken in the centre by a series of metopes telling the myth of the first king of the city, Erechtheus, its benefactor and the founder of the Panathenaic festivals.

Those metopes which were visible from the entrance to the Parthenon courtyard, that is those on the north corner, told the story of the fatal night of Troy, the Iliupersis ('Sack of Troy'). This episode of massacre and rapine had been described in art form only in the painting of Polygnotus in the Lesche (a kind of club-house) of the Cnidians at Delphi. It was brought about by the will of the gods, including Athena, whose decision was transmitted by Zeus through Iris. Here too, and perhaps more overtly than in the legend of the Centaurs and the Lapithae, there is an attempt to glorify the victory of civilization over barbarism, of Hellenism over the East, a victory which also has undertones of the tragic destiny awaiting many of the victors. There is also a clear allusion to the benefits and the prosperity brought by peace which we shall find in other scenes portrayed by Phidias. Pericles was well aware of the blessings of peace, as he brought a certain amount of unity amongst the Greek states which had formed an ancient league of war against Persia, and during his reign a long period of peace began both with Persia and with Sparta. The subject of the metopes on the western side was the battle against the Amazons, another example of the triumph of Hellenism against barbarism. The Amazons from distant Asia had invaded Attica and reached the hills surrounding the Acropolis. Here they had been driven off and annihilated by the arch-hero of Attica, Theseus, who always fought under the aegis of Athena. His victories had preserved the people of Athens for their goddess and assured their sovereignty, as portrayed on the pediment above.

THE IONIC FRIEZE, THE PEDIMENTS, THE PARTHENOS

As those in the procession climbed the steps to the platform of the temple they would see, inside and lower down, the Ionic frieze. This was something entirely new, introduced by Phidias for the first time into the compact Doric structure to carry a subject which must therefore have been of exceptional importance. It was over a yard high and 524 feet long and ran round the outside walls of the cella at the top. It was commonly believed, and still is, even by some scholars, that much of this frieze was invisible and that the artist went on to complete his work, regardless of whether anyone could see it, for the mere joy of creation. In fact the whole of it was visible from the platform through the columns of the peristyle, just as visible as the remains on the western side are today.

The subject of the carving on the Ionic frieze was also something entirely new in the history of Greek art. It was the most solemn celebration in honour of the goddess, the procession which took place at the Panathenaic festivals, held every four years, but transposed into a world in which the gods of Olympus mingle with the Athenian crowds. It was like a huge votive offering in which, unlike the usual steles in high relief placed before sanctuaries as single offerings to the deity, the whole population took part, bearing the embroidered robe, not reverently still, but caught in joyous movement as in real life. The various elements in the procession were shown in the order in which they appeared (except for the horsemen and the coaches which stopped outside the walls) as they divided into two sections on the steps before proceeding to walk round the temple. The subject started on the western front of the frieze from the southern corner, with the preparations for the festival, and the procession was shown along the two long sides in correct order, each group being repeated on both sides, as if we were to imagine that the building had no thickness. We can see the *epheboi*, some on their prancing horses ready to join the knights at the end of the procession, others having their horses brought to them, stroking them, putting on their bridles, holding them in check; others are standing around, putting on their tunics (some of them in the act of drawing them over their heads like a shirt), standing with one foot on a stone lacing up their boots; here and there a horse is shown shaking its head to drive off the flies. The festival organizers move about among the participants, urging on the slow ones or calming down those who are impatient. We see before us the flower of Athenian society, the sons of the aristocracy, the elite of the nation, those whom Thucydides, through the mouth of Pericles, called 'the Spring of the country'. The young people who are ready for the procession are the ideal type of Athenian chivalry, such as Xenophon described in his treatise on horsemanship; they ride either with body erect or leaning forward, their thighs gripping the horse's flanks, their feet hanging freely. The type of horse portrayed by Phidias was also to be a lasting model in art: short-bodied, chest thrust forward and slender legs pawing the ground, head lean and nervy with quiver-ing nostrils. The scene does not succeed in capturing any religious solemnity, but it is pervaded with the carefree gaiety of festive preparations on a clear summer's day.

Along the sides, the procession is headed by the archons and other dignitaries of the *demos*, talking amongst themselves, draped in their heavy cloaks and waiting for others to arrive. They are followed by figures of women walking very slowly, head slightly bent, in the hieratic attitudes of those conscious of the divine presence; these are the daughters of the Eupatridae, the hereditary aristocracy, whose tunics fall in vertical folds, with a festive veil reaching down to their shoulders. They carry the baskets containing the implements for the sacrifice and are called *cane-phorie*. With them are the *ergastine* who have woven

Detail of Parthenon frieze: the group of spondophoroi carrying the pitchers of holy water.

the wool of the sacred robe, then other women dressed in cloaks, carrying incense burners, metal jars and other sacred implements. These girls are delightful in their grace and composure and were to be praised at the end of the Hellenistic age for having brought honour to the procession ' by their beauty and the dignity of their bearing '.

Other groups follow, interspersed with heralds: first the youths wrapped up to their chins in flowing cloaks, leading the sacrificial animals, and the *scaphephoroi*, who were metics, carrying the bloodless offerings, meal cakes and honey; then the *spondophoroi*, each one supporting a pitcher on his shoulder, and the *thallophoroi*, chosen from amongst the oldest citizens, moving in a tightly-packed group and carrying olive branches; then the *apobates*, climbing on to a moving cart and finally the horsemen, the first ones in ranks of six, the others more dispersed, wheeling about or turning round to talk to their neighbours.

A great deal of mis-spent energy has been devoted to attempts to prove that the frieze was carved by a large group of artists of different styles and sensibilities. Anyone with experience of a large sculpture workshop knows how wrong this can be. In the relief work, generally low because of the shadows from the columns, as opposed to the pediments and the Doric frieze which caught the full glare of the sun, we can see that some elements are reduced almost to pictorial level, whereas others stand out in higher relief. This would seem to be a deliberate attempt to highlight certain heads on which it was intended that the viewer's gaze should linger. There is a kind of ' staccato ' rhythm in the *ergastine* and in the water-carriers, figures standing fully vertical and practically still, spaced well apart with the air freely circulating about them. Other figures are vertical, but superimposed in one mass, such as the olive-branch bearers; others flow along, interwoven in a compact mass, such as the young people leading the animals. Here the procession moves along in orderly silence, there it is more confused, restless, with unexpected episodes and people involved it conversation; there are gaps between groups caused by the escorts. This only confirms the unity of the inspiration. The whole work, with its varied rhythms, its pauses, sudden stops and unexpected episodes, was clearly designed to avoid the monotony of a uniform and symmetrical procession. One great artist drew up the plan with the relevant sketches and left the execution of the individual panels to pupils and workmen. If he was not content with the workmanship of any particular piece, he could hand it over to a more expert collaborator and he probably put the finishing touches to practically every detail. This artist can only have been Phidias; the work bears the imprint

One of the metopes of the Parthenon: the Centaur and the Lapith. According to legend the story of the battle between the Centaurs and the Lapithae was carved by Phidias round the edge of the sandals of the gigantic Athena Parthenos.

of his style, which we can also admire in the rest of the sculptural decoration.

In the centre of the frieze on the principal façade, we see the procession arrive in front of the temple. A priest and a priestess receive from the hands of an *ergastina* the yellow and violet robe; by their side stand two noble maidens forming the spiritual link of the human procession with the assembly of the immortal gods shown watching the arrival, seven on each side, looking towards the corners of the façade. The maidens are carrying the *diphroi*, or footstools for the divine guests. Amongst the gods seated in their privileged positions, in addition to almighty Zeus, is Athena, the goddess being feasted, dressed in a tenuous *chiton* which reveals the shape of her young body. The gods are not rigid or detached, or haughty in Olympian aloofness; they are a happy family group, talking and gesticulating among themselves in attitudes of carefree abandon. Ares sits with both hands tightly clasped round a raised knee, Hermes and Apollo converse in admirable intimacy, like two graceful *epheboi*. They occupy the same space seated as men occupy standing or on horseback, and seem as large as the latter; they also seem less aware of the solemnity of the occasion than the grave-faced girls approaching them, and look as though they have come down to take part in the festival being held in their honour and to mix amongst the mortals. The mortals, for their part, citizens of the State of Athens, seem to be marching upwards towards their gods, and, whilst glorifying them and their heroes, it is really the apotheosis of the city which they are celebrating. These citizens are proud of their religious display, proud especially of their works which have made them worthy of their gods, of the power of their arms which has enabled them to humble the barbarian, of the power of their genius, and of reason (the *logos*, primordial element of the cosmos, the *logismos*) which has made them victors and virtual interpreters of the will and the thoughts of the gods. In the far-off dawn of Greek history, when the cult of the Olympian gods, celebrated in the family shrines, was reserved for the aristocrats, as also was at first the cult of the patron god of the Mycenaean king and his realm, the people had drawn their comfort from the mystery rites which offered to the initiated in his own lifetime a glimpse of the immortals and to the pious a chance of participating after death in divine blessedness. Now, however, it was the whole populace of Athens which seemed to be proclaiming its intention to rise, whilst still living, by its own thoughts towards its gods.

Sophocles declared, in the years when work on the Parthenon was beginning, that 'there are many wonders in the world, but none so great as man...: word, thought as swift as the wind, aspirations which give rise to cities, all this he has taught himself' (*Antigone*, 332 ff.). Before long this human thought would venture, in the tragedies of Euripides, to criticize the immortals themselves, and lead to corroding doubt and unbelieving anguish.

On the pediment at the eastern end there is the sacred legend of events which took place in Olympus. This told for the first time in large sculpture the story of the birth of the goddess Athena, who sprang fully armed from the head of Zeus in the distant times of the Olympic era, symbolized by the rising sun on the carriage in the left hand corner, and the setting moon on the right.

No trace remains of the central group of figures, which was knocked down in early Christian times to make room for the apse of the church built inside the temple. Very probably the two principal figures were connected with some image of Nike, the personification of victory. The goddess, born without a mother, the exponent and interpreter of the will of the supreme Zeus, the 'goddess of reason', was born to guide, with the supreme arm of her intellect, her people who would be inspired by her. In what is left of the other figures on the pediment, all of them larger than life and carved in the round, we find the hand of the same supreme artist who designed the frieze of the Parthenon. Here we have Dionysus reclining naked on his cloak, Demeter and Kore tenderly embracing each other, Iris and a group of three figures once called the Fates, but probably representing Aphrodite, her mother Dione and Latona, all of them revealing a perfect mastery in the art of portraying the human body, accentuating only the essentials, expressing at once the internal structure and the softness of the exterior.

The metopes on this pediment also show a victory of divine reason over insane bestiality in the battle against the giants. The central position is given naturally to the supreme god hurling his thunderbolts; Athena is not immediately next to him in the Olympian hierarchy, but next to her, in the same panel, again there is Nike. The sense of this victory must have inspired the frieze below in which the goddess welcomes her triumphant people.

In spite of this profusion of ornamentation, this wealth of material, the delicacy of every detail, when seen from the front the Parthenon looks as its creator intended: a virile, authoritative monument, the perfect materialization of the ideal of a people through a work of art. Standing here one can capture the minutiae, the optical corrections by which Greek architecture reached this state of perfection. Because ancient scientists knew that a horizontal line appears concave to the eye, the bedrock of the Acropolis on which it stands and the whole platform of the temple was cut convex and the same convexity was carried up by the columns to the architraves. As vertical lines seem to diverge as they rise, the columns are not parallel, but converge slightly. The corner ones are nearer to their neighbours than those in the centre and, as they were the only ones which stood out freely in profile against the open sky, were made slightly thicker so that they would not appear more slender than the others. The harmonious perspective of the architecture naturally extended also to the sculptural decoration. The lack of proportion in the figures on the pedestals when seen at eye level was deliberate, and seen from below it disappears. There is the same slight distortion in the metopes on the Ionic frieze, and if one looks very closely it can be seen also in the floral and geometric patterns in the highest parts of the building. Many single votive statues also show a certain asymmetry when they stand on high pedestals.

The Parthenon was admired for over twenty centuries 'as intact and as little injured by the passing of time as if it had only just been built', wrote Louis des Hayes, the ambassador of Louis XIII of France in 1630: intact, that is, until the fatal explosion of the Turks' store of gunpowder during the siege by the Venetian forces under Morosini in 1687. It is ironical that the Commander in Chief of Morosini's land forces, Count Königsmark, who gave one of his officers the order to fire on the Parthenon, was a classical scholar of the University of Leipzig who in his youth had composed a work in Latin on 'The Misfortunes of the Acropolis under the Yoke of the Turk'. A letter from the Countess recalls her husband's sincere grief at having to strike at the most venerable temple of Hellenism. It is easy to forget the imperious necessity of the general's action and that the Venetian troops were the dike holding off the Turkish hordes which were about to flood the whole of Europe, and that the intrepid Venetian fortresses of Crete, Suda and Spinalonga were, even as late as the early eighteenth century, the last little islands in the eastern Mediterranean to be overwhelmed by this tide. This was another of those ruthless struggles in which Western civilization faced up resolutely in mortal combat to the destructive fury of the East.

When the worshippers in the Panathenaic procession had passed through the pronaos (the area between the columns and the cella or naos) and stood in front of the huge door of the cella they would see inside, lit only by the dim light shining through the doorway, the gold and ivory goddess around whom and for whom the whole temple had been built. She was standing, not against the back wall of the cella dividing it from the rear hall, but against a row of columns in front of it running across between the lateral columns inside the cella, a duplicate series of Doric. Athena was shown as a warrior goddess wearing her splendid full-dress helmet decorated with a sphinx between two winged horses and two griffins on the side-pieces, and with her shield and lance resting on the ground and held only with the tips of her fingers. On her breast was the aegis, her ornament, its serpents mingling with her soft wavy tresses. Around her was a whole series of legends symbolizing her Olympian power, such as we have admired already in the decorations of the temples: battles with giants and Amazons on the two sides of her shield, battles with the centaurs round the edge of her sandals, whilst around the base of the statue ran a frieze showing the creation of Pandora, a myth in which the Athenians could interpret the creative gift transmitted by the goddess to the artists of their city who had erected this supreme image to her. In the goddess's right palm stood a statue of Victory: this too was huge and sculptured in the noblest and purest human form, full of assurance and dignity. Here was the Victory which had led her people to excel, in valour and in genius, all the Hellenes, against all threats from the barbarians. Here Athena had come down from Olympus to the land of Attica and had become the incarnation of her triumphant city, a link between heaven and earth and the symbol of their common victory.

In this, the highest point of classical art, have we therefore reached the most perfect expression of the total reality of the human form, of divinity, of nature? Outside it and before it did art only represent a skeleton, an idol with the appearance of human form, clothing his magic, his religious expression frozen into a symbol? As far as portraying the human body is concerned, if we look at the groups of the three Fates on the pediment we find that the true material existence of the folded drapery is sacrificed to the voluptuous outline of the female limbs, whose shiny, youthful smoothness shows through the flowing, pictorial folds of the *chiton*. There is more realism in the *kore* of Euthydikos, in which, after the wave of Ionic fashion which caused the representation of the human body to be neglected, not to say distorted, under coquettish and complicated clothing, we have already noted the rediscovery of a rare balance between the material likeness of the dress and the structure of the body striving to show beneath it. Moreover in philosophical art criticism the terms are often reversible: for the old aristocratic religious class of Athens the for-

mally impeccable image of the Parthenos probably did not represent their real goddess, but an abstraction, a symbol of divinity come down from the realm of ideas to identify herself with her people, whose prosperity she embodied, her gold and ivory representing the state coffers. The stiff archaic *xoanon* probably held for them more of the truly divine; with its roughly human outlines it seemed strangely superior to human life around it, endowed with great power of magic, a functioning divinity, dispensing favours and punishment to the devoted. The Parthenos offered herself from afar to the admiration of the Athenians, but in fact no altar was ever erected in front of the Parthenon. Sacrifices continued to be made on the Erechtheum altar, and the Panathenaic robe was laid up before the old idol in its cella in the Erechtheum.

THE ERECHTHEUM

This second great religious building on the Acropolis was begun after the completion of the Parthenon

Another detail from the Parthenon frieze: young men leading the animals to sacrifice.

On the frieze on the east side, seated divinities watch the arrival of the procession. In the centre Apollo, on the right Artemis.

and after the death of Phidias. Work on it continued until the end of the century. It was planned certainly to be included in the general design of Ictinus along the northern edge of the Acropolis near to the walls and running parallel to the Parthenon. The grace and elegance of its Ionic columns formed a contrast with the severity of the larger temple. The Ionic order was chosen not only to offset with its 'feminine' grace the 'masculine' austerity of the Parthenon, but also because it was the style best suited to the strange religious complex of this building and to link its several discordant parts. The ancients themselves emphasized the unique qualities of the Erechtheum, which defies all the canons of Greek architecture. This is due to the need to combine in one building chapels, altars, sanctuaries, and tombs, and also to site them on different levels. The eastern front rises from the rock in slender columns, overlooking the cella of Athena, whereas the western end has a series of half-columns standing on a high pedestal. Outside this western end stood Athena's olive tree in the precinct of Pandrosos; a small doorway led inside the Erechtheum to the cella dedicated to Erechtheus-Poseidon. Under the floor of the atrium was the salt lake which Poseidon caused to gush out in his contest with Athena. Near the doorway and under the west front was the tomb of King Cecrops, an ancient legendary early ruler of Athens. From the east front a stairway against the wall led down to the level of the temple of Erechtheus, but in front of this on the north side

there was a magnificent wide portico whose exquisite Ionic elements have served as models both to Roman architects (such as the designers of the little round temple right in front of the Parthenon dedicated by the Athenians to Rome and to Augustus) and to architects of modern times. Under the portico and adjacent to several altars, one was supposed to be able to see the mark in the rock made by Poseidon's trident when he struck the ground to summon up the salt lake. On the south side there was another small portico, known as the loggia of the Caryatids, its entablature being supported, not by columns, but by six graceful, solemn female statues. This building is far from being a mere juxtaposition of ill-assorted parts, without contrast, without adaptation, as in the Propylaea, to the various levels. On the contrary, there is a unity in its structure and a harmony in its many parts unich show clearly that the canons of art can be adapted to make a building fit the needs of its surroundings. There is such sensitivity in the use of materials and colour (as in the frieze running right round it in which the various scenes of gods and local heroes stand out in white marble against a background of dark Eleusis stone) that several authorities have attributed it to Mnesicles himself.

In place of all this a learned modern theory offers some monstrous original plan, strictly symmetrical but in the form of a long tube with the two disproportionate projections of the two lateral porticoes. Is it credible that this building, so vitally necessary to the balance of the whole plan of the Acropolis, should be hidden, that the delightful loggia of the caryatids should be scarcely visible behind the truncated remains of the Hecatompedon of Pisistratus not only at the very beginning but for all succeeding ages?

The *korai* in this loggia stand motionless, in a hieratic position, each one carrying on her head, like the echinus of the capital, one of the covered baskets containing the implements for the performing of the mysteries which two priestesses brought out from the loggia every year to the nearby sanctuary of Aphrodite of the Gardens. They are dressed in a Doric peplum which shows underneath it the vigorous shape of their young bodies. In this, as also in their serious faces, framed by the soft tresses which fall on to their shoulders, and in the shading of the colours on the surfaces, we can see a clear reflection of the style of Phidias. One knee is extended forwards and the other is covered by the stiff vertical folds of the tunic, the forward knee alternating on the two pairs of figures so that anyone approaching from the entrance to the Acropolis would take the folds to be fluted columns. Here, as everywhere, the artist's main preoccupation was clearly to expose his work from the best viewpoint. There is another example from the opposite side of the street to the Erechtheum in the commemorative statue to Conon, the admiral who was victorious at Cnidos in 394 B.C., and his son Timotheus. The two statues stood on an arc-shaped plinth which was sited, not tangential to the long axis of the Parthenon, but turned slightly as if to welcome the visitor.

THE COLLABORATORS AND SUCCESSORS OF PHIDIAS

The style of Phidias permeated the whole of Pericles' great undertaking. As the short-lived fashion for the Ionic and the Peloponnesian possibly found in certain works of the late Archaic period such as the fair-haired ephebus, passed away, it became identifiable as a distinctly Attic style. Even after the death of Phidias it continued to dominate all Hellenic art from the end of the fifth century and, once the threat of armed invasion from the East was over, spread out to the lands of Anatolia: the kings of Licia took inspiration from it for their funeral monuments

The northern portico of the Erechtheum, where the mark made on the ground by Poseidon's trident could be seen.

and the main structure of the temple of Athena Nike was reproduced on the spur of a hill at Xanthos; the princes of Sidon also had sarcophagi built in the Attic manner.

If the spirit of Phidias permeated the whole of Pericles' grand design and many artists allowed themselves slavishly to copy his style, although they were men of established reputation, this does not mean that Phidias excluded from the Acropolis any independent project by an artist working outside his circle and his range of interest. In addition to Cresila's bust of Pericles, there were several monuments by one of Phidias' greatest collaborators, Alcamene, who is supposed also to have made one of the pediments of the temple of Zeus at Olympia. His Hermetes Propylaios stood right at the entrance to the Acropolis and several Roman copies and variants have been preserved. Probably his also is one of the rarest original works of the great Greek masters which Pausanias said was only 'dedicated' by him. It was found in the northeast corner of the Acropolis, where Pausanias described it, and shows the tragic group of Procne and her little child Itys, whose tender naked body, clinging to the heavy cloth of its mother's tunic and contrasting with the solemn, brooding immobility of the woman, seems to hint at the agony to come (it was shortly to be killed and its flesh served up to Procne's faithless husband, Tereus). At the time when work was beginning on the great building complex on the Acropolis, or shortly before this, several works appeared by sculptors of quite opposite tendencies to Phidias, such as Myron of Eleutherium (the Attic fortress on the borders with Boeotia). Myron was a great artist in bronze who modelled the human body in the image of the great victorious athletes and caught their fleeting action in the uncertain balance of a moment of rapid movement, or by running together several moments which really happen in rapid succession, as in his famous 'Discus Thrower'. In front of the entrance to the little portico leading into the west courtyard of the Parthenon there was another statue by Myron: a group showing Athena and Marsia, caught at the moment when the satyr is looking covetously at the flute which the goddess has just thrown away, irritated at seeing her disfigured face with its cheeks swollen from playing reflected in the water.

Later still than the Erechtheum was the little temple of Athena Nike which we have already men-

The little loggia of the Caryatidis in the southern side of the Erechtheum. The girls in their Doric tunics recall the priestesses of the temple who carried on their heads the baskets containing the implements for the cult to the sanctuary of Aphrodite of the Gardens.

tioned. This stood on the former strong point adjoining the Propylaea and, although planned in 448, was not begun until 423 during the peace of Nicia. Its order, a perfectly canonical Ionic, was probably chosen when the building was first planned, and there was another little temple very similar to it, built on the bank of the Ilissus about the mid-fifth century, which was still standing in the previous century. Its low frieze, which betrays some haste in the decoration probably as a result of financial stringencies at the height of the Peloponnesian War, also shows scenes from human life, in this case a historical event,

enacted in the presence of the gods on the facade: the victory over the Persians on the long side and, at the back, the victory over the Boeotians, the Persians' allies. The balustrade running round three sides of the terrace was intended to glorify symbolically the last brilliant Athenian victories secured by Alcibiades in this terrible war. There are swarms of figures representing victories, flying about, driving animals to sacrifice, crowning naval and land successes, all emanating from figures of Athena; their scanty, almost immaterial chitons, with their flowing folds emphasizing the shape of their bodies, are a later evolution of the so-called ' clinging wet ' style of Phidias. The so-called Midia style of pottery, which was made in the same period, has similar female figures wrapped in transparent tunics with minute softly flowing folds.

The time was now approaching of Athens's humiliating defeat. The erection of public works was over and the teams of artists and craftsmen now had to seek employment in the more humble sphere of private commissions, such as funeral monuments. These appeared in increasing numbers about this time and the best of them have been found along the Sacred Way, the processional route to the Eleusinian mysteries. Let us halt for a moment in front of a stele in the family plot belonging to Corebos of Melites. It is a monument to a girl, Hegeso, and shows the declining Phidian style in the perfection of the human shapes, the noble dignity of their bearing and in its air of suffused melancholy. The girl is seated and is picking a piece of jewellery from a box held by a maidservant, her gaze symbolizing her regret at leaving that which she has loved on earth most dearly. Here too the drapery, thin and clinging, delicately moulds the shape of the two bodies. A few yards further on, inside the same Ceramicus cemetery, is the stele of Dexileos of Thorikos, one of the five Athenian knights who fell in the Corinthian War in 394 or 393 B.C. This work, a decade or so later than the stele of Hegeso, shows an attempt to re-establish the difficult balance between the structure of the young body and the material quality of its clothing.

Thus we come to the end of the century in which Athens, through the voice of Phidias, left for posterity the monolithic, imperious affirmation of its spirit. It is not that the rest of Greece produced no great works of art; in fact there was a profusion of artistic production throughout the Hellenic world from the Peloponnese to Sicily and from the Asian colonies to the shores of Africa. Whereas, however, Ionic art had a certain frivolity, the price it paid for a rather superficial delicacy, and Peloponnesian art a certain rigidity and austerity in facial expression, only Attic art found the perfect fusion of the external form and the inner spiritual content. Having achieved every skill in the representation of the structure and the beauty of the human body down to the finest detail, Hellenistic art in the fourth century felt itself free to attempt to alter and correct them so as to express the internal conflicts of passion. The proportions of the male body were changed to accentuate slenderness, giving it an unnatural length as if to endow its earthly shape with superhuman size or the heroic qualities a man needs to launch himself out on his conquests. This is the Greek hero, in whose footsteps the spirit of Hellas will spread throughout the ages over the whole known world, from the shores of the Aegean to the banks of the Indus.